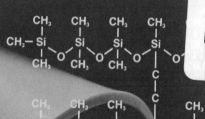

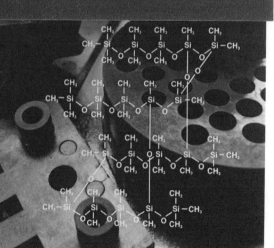

Forty Years
of Firsts

Forty Years of Firsts

The Recollections of a Dow Corning Pioneer

Dr. Earl L. Warrick

Edited by Jeannine Marschner

McGraw-Hill Publishing Company

New York   St. Louis   San Francisco   Auckland   Bogotá
Caracas   Hamburg   Lisbon   London   Madrid   Mexico
Milan   Montreal   New Delhi   Oklahoma City
Paris   San Juan   São Paulo   Singapore
Sydney   Tokyo   Toronto

Library of Congress Cataloging-in-Publication Data

Warrick, Earl L.
  Forty years of firsts: the recollections of a Dow Corning pioneer
  Earl L. Warrick; edited by Jeannine Marschner.
      p.   cm.
  ISBN 0-07-068330-1
  1. Dow Corning Corporation—History.   2. Silicone industry—
United States—History.   I. Marschner, Jeannine.   II. Title.   III. Title:
40 years of firsts.
HD9660.S544D688 1990
338.7′66′0973—dc20   89-36428
                                                                  CIP

1234567890   DOC/DOC   895432109

ISBN 0-07-068330-1

*The editors for this book were Barbara Toniolo and Georgia
Kornbluth, the designer was Naomi Auerbach, and the production
supervisor was Richard A. Ausburn. This book was set in Baskerville.
It was composed by the McGraw-Hill Publishing Company Professional
& Reference Division composition unit.*

Printed and bound by R. R. Donnelley and Sons Company.

*For more information about other McGraw-Hill materials,
call 1-800-2-MCGRAW in the United States. In other
countries, call your nearest McGraw-Hill office.*

Contents

Preface   xi

Acknowledgments   xiii

Chapter 1. The Vision   **1**

The Dreamer and the Organic Chemist   3
    The first experiments • The Rockefeller Center window •
    Corning's Fiber Products Division • General Electric pays a
    visit

The Mellon Connection   7
    Mac comes to Mellon • My "summer" job • The two-
    man fellowship • The glass block project • On the road to
    silicones

Corning and Mellon Team Up   13
    The Mellon fellows meet Dr. Hyde • The joint program
    agenda

The Evolution of Chemical Research   15
    A brief history of organosilicon chemistry • Polymer
    chemistry • The laboratories of the 1930s

Joint Research Begins   20
    The Corning group • The Rickover connection: "I want it
    tomorrow!" • The Corning group expands • Mellon
    studies • Dow Chemical lends a hand

The Research Progresses   27
    Early findings at Mellon • More basic research at Corning

Publishing and Patenting   29
   General Electric's surprise presentation • Corning and
   General Electric publish findings • Accelerating the patent
   effort • The war takes its toll

Dow Chemical Takes an Active Role   32
   Collings heads up silicone research

The Joint Venture Takes Shape   34
   Dow and Corning joint venture meeting • Setting the
   research agenda • The first product: DOW CORNING 4®
   compound

Research Progress at Dow   37
   Dr. Hunter's group • Dr. Barry's group • Scale-up of
   basic production

Formalizing the Joint Venture   41
   Announcement of the Dow Corning Division • The first
   employee • Progress report • The researchers meet •
   The joint venture is born

Chapter 2. The War Years: Building the Business   **47**

Start-Up   48
   Directors and officers • Operating agreements • Report of
   the first fiscal year • Capital funding

Production Begins   50
   Starting materials • Finished products

The Plant Is Built   53
   Rickover visit: magnesium, please • Construction begins •
   Production moves to the new plant site • Official start-up of
   the Dow Corning plant • Expanding the work force •
   Establishing departments • Progress report

The Research Progresses   63
   Corning group • Studies at Mellon • Progress at Dow •
   Translating the research: product development

Chapter 3. The Postwar Years: New Products,
**   New Markets**   **87**

First Postwar Products   88
   Tire-Mold Release: DOW CORNING® 35 emulsion • Rescuing
   the bakeries: Pan Glaze • First consumer product: SIGHT
   SAVERS® • Electrical products

Expansion   101
   Branching out: New York, Chicago, Cleveland • More sales
   offices: Los Angeles, Dallas, Atlanta, Washington •
   International beginnings • Personnel expansion •
   Supervisory training

Spreading the Word: Advertising and Publicity   **113**
  Advertising • Publicizing silicones

More New Products . . .   **118**
  Product engineering labs • Specialty products • Product
  management

**Chapter 4. Chemistry and Production in the
                Postwar Years**   **133**

Production Advances   **133**
  Grignard production • Direct process • Polymer
  production • Fluid bed techniques • Water-repellent
  products • Advances • Trichlorosilane and the Barry
  process

Plant Expansion   **139**
  First plant Outside Midland • New plants

Advances in Silicone Chemistry   **144**
  Pioneers of progress • Patents • Midland groups: research
  and analysis • Pennsylvania State University • Corning
  group • Mellon group   **153**

Chapter 5. The Collings Era: Personal Leadership   **169**

Dr. William R. Collings: The Man   **169**

Product Development and Management   **175**
  Product sales managers • Textile and leather treatments •
  Project Development Center

International Business   **180**
  Dow Corning International S. A. • Dow Corning A. G. •
  Sogesil • Japan • Overseas personnel • Collings's last
  visit to Europe

New Businesses   **184**
  Center for Aid to Medical Research • Silicon business

Chemical Research   **195**
  Chemical Engineering Achievement Award • Mellon
  research • Midland groups

**Chapter 6. Shailer L. Bass: Entrepreneurial
                Management**   **217**

Shailer L. Bass   **217**

Reorganization   **221**

Business Ventures   **223**
  Alpha Molykote Corporation • Ophthalmics • Silicon
  sales • Center for Aid to Medical Research • Medical
  Products Business

Facilities Expansion   **230**
Sealants plant • Medical products plant • Rubber
compounding facility • Carrollton, Kentucky, plant •
Personnel migrations at the sealants plant • Corporate
center

International Business   **235**
Alpha Molykote Europe • Canada: Armet Industries •
Japan: Fuji Kobunshi (Fuji Polymer) • International
restructuring • Shin-Etsu Handotai • Toray Silicone
Company Ltd. • Sydney, Australia • Seneffe, Belgium

Research and Development   **242**
Kipping Award • Patent department • New-product
sales • Bioscience research laboratories • Sealants •
SILASTIC® • Resins • Basic chemistry • Analytical
Department • Organofunctional chemistry

**Chapter 7. The Goggin Era: Multidimensional
               Organization   257**

Dr. William C. Goggin   **258**

The Multidimensional Organization: Evolutionary Steps   **260**
Economic evaluation • The board book • Establishing the
businesses • Corporate objectives • New business
staging • Strike at the Midland plant • Ninth business:
New Projects • "What's New" • Moon products

Further Restructuring: Basic Businesses   **268**
Electronic Products Business • Medical Products Business •
Silicone Rubber Business • Encapsulants and Sealants
Business • Resins and Chemicals Business

International Business   **275**
Pacific area • European area

The Multidimensional Organization: Phase Two   **279**

Dr. Hyde Is Honored   **280**

Facilities   **280**
Alpha Molykote plant • Corporate center planning •
Seneffe, Belgium, plant

More Reorganization   **284**
Area Operating Board • Corporate Business Board •
Evaluation System

**Chapter 8. The Ludington Years: Self-Sufficiency,
               Consolidation, Growth   287**

Corporate Self-Sufficiency   **289**

Growth and Development   **291**
Corporate center • The 1970s • The 1980s: big
opportunities, rapid change

Cultural Sensitivity   296

Silicone Research   297
  C resin • Silicone-organic block copolymers • Emulsion
  polymerization (silicone-based water emulsions) •
  Professional research ladder • Expansion of worldwide
  research efforts • Technical achievement awards

Health and Safety   302
  Ecology committee • Health and Safety Board

Code of Business Conduct   305

The Quality Initiative   306

Taking a Bow   307
  Awards and honors • Research honors

Fortieth Anniversary: A History of Achievement—A Future of Success   311

Epilogue   313

Index of Names   315
Subject Index   323

Preface

The use of history is to give value
to the present hour and its duty.
RALPH WALDO EMERSON

Back in 1943, when Dow Corning was incorporated, a handful of employees produced and sold the company's first products in the midst of World War II. Today, nearly 7000 employees in 12 countries work for the company which leads the world in silicone production.

Many of those who are a part of Dow Corning today may not be aware of the rich and colorful history of the joint venture that has grown and prospered for more than four decades. Few are old enough to recall the early days of Dr. William R. Collings, with his bold leadership style, engaging warmth, and signature bow tie and hat. Only a relative handful remember how Dr. Shailer Bass pushed us into the international marketplace while we were still wet behind the ears—a strategy that paid off far beyond our expectations. Not many recall the excitement we all felt in 1945 when DOW CORNING® 35 emulsion and Pan Glaze became instant successes and we knew we could make it in a civilian marketplace.

Most of the early pioneers are gone now. But the work they did, the contributions they made, laid the foundation upon which the next generation of innovators is building. In the history of the past are written lessons for the future. It is my hope that those who read this history of the first 40 years of Dow Corning will come away with an appreciation of the myriad decisions, struggles, and contributions that go into making a company survive and thrive.

Over the years, thousands of people all over the world have contributed to making Dow Corning what it is today. Many of their stories are told in these pages. But it would be impossible to include everyone who has been a part of the success story that is Dow Corning. This book is dedicated to all of them, to those employees who helped write the story of the company's first 40 years, and to those who are busy writing the history of the next 40.

I wish to thank Jack Ludington for giving me the opportunity to write this book, and for providing ample support from Dow Corning to help me do the job. More than 80 people contributed their stories for the book; their names follow this Preface. Bob Bott deserves special thanks for coordinating the efforts of contributors, working with the publisher, and providing me with plenty of material and moral support. Lee Nelson and the folks in the Dow Corning library provided many useful resources. Mike Daniels sifted patiently through the records retention room to provide me with invaluable historical documents. Jim Dion supplied most of the photographs for the book. Thanks also to Jeff Butcher, who handled the reprinting of the photographs, and to the people at Bradford Riviera. Bill Hargreaves, Bob Bott, and Bob Argyle helped immensely with editing in the early stages of the book.

Maureen Pillepich cheerfully coordinated the substantial volume of correspondence and mailings. Curt Partlo helped me with conversion of Display Write files to Word Perfect, making my work far easier. Thanks to Chuck Lenz, who provided many stories about recent company history, and to Jon Swanson, who assisted with Chapter 7, The Goggin Era. Phil Blumer, Howard Hatchel, and Nancy Higgins contributed vital details for the book.

A number of people reviewed parts or all of the final manuscript. Thanks to Bob Bott, Chi-Long Lee, Don Weyer, Ray Maneri, Bill Hargreaves, Wally Dyste, Forrest Stark, and Jim Jenkins.

I am grateful to Jeannine Marschner, who edited the entire book, improving it greatly in the process. Finally, I wish to thank my wife Jean, who patiently reviewed the many versions of the manuscript.

Dr. Earl Warrick

Acknowledgments

The following people contributed research necessary to the writing of this book.

C. J. Arnold
Wayne Barrett
Dr. A. J. Barry
Don Bartos
Ray Bass
Don Beshgetoor
Bill Betts
Bill Blackburn
Olie Blessing
Phil Blumer
Bob Bott
Si Braley
Eric Brown
Bill Caldwell
Dick Clark
Hal Clark
Joe Closs
Bill Cunningham
Chet Currie
Zeke Dennett

Harry Dingman
Clayt Doremire
Gordon Fearon
Howard Fenn
J. Forder
Don Francisco
Bud Frash
Dr. Cecil Frye
Hoot Gibson
Dr. William C. Goggin
Jerry Griffin
Bill Hargreaves
Bob Hedlund
Dr. Melvin J. Hunter
Ira Hutchison
Dr. J. Franklin Hyde
Jim Jenkins
Ron Johnson
Joe Keil
Charles Kohl

Arnie Kolb
Roger Kolderman
George Konkle
F. A. Kosciolek
Bill Kuhlman
Bud Lankton
Max Leavenworth
Dr. Norman Lloyd
Joe Lubbehusen
Jim McFadzen
Jim McHard
Ray Maneri
Bill May
Jack Moremond
Ray Naegele
Mel Nelson
John Ostahowski
Bill Pedersen
Keith Polmanteer
Mrs. Lew Putnam
Dusty Rhodes

Sandy Sanderson
Fred Saunders
Bob Shipps
K. Shohara
Dr. John L. Speier
Mary Sprague
Bob Springmier
Leo Stebleton
Bob Stewart
Jon Swanson
Clark Swayze
Duane Townley
Dr. Leslie Tyler
Gene Ulanowicz
Carl Voight
Art Webb
Dr. Donald Weyenberg
Don Weyer
Clyde Whipple
Monta Jo Wilson
Dorothy Yates

1

The Vision

Vision: the art of seeing things invisible.
JONATHAN SWIFT

Every new technology, each new field of scientific endeavor, can trace its roots to the stirrings of someone's imagination. The most complex of organizations once existed as nothing more than a concept. All great undertakings begin with an idea—a dream of something new, a hope for a better way, a vision of what might be....

The year was 1930. Dr. Eugene C. Sullivan, a prominent glass chemist, was vice president and director of research at Corning Glass Works in Corning, New York. The $9 million company was engaged in the production and sale of durable glass cookware.

The plastics industry was in its infancy at the time, but already it was clear to Dr. Sullivan that one day, perhaps in the not too distant future, plastic products might replace their glass counterparts, with unhappy consequences for glass manufacturers such as Corning. As he pondered this sobering prospect, Sullivan began to formulate an idea. What if it were possible to combine the advantages of the age-old glasses with the superior properties of the emerging plastics and produce materials that were stronger and more heat-resistant than plastic, but more flexible than glass?

While plastic chemistry held bright promise for the future, the plastics of the day were few in number and weak by any measure. Their uses were limited to small objects: billiard balls, electrical plugs and sockets, picture frames, sunglasses. One day, plastics would proliferate; nylon stockings would largely replace silk, Teflon® would become the

1

Dr. Eugene C. Sullivan, *Vice President and Director of Research, Corning Glass Works.*

predominant material for baking utensils, and a flood of plastic compounds—urethanes, nylons, polythenes, polyesters, polyimines, polycarbonates, polyfluorocarbons—would be unleashed. In 1930, however, the dominance of the plastics was years away. There was still time to ward off the threat.

Dr. Sullivan's conception of a new type of material that would combine the best features of glasses and plastics represented a radical departure from the industrial chemistry of the day. No one had attempted to develop the hybrids Sullivan envisioned. To realize his vision would mean entering an uncharted territory of chemical technology.

Pursuing such an experiment in the best of times would require a singular vision to guide the way into the unknown. Following such a research path in the midst of the great depression, however, would require courage in addition to vision. Money was tight, resources scarce. Prudence would dictate riding out the storm, maintaining the status quo until the economic picture improved. But the question persisted in Dr. Sullivan's mind: "What if it were possible...?"

With the aftermath of "black Friday" casting a pall over corporate America, in the spring of 1930, in the midst of the great depression, with insufficient resources, guided only by an educated hunch, Dr. Eugene Sullivan of Corning Glass Works forged ahead with his unorthodox vision of glass-plastic hybrids. He began by making a most unorthodox move: hiring an organic chemist.

Dr. J. Franklin Hyde,
Corning Glass Works.

The Dreamer and the Organic Chemist

Because glass is an inorganic substance,[1] glass factories of the day hired inorganic chemists to research and produce their products.[2] The idea of employing an organic chemist was unheard of until the day Dr. J. Franklin Hyde began his research at Corning Glass Works.

Dr. Sullivan's reasoning was simple. If Corning were to produce new substances that combined glass technology with the organic chemistry of plastics, an organic chemist must help lead the way. Dr. Hyde seemed the ideal candidate.

After receiving a Ph.D. in organic chemistry from the University of Illinois (one of the country's most prestigious schools in the area of organic chemistry), Frank Hyde had accepted a 2-year postdoctoral fellowship under Prof. J. B. Conant at Harvard University. In the spring of 1930, Dr. Sullivan sent Corning's chief chemist, Dr. W. C. Taylor, to Harvard to search for an organic chemist, at the same time Hyde's fellowship was ending.

Dr. Hyde had just returned from an interview with duPont when Conant informed him of Corning's interest, encouraging him to visit

---

[1]Inorganic substances in most cases contain no carbon; organic compounds are those which do contain carbon.

[2]Glass is formed in large tanks lined with refractory blocks where inorganic oxides and carbonates react and melt at high temperatures to form a molten mass. The molten material is formed into many different objects by a variety of techniques, then cooled to yield solid glass products. Glass plants hired inorganic chemists to monitor the process and develop new compositions. Up to this time there seemed to be no place for an organic chemist in the process.

New York and talk with the company. In Hyde's own words, "I wondered, 'What in the world do they want with an organic chemist in a glass factory?'" Since silicon is one of the basic elements found in glass, Hyde considered that Corning might want to experiment with *organic* compounds of silicon. He had some acquaintance with that field of chemistry from Perkin and Kipping's classic 1894 text *Organic Chemistry*. To prepare himself for the visit to Corning, Hyde reviewed some of Kipping's papers.

At Corning, Dr. Hyde met with Dr. Sullivan and Dr. Taylor. There he learned of Sullivan's dream of compounds that would combine the best of the silicon-based glasses and the carbon-based plastics. After a lengthy interview, Dr. Sullivan offered Hyde the challenge of coming to Corning and developing the materials he envisioned.

The challenge was accepted. In August 1930, Dr. J. Franklin Hyde, the organic chemist, joined the staff of Corning Glass Works in Corning, New York—in the midst of the great depression.

The First Experiments

At the time Frank Hyde joined Corning Glass Works, the company was working to develop glass fibers for use in electrical insulation. In order to provide effective insulation, electrical tapes require a resin to fill up the air space between fibers, as the presence of air pockets causes breakdowns and short circuits.

Glass-fiber tapes are more heat-resistant than cotton. If they could be developed for commercial use as insulators, they would allow the operation of electrical equipment at higher temperatures and greater speeds than ever before.

The resin that would serve as a filler for these new glass-fiber tapes would have to be as thermally stable (heat-resistant) as the glass-fiber tapes they filled. The resins on the market at the time were inadequate. Dr. Sullivan believed that the hybrid materials he envisioned might provide the solution. He assigned the problem to Dr. Hyde.

Hyde's first experiments at Corning thus involved the pursuit of a superior resin filler for use in glass-fiber electrical tape. He began by preparing a number of sample compounds with silicon-carbon bonds, combining the two basic elements of the glasses and plastics, for testing.

Dr. Hyde hydrolyzed the compounds (mixed them with water), and this yielded glasslike, rather brittle, solids. He then heated one of these glasslike products in a Pyrex® test tube until the compound liquefied. Hyde continued heating the tube beyond the melting point, until the Pyrex became so hot that it began to sag and elongate. The product inside the tube, however, remained unchanged, a clear liquid, demonstrating remarkable thermal stability.

This liquid product with the silicon-carbon bond was the first example of the hybrid materials Dr. Sullivan sought—the first compound that combined the basic components of glass and plastic, the first crude laboratory sample of organosilicon polymers, the materials more commonly known as "silicones."[3]

The Rockefeller Center Window

As Frank Hyde continued his resin research, he was called upon from time to time to solve other industrial problems in his lab. In 1932, Corning was asked to solve a structural problem involving a 15- by 40-foot window being installed over the entrance to the new RCA Building in Rockefeller Center in New York City. Corning had prepared 20- by 30-inch blocks of Pyrex glass which would form the larger window. A "mortar" was needed to cement the glass blocks in place and keep them from stressing one another.

Tests had shown that a new polyvinyl acetate resin made by Union Carbide had just the right refractive index for the job (that is, if sheets of the resin were placed between the glass blocks, no "seam" would show; the blocks would bond together and appear to be a single large window). However, because the smaller glass blocks were imperfectly shaped, a mortar made of the resin was needed to fill in any gaps between the sheets.

Dr. Hyde was assigned the task of developing this mortar. He dissolved some of the polymer in a monomeric compound,[4] reasoning that as the monomer polymerized over time, the mortar would adhere to the sheets of resin and form one solid piece of vinyl acetate.

With special dispensation from the glazers' union (a highly unusual concession), Hyde spent 1 month putting the glass blocks in place at the RCA Building, wedging the vinyl acetate sheets between the blocks and using the mortar he'd developed to cement the blocks in place. His reasoning was sound; the monomer did polymerize over time, and the window project was a success.

The problem Dr. Hyde had solved for Rockefeller Center might have

[3]There are a wide variety of *organosilicon* compounds (compounds with carbon-silicon bonds; the term "silicones" includes all the organosilicon *polymers* (compounds formed of large molecules) that have carbon-silicon-*oxygen* bonds.

[4]Monomers are single molecules that can be linked with other molecules to form a polymer; they are the "building blocks" of polymers.

been just another routine industrial project. As it turned out, though, the significance of his work would extend far beyond those glass windows looking down on midtown Manhattan—for the resin Hyde developed for the RCA Building would later become the catalyst that would lead Dr. Rob Roy McGregor and me, out of simple curiosity, to begin our own exploration of the chemistry of silicones.

Corning's Fiber Products Division

By 1935 Corning decided to plunge headlong into the glass-fiber business, encouraged by signs of tremendous growth potential. Others were conducting research in the area, but no company, including Corning, had yet produced practical glass fibers; the field was wide open. A fiber products division was established within Corning, and all the research problems involved in developing the new glass-fiber products were assigned to Dr. Hyde.

Once the division was formed, Hyde continued his work in developing a resin for use with glass-fiber tapes. He believed that the thermally stable liquid silicone compound he'd prepared in the test tube could, with additional work, be transformed into a suitable resin.

Continuing his experiments, Hyde narrowed his focus and concentrated on the hydrolysis product from ethylphenyldichlorosilane. Soon he developed the first crude sample of a silicone resin compound. He tested it by impregnating glass tapes with the resin. The resin proved to be so thermally stable that copper bars wrapped with the impregnated glass tapes withstood heating to between 572 and 752°F. This first practical silicone resin was given the designation 990A resin.

General Electric Pays a Visit

Les Morrow, who managed the Fiber Products Division, was excited about the potential for the new silicone resin Dr. Hyde had developed. He invited two researchers from General Electric, Dr. A. L. Marshall and Winton T. Patnode, to come to Corning and learn what Hyde had achieved.

Corning management thought GE might be interested in working jointly in the new field of silicone resins, since the company was already making resins for motors and other electrical equipment. The visitors, however, departed without discussing cooperative efforts. As it turned out, General Electric realized the tremendous potential of the field as well and decided to pursue silicone research on its own.

This first abortive effort would certainly not be the last attempt at co-operative research. Before long, Corning would link up with some of the finest scientific minds in the country, at the Mellon Institute.

The Mellon Connection

The Mellon Institute of Industrial Research in Pittsburgh, Pennsylvania, was a unique organization, founded in 1913 by Andrew and Richard Mellon at the University of Pittsburgh (Figure 1-1). The Institute filled a need for top-notch research facilities during a time when few companies had the resources for their own research departments.

Mellon operated under an innovative fellowship system. Industrial problems brought to the Institute for study were worked on by one or more persons who were "almost" employees of sponsoring companies. The relationships between the fellows and the sponsoring companies were close.

Figure 1-1. Mellon Institute, 4400 Fifth Avenue, Pittsburgh, Pennsylvania.

Dr. Rob Roy McGregor,
Mellon Institute.

The Mellon system fostered excellent relationships among the fellows as well. No rivalries developed, because no two projects in the same field were ever initiated. So productive were these relationships that in the time I was to spend at Mellon, I would learn more from my association with other fellows than in much of my laboratory work.

Mac Comes to Mellon

Dr. Rob Roy McGregor joined Mellon Institute in 1927 after receiving a Ph.D. in chemistry from the University of Illinois. When I met him, he had been working for the previous year on an opal glass project as a fellow sponsored by the Macbeth Evans Glass Company. It was the summer of 1935, and I was looking for work after having spent a year at Brown University beyond my master's degree in chemistry. At that point I felt I couldn't afford to continue with schooling for the additional 3 or 4 years it might take to earn my Ph.D., so I had written to some 50 companies looking for a position. I didn't receive one reply.

Warrick's "Summer" Job

Then I heard of the possibility of summer employment at Mellon Institute. I interviewed and was accepted for a summer job assisting Dr. McGregor ("Mac" to those who knew him), replacing a man who was leaving to take a permanent position elsewhere. At one point, when Mac left the room, this man said to me, "Do you smoke?" I said "No," to which he replied, "Well, you'd better learn, because Mac's got to borrow from somebody."

The interview went well, I was offered the position, and I began work in July. At the end of that first summer, when I thought my job would be ending, Mac said to me, "We have more than enough platinum to carry on. Why don't we sell enough to fund you for another year?" We did, and I was delighted over my good fortune.

Little did I know, when I joined Mellon Institute in 1935, that the man I planned to assist for one summer would prove to be a major influence throughout my scientific career. We wound up staying together for 21 years. I never did learn to smoke.

The Two-Man Fellowship

Together Mac and I continued work on the MacBeth Evans project. It was a warm relationship, in more ways than one—the melting furnace we used in preparing our compositions required heating to 2900°F. In the heat of July and August, our fourth-floor laboratory sizzled.

Near the end of 1936, Corning Glass Works acquired MacBeth Evans, and Mac and I became a two-man Corning fellowship. Soon afterward, Mac visited Corning to see what projects they might have for us. He returned with glass blocks, each composed of two halves, with a solid glass seal in between. The edges of each block, to which mortar was applied in laying it in a wall, were coated with a resin. Masons were complaining that the resin coating flaked off as they applied the mortar. Our challenge was to develop a coating that would not rub off.

The Glass Block Project

The resin coating, Dr. McGregor had learned, was a vinyl acetate copolymer[5] suggested by Frank Hyde at Corning Glass Works, our sponsor company. It was the same resin Hyde had used with success on the RCA Building window. Mac was familiar with Hyde's name from the days when both were students at the University of Illinois, but he had no idea what sort of research Frank was pursuing at Corning.

When the resin was applied to the windows in the RCA Building, no moisture was present. Once sealed in, the window resisted moisture from the outside, and the weight of the blocks prevented any movement. In the case of the masons, however, the resin coating was immersed in moist mortar before placement, and it simply floated off the glass blocks.

We tried every new coating we could think of to solve the problem. Some 96 coating trials later, however, we looked at each other and said, "Perhaps nothing will stick to glass when water reaches it."

At this point, acquaintances from another Mellon fellowship, sponsored by Union Carbide, suggested we try a new product sold commercially as ethyl silicate, as a possible solution. They gave us 1 gallon of the product for testing.

We partially hydrolyzed the ethyl silicate and spread it on the glass blocks. The coating simply continued to decompose into sand and ultimately flaked off the blocks. Then we tried a different tack, painting

[5]A polymer composed of two or more different monomers.

over the ethyl silicate with the polyvinyl acetate resin while the resin was still sticky, before it had time to decompose. This time there was no flaking at all. The polyvinyl acetate resin effectively "waterproofed" the underlying ethyl silicate, preventing further hydrolysis from occurring and thus stopping the flaking.

We then baked this composite coating, and it continued to adhere to the glass blocks even after they were immersed in water for many days. Our experimentation had finally paid off. Much testing and formulation followed, but all our original findings were confirmed. Years later we went through the Port Allegheny plant of the Pittsburgh Corning Corporation where these glass blocks were made, and the company was still using a modification of our original formulation for the coating.

On the Road to Silicones

The glass block project had sparked our imagination. The ethyl silicate we'd tested as a resin for the blocks contained carbon-oxygen-silicon bonds, which are broken when the compound is hydrolyzed, causing the compound to decompose into sand. We were fairly certain that if the resin we'd used had had a silicon-carbon bond instead, it would not have continued to decompose, as these bonds do not hydrolyze except under extreme conditions.

As we completed the report of our project results for Corning in November 1937, we speculated about what might happen if we could create nonhydrolyzable compounds with carbon-silicon bonds. We knew that if it were possible to do this, we could create a whole array of new polymers. We had no idea where such experiments might lead, how such new polymers might react, what uses might be found for them. Without realizing it at the time, we were about to plunge ourselves into a vast unknown territory of chemical technology: silicones.

Kipping Leads the Way.   Our curiosity pointed us in the direction of the library and the papers of F. S. Kipping.[6] Kipping, a British chemist born in the mid-1800s, had made many compounds with nonhydrolyzable groups on silicon and had developed many polymers as the unwanted by-products of his research. In the course of his experimentation, Kipping had published 54 papers covering the period 1899 through 1944. For many years this collection of papers was virtually the

---

[6]F. S. Kipping, first paper. F. S. Kipping and L. Lloyd, *Chem. Ber.* 15:174 (1899). Final paper, F. S. Kipping and J. Abrams, *J. Chem. Soc.* 1:81 (1944).

Bible for silicone researchers. It provided an excellent starting point for us.

In reviewing Professor Kipping's writings, we found that he had made many organosilicon compounds with different organic groups on the silicon atom, using the Grignard reaction.[7] In simple terms, the Grignard reaction is used to place groups of atoms on molecules. The reaction allowed us to create a carbon-silicon bond.

Grignard Preparations. We carried out our first Grignard reaction at Mellon Institute on February 28, 1938, following the procedure Kipping had suggested. This process generated a fluid containing a variety of silicon compounds. These compounds had to be separated into their "fractions," or components, by distillation. To do so, we had to design distillation columns (Figure 1-2) and learn how to operate them effectively, a new adventure for us.[8]

Resin Experiments. The first attempt to use the new silicon compounds distilled from the Grignard reaction came in trying to prepare film-forming resins. Such resins are used in a variety of applications, from painting houses and cars to insulating motors.

As we experimented with the resins and our research progressed, we kept Dr. Sullivan apprised of our progress. Every 2 months or so Mac and I would make the trip to Corning to present our progress reports in person. During one of our visits, Mac spoke to George Macbeth, who had joined Corning following the Macbeth Evans acquisition. Macbeth told Mac that what we were doing at Mellon was similar to research being done at Corning by Dr. Hyde.

Until that conversation between Mr. MacBeth and Dr. McGregor, we had no idea that we at Mellon and Dr. Hyde at Corning were converging on the same research path. We decided it would be a good idea to

---

[7]The Grignard reaction is named after M. V. Grignard, a French Nobel prize–winning organic chemist who published his technique in 1901. He took metallic magnesium in the form of shavings or chips and placed it in a flask covered with ethyl ether, C_2H_5—O—C_2H_5. To this flask he slowly added an organic halide, e.g., C_2H_5Br, ethyl bromide. A reaction ensued on slight warming of the flask, forming a very reactive intermediate—C_2H_5MgBr, ethyl magnesium bromide. This reactive intermediate could then form a reaction with any organic compound containing a halogen—chlorine, bromine, or iodine—to put organic groups onto the compound. Kipping had shown that this reaction could be used to put organic groups onto silicon, a primary step in forming silicones.

[8]Distillation (also called "fractional distillation") is a process by which compounds are separated into component parts or "fractions" according to their boiling points. The process is carried out in a distillation column, where vaporization and condensation occurs repeatedly, so that higher-boiling-point components are continuously washed back down the column, while the rising low-boiling-point vapors leave the top of the column, thus effectively separating the components according to their relative boiling points.

Figure 1-2. *Left:* Distillation columns, 6 feet tall, were used by the Analytical Department in the early days to separate silicone compounds by their boiling points. *Right:* Distillation towers outside the Midland plant today stand 60 feet tall.

12

visit Hyde in the Fiber Division laboratories at Corning to learn more about his work.

Corning and Mellon Team Up

The Mellon Fellows Meet Dr. Hyde

Dr. McGregor and I spent 2 days with Dr. Hyde, in April 1938. As a result of this meeting, the Mellon and Corning groups resolved to collaborate and build on the work already begun at the two institutions, with each group focusing on different aspects of the research. The study of silicones logically divided itself into two classes of carbon com-

"I see by the current issue of 'Lab News,' Ridgeway, that you've been working for the last twenty years on the same problem I've been working on for the last twenty years."

Drawing by Opie; ©1976 The New Yorker Magazine, Inc.

pounds, alkyl and aryl.[9] We agreed that Hyde's group would concentrate on resins and aryl substituents (e.g., phenyl, xylyl) on silicon; the Mellon group would focus on alkyl substituents (e.g., methyl, ethyl, butyl, amyl) on silicon.

The Joint Program Agenda

The joint program developed at the Corning-Mellon meeting in Frank Hyde's lab in April 1938 guided the groups' research efforts for many months. The program was divided into three sections. One section focused on the development of improved plastics; another involved broad-ranging basic research into organosilicon compounds; the third section was devoted to developing practical applications of the research. A complete outline of the program is included here to illustrate the breadth and ambition of the objectives set for the two groups:

JOINT PROGRAM OF RESEARCH
CORNING GLASS WORKS AND MELLON INSTITUTE
April 5, 1938

Program Section 1

Development of improved plastics with regard to:

1. Chemical stability
2. Heat resistance
3. Waterproofness
4. Hardness
5. Flexibility
6. Adhesion to glass
7. Electrical properties
8. Impact resistance of glass coated with resin

Program Section 2

Detailed study of organic silicon (organosilicon) compounds:

1. Internal plasticizing: study of the effect of addition of alkyl and aryl groups to the silicon atom. As one changes the nature of the groups on silicon, one changes the nature of the polymer formed. We wanted to know the properties of the various possible polymers. The term "internal plasticizing" meant that the organic groups we proposed to add to the

[9]Alkyl compounds are those with the general formula C_nH_{2n+1}; aryl compounds, those with the general formula C_nH_n.

chain of silicon atoms would transform the polymer from the hard, brittle quartz to something less brittle and more useful.
2. Study of effect of modification of the alkyl and aryl groups by:
   a. Introduction of polymerizable bonds
   b. Chlorination (the replacement of hydrogen by chlorine)
   c. Reactions with other molecules such as formaldehyde and ammonia
3. Further study of silicate esters (continued from our work at Mellon) to determine:
   a. Behavior in combination with other materials, e.g., other esters
   b. Behavior in combination with lacquers or plastics, e.g., vinyl acetate, styrenes, and methacrylates
   c. Conditions for hydrolysis
   d. Nonaqueous polymerization reactions
4. Study of the combination of organic silicon compounds with metals.
5. Study of the phenomenon of adhesion to glass.
6. Study of all possible methods of synthesis of organic silicon compounds.
7. Survey to determine the possibilities of resin formation by organometallic compounds, other than silicon; we knew that other organometallic compounds existed, and we wanted to know how useful they might be.

Program Section 3

Study of properties of organosilicon compounds from the point of view of practical applications:

1. As protective coatings for plastics
2. As decorative coatings for glass

A particularly interesting omission from this program is any reference to fluids or rubbers, which would figure so prominently in later work. There was so much to explore, and the field was so new to us, that initially we chose to narrow our focus and devote our attention strictly to the development of resins and improved plastics. Later, we would adopt a much broader approach, examining the products of our basic research with no preconceived objectives in mind.

The Evolution of Chemical Research

Before looking ahead to the progression of silicone research at Corning and Mellon, it is important to step back and review the historical development of organosilicon and polymer chemistry, the backbone of silicone research. While the field of silicones was a new one in 1938, by no means were we starting from scratch in our explorations. Rather, we were building upon a solid foundation of chemical research dating back to the early nineteenth century.

A Brief History of Organosilicon Chemistry

The field of organosilicon chemistry was explored and developed by some of the giants of early chemical discovery. Only a few are cited here; a more complete history of this chemistry can be found in Dr. R. R. McGregor's book, *Silicones and Their Uses*,[10] and in Dr. E. G. Rochow's primer, *An Introduction to the Chemistry of Silicones.*[11]

Berzelius. Johann Berzelius was a Swedish chemist born in 1779. He was the first chemist to isolate the element silicon, a basic component of silicones, from the compound potassium fluosilicate, K_2SiF_6, in 1824.[12] Before Berzelius's discovery, silicon was not recognized as a separate element, as it had been very difficult to separate from chemical compounds.

In his experiments, Berzelius exposed silicon to acid at room temperature. The silicon didn't seem to react with the acid, but when he put it into a stream of chlorine, it ignited and burned vigorously. He then condensed this vaporized product to a liquid, silicon tetrachloride, $SiCl_4$. Today silicon tetrachloride, the compound Berzelius first prepared, is still used as a starting material for preparing silicones.

Wohler. Another famous chemist, Frederick Wohler, born in 1800, carried out a historic experiment in which he synthesized urea.[13] This destroyed a generally accepted belief of the time that bodily products, such as urea, came only from animal or plant sources. Until the time of Wohler's experiment, it was thought that chemical changes undergone in living, carbon-based organisms were different from other chemical reactions and thus could not be created in the laboratory. Wohler disproved that theory, and synthetic organic chemistry was born. Wohler

---

[10]R. R. McGregor, *Silicones and Their Uses*, McGraw-Hill, New York, 1954.

[11]E. G. Rochow, *Introduction to the Chemistry of Silicones*, Wiley, New York, 1946, 1951.

[12]J. J. Berzelius, *Pogg. Ann.*, 1:169 (1824).

[13]F. Wohler, *Ann. Physik*, (2) 12:253 (1828).

prepared silane, SiH_4, and trichlorosilane, $SiHCl_3$,[14] which are still used today in preparing high-purity silicon and compounds of silicon. He also showed that these compounds, used in forming silicones, could be prepared by starting with the element silicon.

As Dr. McGregor notes in *Silicones and Their Uses*,[15] "had Wohler gone just one step further and used an organic chloride, RCl[16] instead of HCl, to make the trichlorosilane, he would have anticipated by nearly a century a useful development in silicon chemistry," that is, the Rochow direct process for preparing silicones (which will be discussed in Chapter 2).

Wohler is also recognized as the first chemist to introduce the term "silicone," but the compound to which he referred was not a silicone as we know it today but rather an oxygen-containing silicon complex, hydrosilane. To describe this complex, Wohler used the German word *silicon*, a word whose closest English translation is "silicone."[17]

Ebelman. J. J. Ebelman in 1844 recognized the acidic character of silicon tetrachloride, $SiCl_4$, and combined it with ethyl alcohol to prepare esters, $(C_2H_5O)_xSiCl_{4-x}$.[18] Ebelman was the first to prepare silicon esters, which are used as starting materials for many chemical reactions and proved to be important in our early work at Mellon in preparing silicones.

Friedel and Crafts. The first true organosilicon compound, that is, one with a carbon-silicon (C—Si) bond, was prepared by Charles Friedel and James Crafts in 1863.[19] They combined diethyl zinc, $(C_2H_5)_2Zn$, which is highly flammable, with silicon tetrachloride, $SiCl_4$. The reaction created a far less flammable fluid, tetraethylsilane, $(C_2H_5)_4$. Ladenburg joined the two experimenters and expanded on the work Ebelman had done, preparing many of the possible esters, some of which are useful in the in situ Grignard process for making silicones.

Kipping. Other researchers produced organosilicon compounds, but it remained for Frederick Kipping, the British chemist introduced earlier in the chapter, to prepare compounds with carbon-silicon bonds us-

---

[14]H. Buff and F. Wohler, *Ann.*, 104:94 (1857).

[15]McGregor, op. cit, p. 7.

[16]"R" in the formula "RCl" represents an organic material.

[17]F. Wohler, *Annalen der Chemie*, **127**(3):257–274 (1863).

[18]J. J. Ebelmen, *Compt. rend.*, 19:398 (1844).

[19]C. Friedel and J. M. Crafts, *Compt. rend.*, 56:592 (1863).

ing the new Grignard reagent, developed around the turn of the century. This was a far easier method of producing organosilicons than Friedel and Crafts had developed and is still in use today.[20]

In his experimentation, Kipping was interested in pursuing the chemistry of silicon; he hoped to show that silicon compounds could be developed that would be similar in many respects to their organic, or carbon-based, counterparts. During the course of his work, Kipping prepared silicon-based compounds that he expected to be similar to ketones, a type of carbon compound. But they didn't respond to any of Kipping's tests for identifying ketones. He called these organosilicon materials "silicones," a contraction of "silicon" and "ketone."

Kipping was thus the first to develop a true silicone compound and the first to use the term "silicone" as we know it today. Kipping was not interested in these polymeric products of his research, the "sticky messes" for which he recognized no use; he was interested only in the pure chemistry of silicon. But ironically, as a result of his work, Frederick Kipping is considered the father of silicone chemistry.

Polymer Chemistry

All silicones are polymers, and in order to appreciate our efforts in producing them, it is necessary to understand a bit about the chemistry of polymers.

The field of polymer chemistry was embryonic in the 1930s. Before 1920, the existence of polymers was not even recognized. The prevailing view in the chemical research community before 1920 was that natural substances such as rubber, cellulose, and starch were formed from unlinked small molecules. In fact, they are all polymers.

Two twentieth-century chemists made important contributions to silicone research through their work in the field of polymer chemistry. Hermann Staudinger hypothesized that certain naturally occurring substances were polymers, and Wallace Carothers developed a useful method of forming silicone polymers.

Staudinger.   Hermann Staudinger,[21] a German organic chemist, was the first to suggest, in 1920, that certain naturally occurring compounds, such as rubber and starch, were indeed polymers—large molecules—rather than groups of unlinked small molecules. His views were

---

[20]F. S. Kipping, *J. Chem Soc.*, 91:209 (1907).

[21]H. Staudinger, *Ber.*, 59:3079 (1926).

not accepted immediately, but after a while his findings were confirmed by scientists who began measuring molecular weights.

Carothers. A decade after the German chemist Staudinger recognized the existence of naturally occurring polymers, an American organic chemist developed a useful technique for forming polymers in the laboratory. In 1929, Wallace Carothers began a study of condensation polymers, formed by building large molecules (polymers) from known small molecules.[22] This led to the development of polyesters and polyamides (nylons) and later to Neoprene, one of the first synthetic rubbers. This important polymerization technique was also used in preparing silicones and at the Mellon Institute in attempts to form silicones.

From the foregoing discussion it should be clear that an enormous amount of work done by distinguished chemists of earlier times provided a starting point for the research efforts of the Corning and Mellon groups. While silicone chemistry represented an entirely new avenue of exploration, the silicone products of the future would build upon the foundation of the past. The achievements of our joint program, and of the many silicone researchers who were to follow, would be attained by standing on the shoulders of giants.

The Laboratories of the 1930s

To get a clearer perspective on the joint program begun at Corning Glass Works and Mellon Institute in 1938, it is helpful to understand the circumstances under which we were attempting to carry out our experiments, to examine the laboratory equipment and analytical techniques available to us as we began our silicone research in mid-1938.

The laboratories of the late 1930s appeared much like laboratories of today, but the equipment and processes available to the scientist were much more limited. Most of what a good researcher considers essential today was not yet available. For example, in 1938, many of the basic instruments, techniques, and physical phenomena used in identifying, measuring, and separating chemical compounds—infrared spectrometers, gas-liquid chromatography, gel permeation chromatography, Instron testing machines, atomic absorption spectra, light-scattering molecular weight (MW), scanning electron microscopes, electron spin resonance, dynamic viscosimeters, x-ray fluorescence, laser Raman

[22]W. H. Carothers, *J. Am. Chem. Soc.*, 51:2548 (1929).

spectra, differential thermal analysis, and nuclear magnetic resonance—had not yet been developed or discovered. Computers, which would become so vital in designing and studying chemicals, and in searching for literature and patents, were still far in the future.

Money was also in short supply. As a result, much of the equipment in our laboratory at Mellon was fabricated on the premises rather than purchased. We had to be machinists as well as chemists; when a distillation column, an oven, or a pressurizable vessel was needed, we had to construct it ourselves.

Obviously, the conditions we faced as we began our silicone research were far from ideal, but in no way did we feel deprived. On the contrary, we were enormously enthused, exhilarated by the possibilities that lay before us. Although our research was still in the embryonic stages, we had done enough work to recognize the vast potential of the new chemistry we were developing. The more we learned, the more obvious that potential became. Dr. McGregor summarized the feelings of both groups in those early days when he commented that the field of silicone research was "large enough for a lifetime of work."

Joint Research Begins

The Corning Group

Frank Hyde continued his resin experimentation under the joint program. Samples of the new 990A resin were provided to various glass-fiber customers, who were pleased with its performance. It wasn't long before Hyde was committed to preparing a quart of the product. While this was a small amount, with the limited personnel and the elementary equipment available, to Dr. Hyde, production took weeks. Bodying the resin (bringing it from a liquid to a resinous state) requires time and patience. Furthermore, the flasks used in preparing the resin had a very small capacity. Thus the procedure had to be repeated many times to produce a sufficient quantity of the final product.

Dr. Hyde made a useful discovery in the course of preparing the first quart of resin for commercial use. The final stages of bodying involved adding a solvent just before the resin reached a gelation stage.[23] Hyde

---

[23]Gelation is the stage at which a resinous composition becomes insoluble.

returned from lunch one day to find that this large batch of resin had gelled before he'd had the chance to add the solvent; the bodying step had been carried too far.

Not wishing to lose the weeks of work he'd spent preparing the mixture, Hyde added a small amount of alcoholic alkali. He reasoned that breaking the last few cross-links with alkali would solubilize the gel. His reasoning was sound, and he soon recovered his resin. It was a fortunate incident. Dr. Hyde's technique was invaluable in controlling resin production and providing a method of salvaging what would otherwise become wasted material.

In the course of this experimentation, Hyde developed a wide variety of silicone compounds that would later become a part of the first major patent effort of the joint research program, the Hyde 19 case.

The Rickover Connection:
"I Want It Tomorrow!"

The Navy expressed an interest in Dr. Hyde's 990A resin for use in electric motors insulated with glass tapes. Harold Boeschenstein, president of Owens-Corning Fiberglass, tried to convince Hyman Rickover, then head of the electrical section of the Bureau of Ships, that Fiberglas insulating tape represented a major improvement over other insulators for electrical equipment. Under Boeschenstein's direction, a motor had been wound using Fiberglas insulation with no resin varnish, and he demonstrated that it could be operated at very high temperatures without failure.

Hyman Rickover could see the potential use for fiberglass insulation in submarines. Without varnish or resin protection, however, electrical wires were vulnerable to water, abrasion due to vibration, or both. Rickover rejected the idea of a motor without varnish protection, whereupon Boeschenstein showed him a piece of glass tape coated with varnish made from 990A resin. Rickover examined the tape and said, "Now you've got something. I want it tomorrow."

The Corning Group Expands

Dr. Johannson. As Dr. Hyde's work proceeded, others joined him in the Corning laboratories. Dr. Kenneth Johannson, a physical chemist working on a glass project at Corning, was the first to assist Dr. Hyde with his silicone research. Johannson had been developing a process to treat the surface of glass to increase its strength. He became interested in Dr. Hyde's organosilicon compounds as possible primers for ethyl cellulose, which was being tested as a strengthening agent. While the glass project was subsequently dropped, Ken Johannson retained his interest in organosilicon chemistry and soon was working with Dr. Hyde on resin development and a variety of basic research projects.

Delong. With the Navy's request for large amounts of 990A resin, and with the expansion of the basic research effort, Hyde asked for more help. Soon Richard Delong joined him after graduation from the Massachusetts Institute of Technology (MIT). Together, Hyde and Delong developed a Grignard machine to produce larger quantities of resin starting materials. The machine was a tubular reactor with a stirrer in which bromobenzene in ether passed over magnesium chips to prepare phenyl Grignards continuously.

The continuous Grignard machine generally worked well, but one day, while working with the machine, Dr. Hyde noticed that the water bath in the reactor was steaming and asked Delong, "How come there's no ether distilling?"

Just as a cork popped out of the reactor, it occurred to Delong what had happened. He had left the cork in the system, probably the previous day; as a result, the ether which normally distilled out of the reactor had nowhere to go, and pressure had developed in the system. Eventually the pressure blew out the cork, spraying the highly volatile ether all around. If there were an Olympic event for racing down a 50-foot hallway, down three flights of stairs, and across a 300-foot stretch of land (to the main gate), Dick Delong's record would still stand.

There was a glass-blowing lamp on one side of the lab, which had a pilot light that Frank Hyde fortunately thought to snuff out with his hand as he departed. When the vapors reached the stirring motor on the Grignard machine, the room was sufficiently full of vapor that, instead of a great explosion, a "whooshing" sound was heard. Dr. Hyde ran out the door under a billow of flame and black smoke.

Fortunately, he escaped with just a few small blisters on the backs of his ears. The sprinklers went off, and the resulting mess took several days to clean up. Dick Delong never again forgot to remove the cork.

Once the continuous Grignard machine was producing adequate amounts of materials for experimentation, Delong, who was interested in fractional distillation, worked hard to separate the mono-, di-, and trimethylchlorosilanes—silicone starting materials—from silicon tetrachloride, $SiCl_4$. This was an extremely difficult process, because the boiling points of these compounds are very close (Table 1-1); many repeated distillations had to be made in order to separate them.

Delong's efforts paid off. His successful separation and characteriza-

Table 1-1. Boiling Points of Silane Derivatives

Compound*	Boiling point, °F
Monomethyltrichlorosilane, CH_3SiCl_3	150.26
Dimethyldichlorosilane, $(CH_3)_2SiCl_2$	158.00
Trimethylchlorosilane, $(CH_3)_3SiCl$	135.14
Tetrachlorosilane, $SiCl_4$	135.68

*All compounds are named as derivatives of silane, SiH_4.

tion of these products enabled Hyde's group to patent the materials later. These patents were important to our early efforts, as they covered the processes for making starting materials for a large number of silicone products.

Lubrication Tests. As the basic research proceeded, Dr. Hyde's group periodically tested the new compounds for use in various applications. Around 1940, the group tested the fluids they'd been developing for possible use as lubricants. Certain of these fluids, the phenyl-containing siloxane hydrolysates, had an oily appearance, and it seemed possible that they would be good engine lubricants.

To test this theory, Dr. Hyde bought a 1½-horsepower Briggs and Stratton gasoline engine. Early in the test, with the silicone fluid being used as the only lubricant, the engine began to plug up with sand; eventually the engine stopped completely because of sand formation. Later, more formal lubrication tests confirmed that simple aryl- or alkyl-substituted siloxanes, the basic types of fluids the group had developed, were not good lubricants, and the group moved on to explorations of other possible applications.

Mellon Studies

Resin Experiments. While Dr. Hyde's group at Corning was refining the basic Grignard process, developing larger quantities of 990A resin, and separating and studying silicone compounds and testing them for possible industrial applications, we were pursuing our half of the joint research effort at Mellon Institute.

We also tried to develop silicone resins. We began preparing methyl, ethyl, isopropyl, butyl, and amyl silicon compounds by the reaction of Grignard reagents with ethyl silicate (these were the alkyl compounds that were the focus of our half of the joint research program). We then distilled these starting materials to get the silicon esters used in the Grignard process to produce resins. We first tried to apply our newly developed resins to the problems of plastics used in optical lenses, which were subject to scratches. As pointed out earlier, the few plastics available at this time were soft; they were easily scratched.

We decided to try placing coatings of our newly developed resins on various plastic sheets in an effort to increase the surface hardness enough to improve the scratch resistance of the plastic. Unfortunately, even the hardest resins we developed did not raise the scratch resistance of the plastic sheets, and we turned our attention to other experiments.

Next, attempts were made to prepare a molding resin from mono methyl ester. "Molding resins" are so named because they can be placed in a mold and cured in a relatively short time to produce an object such as an electrical plug for an extension cord. We were able to prepare a molding resin from silicone polymers, but as in the case of the first resin we'd tried, we were not completely satisfied with our results.

Fluid Production.   Since resin exploration did not live up to our expectations, we abandoned that line of research for the moment and turned our attention to silicone fluids, an area of research not included in the joint program, but one that appeared to have great potential for industrial applications. We developed a series of fluids from the materials left over from resin making, and studied dimethylsiloxane fluid to learn more about its properties as well as to measure its silicon content. We spent a lot of effort in characterizing (determining the properties of) these fluids. We also attempted to further polymerize the fluids to the higher molecular weights needed to develop high-viscosity fluids and rubber.

In Situ Etherless Grignards.   In 1938 we got some help from the Russians. The Grignard reaction used to produce our silicone compounds was a dangerous one, as it involved the use of diethyl ether, a highly volatile substance that posed a great explosion and fire hazard. In October 1938, two Russian scientists, K. A. Andrianov and O. Gribanova, writing in the *Journal of General Chemistry*, described "etherless" Grignards, and an in situ Grignard reaction that eliminated one step in the process.[24]

These papers showed us how to carry out the Grignard process more efficiently and safely. Within a week after the papers appeared, we ran our first etherless Grignard at Mellon, using the new in situ reaction.

[24]K. A. Andrianov and O. Gribanova, *J. Gen. Chem. (USSR)*, 8:552 (1938); also *J. Gen. Chem. (USSR)*, 8:558 (1938).

When we distilled the product of the reaction, we found that we had a much broader range of compounds than the Russian scientists had reported. Because of this we were able to obtain a patent on our process.[25]

This process was good for producing ethyl compounds, but we were also interested in methyl materials, which involved a different production technique. In May 1939 we succeeded in running a methyl Grignard using an etherless method.

To do this we used a borrowed 1-pint container that could withstand high internal pressure. The container was filled with ethyl orthosilicate and magnesium. Another transfer vessel was filled with methyl bromide gas and connected with the reaction container. The gas spread to the reaction vessel so that when we shook it, the Grignard reaction proceeded.

While the procedure worked, the tiny vessel we used produced only minimal amounts of product. In order to prepare larger amounts of methyl compounds, the Mellon machine shop built a bigger, 1-gallon reactor for us. With our basic production processes in place, our research group began to expand its efforts.

The Mellon Pilot Plant.   As we continued our fluid research at Mellon in 1939, we began attracting interest among the other fellowships at the Institute. We had limited amounts of silicone fluids and were busy characterizing them. The 1-gallon reactor yielded more product than we'd had before, but our capacity was still limited.

As a result of the interest generated by the other Mellon fellowships, a meeting was held in January 1940 between the managements of Corning Glass Works and the Mellon Institute. The group discussed possible cooperative studies with other fellowships at Mellon. All agreed that such efforts could proceed, so long as the managements of Corning and Mellon were kept informed about the studies.

In order to develop more product for use in cooperative testing efforts, Dr. Sullivan agreed to install a pilot plant in the basement of Mellon Institute. The first-year budget for the plant included $1500 for equipment, $1800 for operator salary, and $2700 for supplies and overhead—a grand total of $6000!

Ed Mease, a chemical engineer, began work as our pilot plant operator within a month. Working with people from the Blaw-Knox Corporation, he designed a 20-gallon jacketed kettle[26] that could withstand

---

[25]R. R. McGregor and E. L. Warrick, U.S. Patent 2,380,057, 1948.

[26]A jacketed kettle works something like a double boiler. A chemical reaction is carried out in a kettle, which sits inside another larger kettle. The larger kettle is filled with steam and helps to trigger the reaction in the main kettle.

100-pounds-per-square-inch internal pressure. The other piece of equipment needed for production was a 10-foot distillation column, and with this in place, the pilot plant was ready for production.

Pilot Plant Production. The first Grignard reaction in the new unit was carried out on July 20, 1940, and soon there was enough fluid polydimethylsiloxane, the basic silicone "product," available for cooperative testing. Westinghouse and Gulf fellowships were among the first to request samples of these dimethyl fluids for basic research studies. Gulf researchers had a specific application in mind; they wanted to test the new fluids as possible additives for their petroleum oils.

At the same time that we were expanding our capacity at Mellon, Corning was searching for more ethylphenyldichlorosilane for Hyde's 990A resin, to meet the Navy's demand. Hyde's group asked if there would be any possibility of preparing the material in our pilot plant. At the time, a rubber reserve fellowship at Mellon was discontinuing some operations, and we purchased from them a 50-gallon unjacketed kettle. We also acquired a 12-inch-square plate-and-frame filter press. With some other miscellaneous tanks and piping, Mease put together an operating system to produce the materials Corning needed.

One of the first tries at preparing a phenyl Grignard for the production of ethylphenyldichlorosilane was made in the 20-gallon kettle. Shortly after he started up the operation, Ed Mease appeared in Dr. McGregor's office and calmly told him, "There is a fire in the pilot plant." Mac replied, "Why aren't you down there putting it out?" Mease said, "I tried; the kettle is partly full of dry ice, so the whole operation is blanketed. But the dry ice is reacting with the Grignard which formed, and we'll have to wait until that is all consumed." (Dry ice is frozen carbon dioxide, CO_2, which can generally be used to extinguish fires. In this case, although the original fire was out, the kettle was still red-hot because of the unanticipated reaction).

Once the reaction was spent, Mease returned to the plant and found that the heat of the reaction was so great that it had caused bits of magnesium to be fused to the stirrer on the reactor. This approach to producing phenyl Grignards was wisely abandoned.

A phenyl Grignard was finally made in butyl ether in the large kettle, but this proved to be an unworkable and dangerous process as well. Clearly the basement of Mellon Institute, in the heart of the University of Pittsburgh campus, was not the place to conduct even medium-scale chemical reactions. We would have to find another means of producing more starting materials.

Figure 1-3. The "bouncing putty" developed in the labs of Mellon Institute in 1940 became the basis for the popular children's toy SILLY PUTTY®.

Dow Chemical Lends a Hand

In search of larger amounts of product, Frank Hyde asked Eastman Kodak's Chemicals Division to produce 25 pounds of phenyl-trichlorosilane, another silicone starting material. Hyde knew this was only a stopgap measure, and at this point, he suggested to Dr. Sullivan that Dow Chemical might be able to provide assistance. Dow had the chemical engineering know-how and size to develop large amounts of product for Hyde's group, and it had the magnesium and organic ha-lides needed for the Grignard reaction.

Dr. Sullivan knew Dr. Edgar C. Britton, director of research of Dow, and invited him to come to Corning to discuss the proposed production efforts. As a result, Dr. Britton called Mac at Mellon, and in mid-September 1940 we sent Britton the procedure for our pilot-scale etherless Grignard reaction. Soon afterward, Britton's lab began supplying Corning with the ethylphenyldichlorosilane it had requested from Mellon.

The Research Progresses

Early Findings at Mellon

Our work in the Mellon pilot plant yielded many interesting and useful findings in those early days. We were learning much about the basic chemistry of silicones, and our road to discovery took some unexpected detours and interesting turns.

SILLY PUTTY®. Our studies of hydrolysis and polymerization techniques had shown that sulfuric acid increased the molecular weight of polydimethylsiloxane fluids; the higher-weight fluids were more viscous, thicker. We were always looking for higher-molecular-weight materials, which were needed to produce silicone rubber, one of our goals.

By late summer 1940 we knew how to carry fluids to a "gummy" or rubbery state, but we still had not developed a silicone rubber. One of our attempts produced instead a curiously resilient material which we called "bouncing putty." We knew the substance was not the polymer we were looking for, but we added fillers to it and took advantage of its unique properties to astound visitors by bouncing it off the ceilings and walls of our laboratories. We decided to patent this unusual material[27] even though no use was apparent at the time. Later it would be marketed as a popular children's toy, SILLY PUTTY® (Figure 1-3).

Viscosity Index. The Gulf fellowship had been testing our polydimethylsiloxane fluid as a petroleum oil additive at its laboratories near Pittsburgh. Gulf found that the fluid acted as an effective defoamer for petroleum oils. This finding led to an important product for the war effort; it was used in airplanes which flew at high altitudes, to prevent oil from foaming out of the engines.

Gulf also reported that our dimethylsiloxane fluid seemed to have the lowest "viscosity index" of any fluid it had ever tested; that is, its viscosity changed very little under extremes of cold or heat. When we found this out, we began measuring the viscosity of our fluids. Our measurements verified Gulf's research results.

This finding led to the hope of developing more versatile lubricating oils. The oils on the market at the time thickened so much in cold weather that thinner, or lower-viscosity, oils were necessary in winter. Silicone fluids held out the promise of all-weather lubricants.

Resistance to Oxygen. Another important research finding came about through a cooperative study in March 1941. Mine Safety Appliance Company was seeking a lubricant for pumps using oxygen under high pressure in mines. We provided the company with a nonvolatile fluid sample, and its tests showed that the fluid could be exposed to oxygen at high temperatures and at high pressure without oxidizing.

---

[27]R. R. McGregor and E. L. Warrick, U.S. Patent 2,431,878, 1947.

The use of the fluid in oxygen pumps later was dropped because the product was not a good lubricant. However, our discovery of the fluid's resistance to oxidation was important to later work, as most of the uses of this product (which would later be marketed as "DOW CORNING 200® silicone fluid") required that it hold up under high air temperatures.

More Basic Research at Corning

Dr. Hyde continued his research efforts with the aid of the additional resin starting materials prepared at Dow. He recruited Joe Domicone, who had been working in the Corning main plant, and Mary Purcell Roche to assist in the research effort.

At the same time, one key member of the group, Dick Delong, decided to return to school for a Ph.D. degree. To replace him, Bob Fleming, who was just graduating from Cornell with a degree in chemistry, was recruited. Soon the group was filled out by Dr. William Daudt from Harvard.

At Corning, Bill Daudt and Bob Fleming carried out more exploratory research in Hyde's lab. Daudt worked on synthesizing compounds using the normal Grignard reaction and sodium fluosilicate, and Fleming experimented with lithium in the synthesis of organosilicon compounds, an attempt at replacing the expensive Grignard technique for producing starting materials. While the process was technically successful, it too proved to be very costly and was dropped.

One early piece of work by Fleming proved to be a very important contribution to the silicone effort. This was his research into the isolation and characterization of cyclics (compounds with atoms arranged in a ring or closed-chain structure) from dimethylsiloxane compounds. These cyclics later became the starting materials for the silicone rubbers we developed in the labs at Mellon.

Publishing and Patenting

General Electric's Surprise Presentation

At this point, the results of basic research Hyde was carrying out in the Corning labs and experiments we were conducting at Mellon Institute had not been published. In September 1940, however, the presentation of two papers at a professional meeting prompted Hyde quickly to go public with his findings.

The one-hundredth meeting of the American Chemical Society (ACS) was held in Detroit on September 9 to 13, 1940. At that meeting,

"I've found it! It's a cure for the common cold, or it will increase fuel efficiency five hundred per cent, or it will make washday brighter!"

Drawing by W. Miller; ©1984 The New Yorker Magazine, Inc.

two papers were presented in the ACS Division of Inorganic Chemistry. One, by Dr. E. G. Rochow and W. F. Gilliam of General Electric, was called "Polymeric Methyl Silicon Oxides." The other was by W. F. Gilliam, H. A. Liebhafsky, and A. F. Winslow, also of GE; it was entitled "Dimethyl Silicon Dichloride and Methyl Silicon Trichloride."

These papers created quite a stir in Corning, as both presented findings similar to those of Hyde's research group, involving silicone starting materials. Dr. Sullivan called his friend Dr. Coolidge, General Electric's research director, who came to Corning to discuss publication plans. Because of their friendship, Coolidge agreed to hold up publication of the General Electric papers to give Frank Hyde and his people time to publish a paper simultaneously.

Corning and General Electric Publish Findings

As a result, a paper written by Frank Hyde and Dick Delong outlining the findings of their research into silicone starting materials was published in the same issue of the *Journal of the American Chemical Society* as the two GE papers that had been presented at the ACS meeting.[28]

These articles by the General Electric and Corning researchers were the first papers on industrial silicones to appear in a professional journal, and as much as any other event, their publication signaled the beginning of industrial silicone production. The only prior silicone research reported in the journals had been Kipping's reference to the by-products of his research, the products in which he had shown no interest. Little did Kipping know what a world of applications would one day be found for the materials he referred to as "uninviting glues" and discarded as useless.

Accelerating the Patent Effort

It was important for the Corning and Mellon groups to patent the new processes and materials they were developing, in order to remain competitive, particularly with the knowledge that General Electric was also actively pursuing silicone development. Almost from the start of the Corning-Mellon joint research program, this issue was discussed with Walt Rising, one of Corning's patent attorneys.

Rising's experience had been in the glass business, and he was not comfortable dealing with patents involving organosilicon chemistry. This, coupled with the newness of the field of silicone technology, meant that progress was slow in writing definitive patents for the two groups.

The concern over delays in the patent process was heightened when five General Electric patents were issued in October 1941.[29] These covered in some ways methyl, ethyl, and phenyl silanes—silicone starting materials we had also been developing in our labs. Much of the work at both Corning and Mellon Institute was covered by the patents. Both groups were dismayed by this preemptive move.

Shortly after this setback, Hyde and McGregor met with Walt Rising and Fred Knight, Corning's general counsel. The discussion centered on ways to speed up the patent work in Corning. Someone with a very special set of credentials would be needed to handle this new area of patent law.

After a search process that lasted several months, Dr. D. Leigh Fowler, an organic chemist from Brown University, was selected to join Corning's patent effort. Fowler had obtained a law degree in addition to his Ph.D. in chemistry, and he moved quickly to bring his organic background and legal training to bear on the problems of silicone patents.

---

[28]J. F. Hyde and R. Delong, *J. Am. Chem. Soc.*, 63:1194 (1941); E. G. Rochow and W. F. Gilliam, *J. Am. Chem. Soc.*, 63:798 (1941).

[29]E. G. Rochow, U.S. Patents 2,258,218, Oct. 7, 1941; 2,258,219, Oct. 7, 1941; 2,258,220, Oct. 7, 1941; 2,258,221, Oct. 7, 1941; 2,258,222, Oct. 7, 1941.

Despite Leigh Fowler's efforts, however, the patent process continued to move slowly, for just as Corning was accelerating efforts to hasten the process, the government stepped in and placed under secrecy all patents deemed vital to the World War II effort. The new restrictions were broadly applied to any patent application involving materials that the government thought *might* be useful in the war—including those covering some of the early discoveries at Corning and Mellon.

The War Takes Its Toll

The war exacted its toll in other areas as well. Bob Fleming's promising research at Corning was cut short by a call from Uncle Sam. Earlier, when requesting to have his reserve commission status clarified, Fleming had been informed that he'd never be activated "because you are color-blind and underweight." Later, when he received notice to report to New York for induction, Fleming confidently told Dr. Hyde he would be back by Monday. When Monday came, however, Hyde received a call from Fleming saying he was in the Army and was qualified for combat duty. He wasn't to return until the war was over.

The Mellon Institute also felt the effects of the war, when Ed Mease was sent overseas in March 1941. John Goodwin was soon hired to replace him as pilot plant manager.

Dow Chemical Takes an Active Role

Around the time Ed Mease was sent overseas in the spring of 1941, Dr. Clarence Moyle from Dow's Britton lab came to Mellon to learn more about the pilot-scale etherless Grignard process Mease had been managing. He returned to the Britton lab armed with the information, and at this point Dow began to carry out the Grignard process for us, in addition to supplying us with starting materials. Soon Dow would become involved in silicone research efforts of its own.

Collings Heads Up Silicone Research[30]

Early in 1942, Dr. Willard Dow, then president of Dow Chemical, learned of Dr. Britton's project to produce resin starting materials for

---

[30]Much of this information is taken from Robert S. Karpiuk, *Dow Research Pioneers*, Pendell, Midland, Mich., 1984.

Corning and asked Bill Collings to take charge of Dow's silicone developments. Willard Dow had great confidence in Collings, for he had a solid record of accomplishment at Dow.

William R. Collings had joined Dow in 1915, taking a summer job before his senior year in college; after graduation he became a permanent employee. Over the years, Collings had compiled a list of impressive accomplishments within the company. By 1942, when Willard Dow singled him out to head up silicone research and development, he was managing the Cellulose Products Department. His charge was to branch out into the field of silicones while continuing the department's cellulose research efforts.

The Cellulose Products Department. Bill Collings had a strong group of researchers working under him. He had selected Dr. Shailer L. Bass from Dow's organic laboratory to direct the cellulose research effort (Figure 1-4). Dr. Bass had come to Dow in 1929 with a Ph.D. in organic chemistry from Yale University. Melvin J. Hunter also joined the group, with a bachelor's degree in chemistry from Antioch College.

Several others who joined the Cellulose Products Department when it was formed—Toivo Andrew ("Andy") Kauppi, head of Technical Ser-

Figure 1-4. *Left:* Bill Collings, manager of the Cellulose Products Department within Dow Chemical, was selected by Willard Dow to head the silicone project. *Right:* Collings selected Shailer Bass to direct the research effort.

vice and Development (TS&D); Firth ("Zeke") Dennett, in the production group; Howard Fenn, who worked in experimental production of cellulosic derivatives; John Gilkey, Art Gordon, and Roger Kolderman in research; Olin (Olie) Blessing, in the inspection and purification group; and Jim McHard in the analytical and control group—would one day become part of Dow Corning's silicone operation when it was formed as an outgrowth of the Cellulose Products Department.

The Joint Venture Takes Shape

Dow and Corning Joint Venture Meeting

In order to meet Hyman Rickover's demand for 990A, Dr. Hyde's group since 1939 had been trying to expand production of the resin. Dow Chemical had first been called upon to assist with the effort in 1940. By 1942, with production still not up to the Navy's demand, top management from Corning Glass Works and Dow Chemical decided to meet and discuss joint development efforts for the resin.

By this time, it was clear that the field of silicone chemistry had tremendous growth potential that would lead far beyond production of a single resin to solve a wartime problem. The proposed meeting between the two companies would also cover discussion of the broader field of silicone research and development.

On April 1, 1942, five men met in Detroit, Michigan, to discuss the possibility of cooperative research and development of silicone technology: Willard Dow, president of Dow Chemical Company; Glen Cole, president of Corning Glass Works; Harold Boeschenstein, president of Owens Corning Fiberglas; Dr. William R. Veazey, Dow's research coordinator; and Bill Collings, general manager of Dow's Cellulose Products group.

Collings reported on what transpired at this meeting:[31]

> Mr. Boeschenstein was the principal spokesman and he presented many ideas relating to potential uses of silicones. He dwelled at length on the need for heat resistant resins to be used with Fiberglas yarn and fabrics in electrical applications. He thought also that the unusual properties of silicone fluids would find use in other defense applications.
>
> Finally, Corning's President, Glen Cole, proposed in about these

---

[31]Dow Corning, internal memo dated November 13, 1967.

words, "I suggest that Corning Glass Works and The Dow Chemical Company form an equally owned company. We have some inventions and you have chemical know-how. Let's not take stock for these; just consider them of equal value. I propose that we form a new company into which we agree to invest equal amounts of money and then we take equal numbers of shares." As I remember it, Willard Dow readily agreed and there was little further discussion of this proposal.

Glen Cole suggested that a competent man, George Murnane, prepare the formation agreement, and Willard Dow agreed. Mr. Murnane had a national reputation as a business negotiator.

Setting the Research Agenda

Following this "handshake" agreement, a second meeting was held in Corning, New York, on April 9, 1942, among principals of the companies involved to discuss the program of research to be pursued by the new company. The meeting agenda covered four issues:

1. Prospects for use of the new silicone materials being developed

2. Developments under way in the laboratory, and sales to date

3. Expedition of tests on further applications

4. By-products of the manufacture of resins and oils

The first item was the focus of the entire meeting. Discussion centered on the advantages of 990A resin and the current prospects for the sale of 990A and polydimethylsiloxane fluid. Twelve companies were exploring various uses for the resin, and five companies or government agencies were interested in the polydimethylsiloxane fluid (which we referred to as "200 fluid"), which was being used as a defoamer in military aircraft and as a means to dampen the movement of instrument needles to prevent damage to the instruments.

The First Product:
DOW CORNING 4® Compound

An informal joint venture proceeded on the basis of the handshake agreement between Corning Glass Works and Dow Chemical. As it turned out, the first product sold by the new venture was not even on the agenda at the Corning meeting. It was a greaselike compound developed in the Mellon labs in May 1942 by the reaction of aluminum trichloride, $AlCl_3$, with the cyclic pentamer of one of our dimethyl-siloxane fluids.

That same month, Dr. McGregor made a visit to Midland to conduct lubrication tests on our polydimethylsiloxane fluid. At that time he showed Shailer Bass the new compound he'd developed at Mellon. Bass was interested in its potential as a solution to a pressing wartime problem.

Shailer Bass had been a member for some time of a government committee which had been seeking an ignition sealing compound for the rotary engines used on aircraft flown in the war. The aircraft engines were piston-driven with spark plugs, and at high altitudes corona tended to form around the high-voltage lead to the spark plug, causing a loss of ignition. Bass thought the compound Mac had shown him might provide the solution to the ignition problem.

During McGregor's 2-week stay in Midland, efforts were made back in Pittsburgh to duplicate the grease, but all the Mellon attempts failed. Dr. Bass then tried to prepare and succeeded in preparing a similar grease in the Cellulose labs at Dow, by adding silica filler to some of the polydimethylsiloxane fluid Mac had brought along for the lubrication tests. The resulting product was given the name DOW CORNING 4® compound and was patented a few years later.[32] A sample of the compound was submitted to Shailer Bass's committee for testing in aircraft ignition systems.

The committee compared the compound with one of the organic ignition sealing compounds (Scintilla 47) on the market (Table 1-2). The silicone-based DOW CORNING 4® compound demonstrated its superiority to the organic compound in many ways.

The compound worked beautifully in tests. It was forced into the ignition harness of pipes which surrounded the high-voltage leads to the plugs in the aircraft. The compound had good dielectric properties and prevented the corona discharge that caused the ignition failure. By using DOW CORNING 4® compound in the ignition system, an aircraft could remain at 35,000 feet for a full 8 hours; without the aid of the compound, it could safely remain at that altitude for just a few minutes.

The Grease That Helped Win the War. From this point on, the first product of the new, unofficial venture would occupy much time and attention. DOW CORNING 4® compound made a major contribution to the war effort. It made possible the flight of airplanes, B17s and subsequent models, to England and north Africa at a time when the United States

[32]S. L. Bass, U.S. Patent 2,428,608, 1947.

Table 1-2. Properties of Aircraft Ignition Sealing Compound

Property	Scintilla 47	DOW CORNING 4®
Color	Green	Colorless
Reaction to litmus	Neutral	Neutral
Specific gravity	1.2	1.0
Consistency:		
77°F	Sticky plastic	Soft grease
−25°F	Too stiff to apply	Easy to apply
300°F	Flows out	Soft gel
Flash point, ASTM*	370°F	620°F
Fire point, ASTM	470°F	Over 670°F
Water absorption	1% maximum	0.25%
Arc resistance, ASTM	Carbon track; 145 seconds	No carbon track; 81 seconds
Spark resistance:		
1500 sparks/minute	OK for 2 hours	OK for 2 hours
8800 sparks/minute (magneto, 7-mm gap)	Carbon track; 1 minute	Burns to white ash in 10 seconds; no track
Volume resistivity:		
70°F	10^9	1.1×10^{13}
200°F	10^7	9.7×10^{13}
Dielectric strength, volts/mil	275 minimum	300–850
Dielectric constant (at 1000 cycles, 77°F)		2.6
Power factor (at 1000 cycles, 77°F)		2.73%

*American Society for Testing and Materials.

was beginning to lose many aircraft through submarine attacks on the shipping convoys that carried our airplanes across the sea (Figure 1-5).

Research Progress at Dow

Once the informal joint venture was arranged, silicone research accelerated within Dow Chemical. When Willard Dow assigned Collings the

Figure 1-5. *Above*: Crew before one of the B series of airplanes, all of which had rotary engines like the one shown here. *Left*: The ignition harness, not visible, is inside the circular cowl and is filled with DOW CORNING 4® compound to permit high-altitude flights over water.

Figure 1-6. Dr. Melvin J. Hunter (*left*) and Dr. Arthur J. Barry (*right*) managed two groups working on silicone research within Dow Chemical's Cellulose Products Department in the early 1940s.

task of pursuing silicone development early in 1942, much of the cellulose work was discontinued. By mid-1942, after the Detroit meeting, the focus of Dow's Cellulose Products group was exclusively on the new field of silicones. In Collings's July 1942 report to Willard Dow, he listed some of the accomplishments of the Cellulose Products Department since the focus had been shifted to silicones:

- Development of a continuous ethyl Grignard machine
- Shipment of 30 gallons of DOW CORNING® 990A additive (Dr. Hyde's resin)
- Strong demand for DOW CORNING 4® compound as a spark plug sealant
- First draft of George Murnane's proposals for the joint venture completed

Dr. Hunter's Group

Within the Cellulose Products group, two groups of researchers, under Dr. Melvin J. Hunter and Dr. Arthur J. Barry (Figure 1-6), had made considerable progress since the group had been given the task of producing silicones.

Dr. Hunter's group in the early stages of silicone research consisted of Wayne Barrett, Harold ("Hal") Clark, Dick Clark, Don Kime, Larry Rauner, Chester ("Chet") Currie, Zeke Dennett, Jim Fletcher, Earle Smith, Phil Servais, Gerry Van Dyke, and Jean Whiting.

Characterization Studies. Beginning in the fall of 1942, Mel Hunter's group studied the in situ Grignard process developed at Mellon Institute to produce methyl-substituted silicon esters. They progressed from a 2-gallon pressure reactor to a 15-gallon reactor and then turned the production over to Dick Freeman.

The group studied the hydrolysis of the esters and the distribution of product within the cyclic, linear, and high-polymer fractions. They clearly demonstrated the ability to repolymerize cyclics to high polymers and carefully fractionated the distillable low polymers. From these cuts Currie and Hunter identified cyclics, from the trimer through the octamer. Hyde had earlier characterized the trimer and tetramer, but the higher members of the series were new. The group's work on characterizing cyclics expanded on Bob Fleming's earlier experiments and was utilized in later polymerization processes, including my subsequent development of silicone rubber.

Distillation: The Arctic Project. Dick Clark did much of the fractionation of the mixed cyclics in a still located on a porch outside the 298 building in Dow Chemical Company. The column was 5 feet high and 4 inches in diameter and was steam-traced on the outside. The still pot was a 22-liter flask resting in a container of sand and heated with a gas flame. Clark wore his warmest deer hunting clothes and referred to his work as the "arctic project," as it was winter when much of this distillation took place.

More than 50 gallons of mixed cyclics were distilled through this column and later refractionated in smaller stills. The cuts were given to Jim Fletcher, whose desk was near an outside wall. By morning, crystal had formed on the bottom and side of the sample bottles.

Mel Hunter had a great interest in crystals and quickly took these to Dr. Ludo Frevel in Dow's x-ray laboratory, where they were identified as the cyclic octamer. These findings were later published in the *Journal of the American Chemical Society*.[33]

Dr. Barry's Group

Water Repellency. Before pursuing silicone research, Art Barry's group finished work that had been started before the silicone project

[33]L. Frevel and M. J. Hunter, "The Structure of Hexadecamethylcyclooctasiloxane," *J. Am. Chem. Soc.*, 67:2275 (1945).

was announced early in 1942. Dr. Barry had been working on hydrophobing cellulose, making it water-repellent by mixing it with esters and chlorides. He succeeded, but when the question of patenting these materials came up, Dr. Veazey wisely counseled waiting until after the joint venture negotiations were completed, so that the Corning people would not think Dow had been trying to preempt any part of the field.

Direct Processes.   After this early work, Dr. Barry's group turned its attention to silicones and began to study a series of direct processes, those which started with elemental silicon to make silicones (before this, silicones were produced by starting with silicon compounds). If a direct process could be developed, it would be far less expensive than silicone production by means of the Grignard reaction.

Barry's group came close to developing a direct process, but never quite achieved it. While the etherless Grignard process was quite expensive, it was used to prepare diethoxydimethylsilane until after the war ended. Shortly thereafter, General Electric began licensing the first successful direct process.

Scale-Up of Basic Production

As silicone research proceeded in the Cellulose Products Department, many of the group's members got involved in finding ways to prepare ethyl silicate and silicon tetrachloride for the Grignard process. Clarence ("Bud") Lankton, one of the pilot plant people in the Cellulose Products Department, began to form the esters needed in making ethyl silicate through the reaction of alcohol with purchased $SiCl_4$. At some point a process was worked out to prepare the basic $SiCl_4$ by mixing silicon carbide, SiC, with chlorine in a tubular reactor. With these techniques perfected, the group no longer had to rely on outside sources to supply the starting materials needed for silicone production.

Formalizing the Joint Venture

Announcement of the Dow Corning Division

While the three groups at Corning, Mellon, and Dow Chemical were expanding their research efforts, arrangements for the joint venture were proceeding. In August 1942, George Murnane and Corning representatives met again with Dow people in Midland to discuss the details of

Olie Blessing, *Sales Manager,*
became the first employee of the
Dow Corning joint venture.

the joint venture agreement. By this time, demand for the DOW CORNING 4® compound had mushroomed to 1000 pounds per month.

On September 15, 1942, a meeting was held at the Buffalo Club in Buffalo, New York, with Corning Glass Works represented by Glen Cole and Dr. Sullivan, and with Dow represented by Willard Dow, Dr. Veazey, Dr. Britton, and Bill Collings. At this meeting the formation of a joint venture between the two companies was confirmed, and attorneys from each firm were instructed to proceed with preparation of the required legal instruments.

It was agreed that the new organization would begin to function immediately as the Dow Corning Division of the Dow Chemical Company, until a separate legal entity could be established. Management of the division was to be vested in the Management Committee, which had six members: Glen Cole, Dr. Sullivan, and Amory Houghton (chairman of the board of Corning Glass Works) for Corning; Willard Dow, Dr. Veazey, and Bill Collings as Dow representatives. The two companies agreed to invest an initial sum of $500,000 each and a maximum of $100,000 more per year for the next 5 years.

Later in September 1942, at the annual meeting of the American Chemical Society in Buffalo, New York, representatives from Corning Glass Works, Mellon Institute, and Dow Chemical met in the Statler Hilton Hotel and formally announced the formation of the Dow Corning Division of Dow Chemical Company.

The First Employee

Shortly after the September 15 meeting which established the Dow Corning Division, Bill Collings recruited Olie Blessing for the position of division sales manager. Blessing had worked with Collings in developing calcium chloride and cellulose products at Dow and had proved himself a capable, effective sales representative.

Collings knew that Olie Blessing would be the perfect person for the job and called his office on a Friday afternoon to offer him the position. He was told that Blessing was out playing golf. Collings drove with Don Williams, Dow's vice president of sales, to the Midland Country Club golf course. They found Blessing on the fifth green and informed him that he was to head up sales of the new division, and that the job would begin on Monday. Olie Blessing thus became the first official Dow Corning employee.

Progress Report

By December 1942, Collings was able to report that the new division was equipped to produce its own silicon tetrachloride and its own ethyl silicate, thanks to the work done by Art Barry's group. In addition, the division was studying the possibility of using normal Grignards on silicon tetrachloride, was studying the use of a mixed ester chloride, $(C_2H_5O)_2SiCl_2$ to overcome the problems with the close boiling points of the methyl chlorosilanes, was making 200 pounds of fluid for the DOW CORNING 4® compound every week, and was producing 1000 pounds of resin 990A resin per month. A considerable amount of progress had been made in the division which had been formed just 3 months earlier.

The Researchers Meet

In mid-December 1942, the first of a series of research meetings was held in Midland, in the auditorium of the 47 building just outside the Dow Chemical plant. The purpose of the meetings was to provide the three groups of researchers a forum for exchanging information and ideas.

We recorded these research meetings on some of the new long-playing records made from ethyl cellulose. As we listened to a playback of the record of that first meeting in December, many of us were astonished at the intensity in our voices. One member could not believe that he emphasized his points so forcefully as to leave regular loud clicks on the record from his chalk on the blackboard. We were like kids in a candy store, bursting with enthusiasm, filled with excitement over the discoveries we were making and eagerly anticipating the mysteries yet to be unfolded.

The Joint Venture Is Born

Following the initial meetings between Dow and Corning, the boards of directors of both companies discussed the details of the proposed joint venture. Calvin Campbell, general counsel of The Dow Chemical Company, was concerned about the possible antitrust implications of such a venture. As silicones were important to the war effort, and because of this concern, Campbell contacted Under Secretary of War Robert P. Patterson, who subsequently sent a letter to Willard Dow on January 22, 1943, urging that such a joint venture be formed to make products needed in the war effort.

Few companies are "urged" by a government official to form a joint venture, but as a result of Robert Patterson's letter to Willard Dow

(Figure 1-7), on February 9, 1943, a formal agreement was signed by representatives of Corning Glass Works and The Dow Chemical Company to form Dow Corning Corporation.

Each company agreed to subscribe for $50,000 of the capital stock of the new company, with the understanding that additional subscriptions would be needed from time to time. Only $5000 was paid in by each company at the time of incorporation.

WAR DEPARTMENT
OFFICE OF THE UNDER SECRETARY
WASHINGTON, D. C.

JAN 22 1943

Wright, Gordon, Zachry, Parlin & Cahill
63 Wall Street,
New York

Attention: Mr. William E. Dulles

Gentlemen:

You have presented to my office memorandum concerning proposed arrangements by the Dow Chemical Company and your client, Corning Glass Works, for the production of organo-silicon compounds under which the two companies are considering a joint enterprise through the formation of a corporation to further both research and production techniques and to undertake the commercial manufacture and sale of such compounds and products made therefrom.

The Air Forces have conducted comprehensive laboratory tests and full scale engine tests on one of the Dow-Corning compounds, the use of which is eliminating flashover and moisture difficulties encountered in airplane ignition systems. Results of the tests have shown this compound to be superior to any other compound previously developed.

At the present time one of our engine manufacturers is incorporating this compound in engines installed for high altitude planes while other manufacturers are contemplating adoption thereof as soon as adequate manufacturing facilities are available.

Since the development of the compound has resulted from the joint efforts of Corning Glass Works and Dow Chemical Company, I believe that it would be advantageous to the war effort if a corporation was formed by the two concerns in the furtherance of additional research and production technique and practice.

Yours sincerely,

Robert P. Patterson
Under Secretary of War

Figure 1-7. With the approval of the War Department, Dow Chemical and Corning Glass Works were able to proceed with joint venture plans.

William Groening, assistant general counsel of Dow Chemical, drew up the articles of incorporation. These articles were signed on February 1, 1943, and Dow Corning Corporation was granted a charter to operate by the State of Michigan on February 17, 1943.

What began as a concept, a vision, the product of a single imaginative mind, had blossomed over the course of a decade into a viable, growing enterprise with boundless possibilities for the future. Dr. Sullivan's dream of something new, his hope for a better way, was now being realized.

The transformation from the conceptual to the concrete was not an easy one. Looking back at those early days that led to formation of the joint venture, the high spirit of Dr. Hyde's researchers in Corning Glass Works was astounding. The conditions under which the group worked in those pioneering years of silicone research were abysmal by today's standards. The research laboratory, which was not air-conditioned, was situated next to Corning A factory, so that , noise, heat, and dust came through the windows in the summer. The lab had inadequate ventilation and safety standards. The scarcity of resources—the lack of analytical techniques and instruments, and the need for fabricating equipment on the premises—was pointed out earlier.

The obstacles facing the Corning researchers were formidable. But the creativity, the excitement of anticipation, and the sense of satisfaction Dr. Hyde's group experienced far outweighed any inconveniences they faced in carrying out their pioneering work. We experienced those same feelings of excitement and fulfillment in our early research at Mellon Institute. Our working conditions were a great improvement over those at Corning, but had we been working with the researchers back in New York, I doubt our enthusiasm would have been dampened in the slightest. The power of the vision we were pursuing made us oblivious to our surroundings.

Perhaps more striking than the accomplishments of the researchers, in the face of numerous and serious obstacles, was the excellent spirit of cooperation among the three groups at Mellon, Corning, and Dow Chemical in those early days before a formal joint venture agreement was reached. This solid working relationship would serve the new Dow Corning Corporation well, as it would continue to grow and meet the increasing demands of a wartime economy.

2
The War Years: Building the Business

Heaven is not reached at a single bound;
But we build the ladder by which we rise.
JOSIAH B. HOLLAND

Once incorporation papers had been signed, Dow Corning faced the formidable challenge of establishing itself as a strong, independent company. The first order of business was to establish a sound management team and an operating structure to carry the company through its early years.

As soon as the management team and operating structure were in place, Dow Corning could focus on its key immediate goals: building a new plant, hiring the staff needed to continue and increase production of wartime goods, intensifying the research effort, and translating research findings into new products.

Until a fully functioning plant was operating, research and development work would continue in three separate locations: Corning Glass Works in Corning, New York; the Mellon Institute in Pittsburgh, Pennsylvania; and the Dow Chemical Company labs in Midland, Michigan. A substantial commitment of resources and a major coordination of efforts would be required to transform Dow Corning during the war years from a fledgling operation with a handful of employees to a growing, vital silicones manufacturer employing hundreds of workers.

Start-Up

Directors and Officers

The first board of directors of the newly formed Dow Corning Corporation (Figure 2-1) included Willard Dow, Dr. E. C. Britton, Bill Collings, and Dr. William R. Veazey from Dow Chemical; and Amory Houghton, Glen Cole, Dr. Sullivan, and Eugene Ritter from Corning Glass Works. Dr. Sullivan was named chairman of the board, and Dr. Britton secretary.

The first official meeting of the board was held on February 23, 1943, in New York City, just a week after the company had been granted its operating charter. Officers of the new company (Table 2-1) were named at the meeting. Dr. Sullivan was appointed Dow Corning's first president; Collings was named vice president and general manager.

With the management team in place, it was time to spread word of the new company to the larger business community. Following the first

Figure 2-1. Dow Corning's first board of directors: *left to right*, William R. Collings, Dr. Edgar C. Britton, Amory Houghton, Dr. Eugene C. Sullivan, Glen W. Cole, Eugene W. Ritter, and Dr. William R. Veazey. Willard Dow was not present when the photograph was taken.

Table 2-1. First Elected Officers of Dow Corning Corporation

President	Dr. Eugene C. Sullivan
Vice president	William R. Collings
Secretary	Dr. Edgar C. Britton
Treasurer	Charles LaFollette
Assistant secretary	Eugene W. Ritter
Assistant secretary	Calvin A. Campbell
Assistant treasurer	Burl D. Huber

board meeting, Willard Dow sent telegrams to local and national professional and business journals, formally announcing the formation of the Dow Corning joint venture. At the same time, operating agreements were being negotiated with Dow Chemical Company and Corning Glass Works.

Operating Agreements

Dow Corning officially began operating on March 1, 1943. The new firm's fiscal year was set to mirror Dow Chemical's, ending on May 31. On March 2, Dow Chemical signed agreements to produce silicone compounds, fluids, and resins for resale by Dow Corning. Corning Glass Works and Dow Chemical Company also agreed at this time to conduct research for Dow Corning on a contract basis.

On March 3, Charles LaFollette, Dow Corning treasurer, met in Midland with Earl Bennett, treasurer of Dow Chemical, to discuss the early operating phase of the corporation. The two agreed that Dow Chemical would continue to manufacture materials for Dow Corning to sell until such time as the new company had its own manufacturing facilities.

Under terms of the joint venture, Dow and Corning would make available to Dow Corning "all inventions in the field of organosilicon compounds" which they then owned or might own until 1958. Although ownership of their respective patents would remain with Dow Chemical and Corning Glass, Dow Corning would receive royalty-free licenses and the right to sublicense others.

Report of the First Fiscal Year

Just a few months after joint venture arrangements were formalized and operating procedures established, Bill Collings delivered his first report to the shareholders, for the 3-month fiscal year ended May 31, 1943. In it, he outlined three product areas on which the new company was focusing—resins, fluids, and the DOW CORNING 4® compound—and discussed sales figures and production capacity. A brief financial report for the truncated fiscal year showed a loss of $9000 on sales of $75,000.

Even before the new firm was incorporated, Collings had been working with Bill Caldwell in Dow's engineering group on plans for a new plant for silicone research and production. Collings pointed out in his year-end report that such a plant for Dow Corning was in the design stages and would require the approval and support of the board of directors.

Capital Funding

The new joint venture got off the ground with an initial $10,000 investment in February 1943. The total capital funding required was estimated at $750,000, but this sum proved to be inadequate. By the end of 1944, $1.7 million had been invested in Dow Corning, the bulk of the funds being allocated for construction of the new plant. The combined investments of the two parent companies were translated into shares of Dow Corning stock as shown in Table 2-2.

Production Begins

Until the new plant was built, Dow Corning relied on facilities set aside within Dow Chemical to meet its production needs, as Bennett and LaFollette had discussed. The Britton laboratory in the 20A building developed a pilot plant for Dow Corning, where the DOW CORNING® 990A additive was made. The Cellulose Products Department was given

Table 2-2. Initial Investment by Dow Chemical and Corning Glass Works

Date	Investment	Shares of Dow Corning stock
February 1943	$ 10,000	100
June 1943	90,000	900
August 1943	700,000	7,000
June 1944	200,000	2,000
October 1944	700,000	7,000

responsibility for producing fluid products and compounds for Dow Corning.

Starting Materials

Ethyl Silicate (Etherless Grignards). With the operating agreements in place and resin production proceeding in Dr. Britton's lab, Dow's Cellulose Products Department turned its attention to developing silicone fluids and compounds for Dow Corning. Ethyl silicate was one key material needed for the etherless Grignard production process. The only source for the material at this time was the Union Carbide Corporation. Delivery of ethyl silicate

Howard Fenn, *Dow Corning's first production manager.*

from Union Carbide was slow, several weeks for even the smallest of orders, and these delays prompted the production group, under Howard Fenn, to establish an ethyl silicate plant within Dow.

The production of ethyl silicate was supervised by Bud Lankton, who reported to Howard Fenn. The operation proceeded quite smoothly, although on one occasion a 55-gallon drum, in which silicon tetrachloride was received, escaped from the operator about midnight. The bung popped out, spilling the contents on the floor, forcing the evacuation of all employees from the east side of the Dow plant to escape the acrid, choking odor. If the production of ethyl silicate were to become a permanent process, the 55-gallon drums would have to be replaced and a better means of handling silicon tetrachloride found.

Alkylchlorosilanes (Normal Grignards). At the same time, Gordon Brown and Bill Kuhlman were developing a pilot plant within the Cellulose Products Department to make alkylchlorosilanes used in the Grignard reaction for producing DOW CORNING 200® silicone fluid. The process involved the conventional Grignard synthesis with diethyl ether and pure magnesium chips. Ira Hutchison was assigned the task of developing a method for drying the ether used in the process, and soon he was given responsibility for supervising the entire process.

In addition to finding a way to dry the ether, machinery was needed to process the raw magnesium used in the Grignard reaction. The magnesium supplied by Dow for this purpose came in the form of 12-pound "cell slugs" which looked like loaves of bread. These had to be converted into proper chips with considerable surface area. A special chipping machine was designed and built by Fred Dulmage.

Silicon Tetrachloride. Silicon tetrachloride, $SiCl_4$, was another key starting material needed by Dow Corning, and a project to develop a process for making the chemical was initiated, with Lee DePree in charge. The process was developed just in time to design a silicon tetrachloride unit for the new plant under construction.

Ira Hutchison, who had been responsible for the Grignard process, was given the task of designing the distillation columns needed for the new unit. Because of World War II, outside engineering help was almost impossible to find. This meant, that much of the design for the new plant had to be developed by in-house engineers. Fortunately, Dow Corning had access to a highly capable in-house engineering staff, including Gordon Brown of Dow Chemical, who supervised the distillation calculations.

Calculations were made for the separation of methyl chlorosilanes in addition to ethyl chlorosilanes. There was a short period of time during which plans for the new Dow Corning plant focused exclusively on ethyl silicon compound production, primarily because such production was familiar to Bill Collings and the ethyl cellulose researchers at Dow Chemical. However, when it became evident that methyl compounds were superior to ethyl at high temperatures, planning was broadened to incorporate the production of methyl compounds as well.

Finished Products

Fluid Production. Initially the production of dimethyldiethoxysilane, the intermediate product used in making fluids and compounds for Dow Corning, was handled by George Greminger, employing the etherless Grignard reaction developed at Mellon. Distillation and separation of the products of this reaction were carried out in a distillation system built in a corner of the 340 building.

All went well until an implosion occurred within the still pot, ripping it apart. Despite Zeke Dennett's heroic efforts to scoop up what he could, the valuable intermediate product was lost. Investigation revealed that the jacket of the still pot, which was designed for steam pressures up to 15 pounds per square inch, had operated for quite a while at 150 pounds per square inch. The still pot had come from Dow salvage, and its history and design specifications were only vaguely known. A new higher-pressure still pot was obtained, and no further distillation problems arose.

Once the distillation process was complete, the next step was hydrolysis and polymerization of the dimethyldiethoxysilane to produce the fluid products. This process was carried out in a glass-lined kettle in the 340 building and was supervised by Zeke Dennett. The kettle was equipped with a short column and receivers so that volatile products could be removed from the manufactured fluid. The final devolatilization of the fluid was carried out in an improvised molecular still and the production process completed by filtering the fluid through a plate-and-frame press.

Compound Production. While the fluid-production process for Dow Corning was being established within the Cellulose Products Department, Larry Rauner began supervising production of the DOW CORNING 4® compound in Dow's 369 building. Rauner's group had considerable problems early on with gelling of the product after it had been packaged in collapsible tubes or cartridges. Once that problem was solved and production of DOW CORNING 4® compound was well under control, the group began producing a few variations as well: a stopcock grease, a plug-cock grease, and a general-purpose compound named "DOW CORNING® 7 compound."

Quality control was an important aspect of the production process from the inception of the new company, and the task of monitoring quality was given to Larry Rauner. In addition to manufacturing DOW CORNING 4® compound, Rauner tested it against specifications set by the Bendix Aviation Corporation, with Jean Whiting running the materials tests.

The Plant Is Built

Rickover Visit: Magnesium, Please

While the design for the new Dow Corning plant had already been developed, no construction could take place unless magnesium, an essential ingredient in the Grignard reaction, could be purchased. The United States was at war, and magnesium was under priority control. Dow Chemical was producing magnesium at the time; but it was impossible for Dow Corning to purchase the material from Dow without a government allocation.

The problem was soon resolved. In the spring of 1943, while the new plant was still in the planning stage, Owens Corning attempted to fly Hyman Rickover (Figure 2-2) into Midland to see the progress being made on production of DOW CORNING® 990A additive (formerly called "990A resin") in the Britton lab. However, bad weather grounded the plane in Detroit, and a car was sent down to bring Rickover to Midland.

Much time and effort had been spent in preparing for Rickover's visit, including preparations for a formal luncheon at the Midland Country Club. The car bringing him to Midland arrived in time for

Figure 2-2. Dr. Edgar C. Britton, director of organic research, The Dow Chemical Company, with Lieutenant Fluke and Commander Rickover, both of the electrical section of the U.S. Navy Bureau of Ships.

lunch, but Rickover demanded to be taken directly to the 20A building where the resin was made. Dr. Veazey and Olie Blessing arranged to have the lunch sent from the country club to Dow Corning's first office building, where it was consumed during a tour of the building.

After lunch, Rickover returned to Detroit in the Dow car. En route, he asked what the group needed to continue production of its products for the Navy. The answer was "magnesium." Rickover then gave the group an order for 25 motors, 25 pounds of grease for the bearings, and paint to coat the motors. This order carried with it the priority needed to purchase magnesium, allowing construction of the new Dow Corning plant to proceed.

Construction Begins

With Rickover's order in hand, an authorization to provide labor and materials to build the new plant, at an estimated cost of $750,000, was approved by Dow Corning's board of directors in September 1943. Carl Branson, a longtime Dow employee and an expert in plant construction, was named project manager.

Because of Branson's extensive experience at Dow, work on the new plant moved forward rapidly. Construction began soon after the authorization was signed; the 101 building, a modest office unit, was completed and the roadway system under construction before winter. The 80-acre plant site, on Saginaw Road about a mile east of Dow's plant, was owned by Dow and had been used in an unsuccessful attempt to grow aspen trees as a source of cellulose to produce ethyl and methyl cellulose.

Since the government had placed restrictions on all purchases of new materials during the war, the construction group relied on its access to the Bureau of Ships excess property lists to obtain many of the items needed for the plant. Much of this excess property had already seen extensive service before it was sold to industry. For example, the original Dow Corning water tower, obtained from the lists, was 42 years old at the time it was purchased.

Architect Alden Dow, noted for his use of color, open spaces, and natural lighting, designed the main office building (101) and the traffic and shop building (102). A plant protection department also was established in 101, at a time when most of the plant site was still a cow pasture, with an automobile used as the gate house.

Production Moves to the New Plant Site

Production began moving to the new site in the spring of 1944 (Figure 2-3). As the major manufacturing buildings in the new plant—301, 302, 303, and 304—reached the piping stage, the Dow Chemical personnel who had been selected to supervise plant operations were transferred to Dow Corning so that they would be on site to monitor the last stages of construction. These men were:

Bill Kuhlman—301 building (Grignard production)

Ira Hutchison—302 building (distillation)

Zeke Dennett—303 building (fluids and resins)

Bud Lankton—304 building ($SiCl_4$ process)

These building supervisors reported to Howard Fenn, who had been named production manager of the new plant, or to Gordon Brown, assistant production manager. Bill Caldwell was named general plant manager.

Around this time it was determined that more money would be needed to complete construction, and funding was doubled to

Figure 2-3. *Above:* Construction begins at the site of Dow Corning's first plant (fall 1943). *Below:* Office building 101, early 1944, at the Midland plant entrance.

$1,500,000. By the end of the project, the total cost of the new plant had risen to $2,100,000, almost triple the original estimate.

While work was proceeding on the manufacturing buildings, construction of 101, the main office building; 102, the traffic and shop building; and 103, which housed the newly combined Analytical and Resin laboratory, was completed, along with the pilot plant building that stood next to building 103.

Clarence Moyle, who had worked in Dr. Britton's lab, transferred from Dow at this point to take responsibility for the pilot plant. Art

Webb made the move along with Moyle, and soon they were joined by Harry Dingman, also of Dow.

Official Start-Up of the Dow Corning Plant

One by one, the manufacturing processes were begun at the new site. Gordon Brown started the continuous Grignard pilot plant in building 301 in May 1944. A month later the first simultaneous Grignard for the production of phenylmethylchlorosilane was also carried out in 103 building.

In September 1944, Bud Lankton began preparing $SiCl_4$ in building 304. In November, the first Grignard and phenyl-methyl coupling were carried out in 301. In February 1945, production of methylchloro-silanes began in 301. These materials were distilled in building 302, and the pure dimethyldichlorosilane separated was used in the production of the DOW CORNING 200® silicone fluid after hydrolysis. Three men helped to make this early plant operation a success in their new roles as shift supervisors: Ariel Haebler, Harold Locke, and Don Ross.

As soon as the pilot group began to make some intermediate products, Jim Fletcher and Jean Whiting, from Mel Hunter's research group at Dow, joined the pilot effort to prepare batches of resin. The objective of the pilot plant group was to establish optimum conditions for later plant-scale operations.

In the latter part of 1944, Zeke Dennett (also in Hunter's group), with Jim Fletcher's help, began work in 303, the polymer finishing facility. January 1, 1945, was arbitrarily designated as the start-up date for the 303 building, where the products were finished and readied for shipment, and with it the official start-up of production at Dow Corning was established in union contract negotiations.

Expanding the Work Force

Dow Corning needed many hourly workers in its new plant, and it was a natural transition to bring some from Dow Chemical. As the focus of the war effort changed, a chemical warfare complex at Dow was shut down. Many of the skilled employees from this unit elected to transfer to new jobs at Dow Corning, bringing with them the valuable experience in chemical operations they'd gained at Dow. Dow Corning also obtained experienced people from a plant Dow operated in Ludington, Michigan, which was shut down at the end of World War II.

Many of these former Dow employees also operated small farms on the side. Collings liked people with farm backgrounds, because of his feeling that they were hands-on workers, self-reliant and reliable. These were people who, in Collings's words,"knew how to work and fix things themselves when things went wrong." This sort of employee would prove valuable in the new plant, where the start-up of new machinery and new processes almost guaranteed the need for workers who could "fix things."

Collings was an aggressive recruiter. He actively solicited staff from Dow Chemical, often talking to a recruit on Thursday or Friday, asking whether the person would like to transfer to Dow Corning, and explaining the job he had in mind. If the recruit hesitated, Collings would tell the prospective employee to think it over—and report to work on Monday.

Establishing Departments

Engineering and Support Services.   Once manufacturing operations were in place, staff departments were established at the new site. A purchasing service was begun in the new office building, 101. Shop service, receiving, and a traffic department were established in 102. In September 1944 an engineering department was formed; with available space now in short supply, it had to be located in a room in a vacated construction shanty at the site.

Personnel.   Mary Dawson was hired to head up a formal personnel department. Before this time, no one in particular had been assigned responsibility for personnel issues. As a result, job seekers who walked in off the street had routinely been interviewed by several of the top managers and in many cases had been offered jobs on the spot.

Sales.   Following the first abbreviated fiscal year, sales moved at a brisk pace. Revenue for the new company's first complete fiscal year ending May 31, 1944, just surpassed the $1 million mark. By the end of 1945, sales had grown to nearly $1.4 million.

During this war period, demand shifted away from resins. Sales during these last years of the war were mostly of DOW CORNING 4® compound for use as an ignition sealant, some fluid for damping of aircraft instruments, and fluid for antifoaming of aircraft engine oil and submarine diesel oil. Despite the initial focus on resins, demand for resin products did not meet the high level of expectations set for them, partially because the Dow researchers were not able during the war years to perfect the resins Rickover needed to aid the Navy effort.

As sales grew, so did Olie Blessing's sales department. Roger

Kolderman, who had been active in the Cellulose Products Department at Dow, soon joined the department. Charlie Sanford came to the group early in 1944.

Advertising. With operations in place at Dow and Corning, and the new plant in the pilot stages, the sales department began to advertise. As a first step in spreading the word about its unique new silicone products, in June 1944 a series of news releases was mailed to various segments of the local and national news and business media. The releases emphasized the unique properties of Dow Corning's silicone fluids and resin products and touted the fact that a modern chemical plant was under construction and would be functioning later that summer.

After this early announcement, the sales department began to develop print advertising for some of its products. A brochure for DOW CORNING 200® silicone fluid was developed, and a sales bulletin describing stopcock grease was produced, introducing the product as a lubricant for laboratory glassware, as a way of bringing silicones to the attention of chemists.

After these initial promotional efforts, Lou Putnam was hired to manage a full-fledged advertising department, which was formed in January 1945. He in turn hired John Church as his assistant, and the two-man department was housed in a small construction shed along with plant electricians, pipefitters, and construction engineers.

With a minimal first-year budget, it was clear that extensive promotion would not be possible, and the more expensive forms of advertising, such as radio, could not even be considered. The print advertising begun by the sales department could continue, but the department would have to devise other innovative approaches to promoting Dow Corning products.

One approach was indeed innovative; unfortunately, it almost broke the bank. Putnam decided to prepare an exhibit to demonstrate Dow Corning technology at a trade show to be held in the Statler Hotel in Detroit. The exhibit included silicone-insulated electric motors subjected to high heat and humidity.

A good chunk of the meager $400 budget set for the 3-day show went into chain-hoisting the motors to the second floor of the Statler Hotel, where the trade show was taking place. The remainder of the trade show budget, after setup, was placed in a drawing account with the hotel, in John Church's name.

What Putnam hadn't counted on was the enthusiastic response of the salespeople in participating in the show. When the show began, the sales department set up a first-rate hospitality suite in the hotel, with sumptuous hors d'oeuvres and flowing champagne. Late in the afternoon of the first day of the show, the hotel credit manager called, requesting payment for a sizable bill that wiped out the drawing account many times over. Thanks to the enthusiasm of the sales staff, Putnam was forced to call Burl Huber, assistant treasurer, in Midland to bail him out.

This particular innovative approach to promoting Dow Corning products was quickly abandoned, but the advertising department developed a variety of other advertisements and promotions that succeeded in steadily increasing the volume of sales during the war years and beyond (Figure 2-4).

Progress Report

While departments were still being established at the new plant and the transition from manufacturing at Dow to production at Dow Corning continued, Bill Collings submitted his first report on the progress of the new company to Glen Cole, president of Corning Glass Works. In this letter to Cole, dated September 9, 1944, Collings highlighted Dow Corning's achievements and reported on the industry in general as it had progressed since incorporation just 1½ years earlier. The main points of Collings's letter are discussed below.

Profits. Dow Corning had made a profit of $24,000 in its first complete fiscal year ended May 31, 1944, offsetting the $9000 loss of the abbreviated fiscal year 1943.

Products. The new company's products could be divided into three groups:

Group 1: Phenylsilicon Compounds. In group 1 were products containing substantial amounts of phenylsilicon compounds. Primary in this group were the impregnating varnishes for Fiberglas cloth. Four companies—Westinghouse, Anaconda, Phelps Dodge, and Allis Chalmers—were the principal users who were working cooperatively with Dow Corning on developing and applying these new resins.

Group 1 products also included materials for making high-temperature enamels for protective coatings. These coatings were used on such items as boiler stacks, hot ducts, stoves, motor exhaust manifolds, and silicone-glass-insulated high-temperature electric motors.

Finally, group 1 products included the 700 series fluids, which were superior to the existing two series of fluids in heat resistance and lubricating properties.

Group 2: Methyl Substituents. Products in group 2 were of the heat-hardening type, mainly methyl substituents. They were used principally

Figure 2-4. The Paul Bunyan series of advertisements was one of the first efforts of Lou Putnam's advertising department.

for bonding Fiberglas cloth to make laminated heat-resistant structures for a variety of electrical uses. This group also included baking varnishes for rotating coils.

Group 3: Fluids, Compounds, and Rubber. Group 3 products were those which stemmed from the fluid-manufacturing process still being operated within Dow Chemical. This group included the 200 and 500 fluids and various sealing compounds. A new member of this group was silicone rubber.

Competition. The only competition to this point came from General Electric, and very little of its product had been seen in the marketplace. Much of GE's silicone output appeared to be utilized internally, in its own equipment.

General Electric had been reluctant to recommend and build equipment for the Navy, which seemed to indicate it had not progressed as far as Dow Corning had in production of the heat-resistant resin needed in motor insulation. Westinghouse appeared to be leading the electrical industry in the use of silicones in electrical equipment, with the result that even General Electric had begun requesting resin from Dow Corning in order to remain competitive.

Speculation was that it would be a long time before General Electric would be self-sufficient and pose a serious competitive threat. Other competition might arise from chemical companies which had experience with chlorine and chlorine products, used in preparing silicon tetrachloride needed for the Grignard reaction.

Publicity. Collings pointed out that silicones, and Dow Corning, were receiving favorable publicity in a number of magazines:

- *Electrical World* in its July 22, 1944, issue editorialized that:

  [One] profound influence upon the whole field of electrical apparatus design is certain to be the result of the new silicones recently announced.[1]

- An article about postwar markets, which appeared in the August 1944 issue of *Chemical and Metallurgical Engineering,* stated that:

  [The] most propitious single wartime development in the entire resins and plastics field is the recent commercialization of the silicone series of resins by Dow Corning Corporation.[2]

- *The Westinghouse Engineer,* in a September 1944 article about silicones in the electronics field, concluded with this statement:

---

[1]Editorial, p. 84.

[2]"Chloride Industry," p. 121.

Unquestionably the new silicone resins constitute one of the greatest advances made in electrical insulation.[3]

Much progress had been made in the year and a half since incorporation papers were signed. A new plant had been built, employees hired, departments established, and production transferred from Dow Chemical to Dow Corning. In addition, throughout this period the research effort had continued to build and to yield new discoveries about the properties and potential applications of the silicones.

The Research Progresses

Silicone research progressed rapidly once the joint venture was formalized. Dr. Hyde's group in Corning Glass Works in New York expanded and continued its basic studies. The group at Mellon Institute in Pittsburgh entered the new field of silicone rubber. Researchers in Dow's Cellulose Products Department in Midland, Michigan, continued their direct-process work and made many other fundamental contributions to silicone chemistry during these war years.

While the groups worked independently, the research conferences begun in December 1942 continued to bring them together periodically throughout the remainder of the war years. These meetings provided a valuable forum for the exchange of information between the Dow, Corning, and Mellon researchers as they sought to build on their collective base of knowledge about organosilicon compounds.

Corning Group

From 1943 until the end of the war in mid-1945, Frank Hyde's group in Corning Glass Works consisted of Bill Daudt, Ken Johannson, Joe Domicone, and Mary Purcell Roche. Julius Torok also participated briefly in the group's work. As noted earlier, Bob Fleming had entered the armed services and Dick Delong had returned to graduate school (Figure 2-5).

Basic Patents: Hyde 19. Frank Hyde continued to develop new techniques for improving on his DOW CORNING® 990A additive. At the same time, the entire Corning group became involved in developing the comprehensive patent case "Hyde 19."

---

[3]Graham Moses, "New Silicone Resins Boost Insulation Temperature Limits."

"Now, see here, Dr. Smalley! I smell fudge again!"

Drawing by Vietor; ©1982 The New Yorker Magazine, Inc.

The processing of the Hyde 19 patent case, involving some 125 examples of silicone compounds, went on for several years as a result of interference proceedings and separate patent cases that were carved out of it. Issuance of patents was further delayed because of wartime secrecy. Most of the Hyde 19 patents were finally issued on October 25, 1949.

The Hyde 19 case, along with other early copolymer patents,[4] covered a wide range of organosilicon compounds which yielded a great variety of Dow Corning products. These basic patents (which were delayed because of their wartime classification as "secret") also proved useful as leverage in subsequent cross-licensing discussions with General Electric.

Water Repellency and Fiber Dyeing.   As a result of the basic research conducted by Dr. Hyde's group in Corning during the war, a number of

---

[4]W. Daudt, U.S. Patents 2,446,135, 1948; 2,451,664, 1948; 2,468,869, 1949; J. F. Hyde, U.S. Patents 2,438,478, 1948; 2,441,098, 1948; 2,441,320, 1948; 2,449,940, 1948; 2,450,594, 1948; 2,455,999, 1948; 2,456,783, 1948; 2,457,677, 1948; 2,458,944, 1949; 2,460,457, 1949; 2,462,267, 1949; 2,462,640, 1949; 2,470,562, 1949; 2,480,822, 1949; 2,489,139, 1949; J. F. Hyde and W. Daudt, U.S. Patent 2,443,353, 1948.

Figure 2-5. The Corning research group in 1942 (*left to right*): Dr. William Daudt, Dr. O. K. Johannson, Dr. J. Franklin Hyde, and Julius Torok.

applications for silicone compounds were patented, in addition to patenting of the basic compounds themselves.[5] One of the most useful early applications of the work was Frank Hyde's treatment of glass fibers, using hydrolyzed silanes, to create a water-repellent product. Ken Johannson also treated glass fibers with hydrolyzable silanes to form a coating which permitted dyeing of the fibers.

Silaneal Humidity Treatment. Another early application of silicones was the maintenance of high surface resistance to humidity for glass-based electronic components. Ken Johannson had treated glass surfaces with chlorosilanes to achieve water repellency, and this work led to development of the "silaneal" process for treating electrical components for resistance to water. Harry Laudenslager and Julius Torok were also active in this work.

Polymerization Studies: The Road to Rubber. One important study made by Dr. Hyde during the war years was that of the polymerization

[5]J. F. Hyde, U.S. Patents 2,439,689, 1948; 2,467,976, 1949; 2,490,357, 1949; J. F. Hyde and O. K. Johannson, U.S. Patents 2,438,055, 1948; 2,453,092, 1948; O. K. Johannson, U.S. Patents 2,436,304, 1948; 2,466,434, 1949.

of cyclic siloxanes to yield high polymers. Later, this became one of the chief methods used in forming high polymers. In the course of his polymerization experiments, Dr. Hyde produced a gelled solid, useful later on as a raw material in the development of silicone rubber.

Together, Hyde and Johannson conducted another study of importance to the work on silicone rubber, the preparation and characterization of sodium salts of mono-substituted silanes. These salts proved useful by catalyzing the polymerization of cyclic siloxanes, an important step in developing the high polymers needed in silicone rubber. This research was covered by two patents.[6]

X-Ray Studies: Settling an Old Score. In 1945, Frank Hyde and Mary Purcell Roche developed and characterized a series of diphenylsiloxane cyclics in the course of their basic research. The two had clearly identified two forms of the cyclic trimer and three forms of the cyclic tetramer. Dr. Ludo Frevel of Dow Chemical used his expertise in x-ray identification to fully characterize these new cyclic compounds. The results of this research were published 2 years later in the *Journal of the American Chemical Society.*[7]

Publication of the results settled an old disagreement between Professor Kipping and Dr. Hyde. Earlier, Kipping had written the editor of the journal suggesting that Dr. Hyde had "impugned my reputation" by disagreeing with the results of an earlier experiment Kipping had performed. In a paper published in 1941, Dr. Hyde had quoted melting points for diphenylsilane diol as 342°F, whereas Kipping had reported 266 to 270°F.

Dr. Hyde speculated that the difference in reported melting points had probably been due to the fact that Kipping had used soft-glass melting-point tubes rather than Pyrex tubes, and the surface alkali had caused breakdown of the diol. Hyde resolved the dispute by performing two separate experiments and showing that his diol, which melted at 342°F in Pyrex-brand glass melting-point tubes, did indeed melt at 266 to 270°F in soft-glass melting-point tubes. He set the record straight by noting this discrepancy in a letter to the journal *Chemistry and Industry.*

Studies at Mellon

Our research at Mellon during the war years covered sulfuric acid polymerization of siloxanes, including cyclics; mono-tri resins (formed by

[6]J. F. Hyde and O. K. Johannson, U.S. Patents 2,438,055, 1948; 2,453,092, 1948.

[7]J. F. Hyde, L. Frevel, H. Nutting, P. Petrie, and M. Purcell, "Diphenylcyclosiloxanes," *J. Am. Chem. Soc., 69:488 (1947).*

combining monomethylchlorosilane and trimethylchlorosilane); lubrication testing; oxidation studies; physical property studies; and correlation of physical properties with the chemical components of the compounds we were developing. In addition, we continued exploring the new field of silicone rubber.

At the time of incorporation, the Mellon group consisted of three members in addition to me: Dr. McGregor, John Goodwin, who managed the pilot plant, and Helena Corsello, who had been hired the previous September to assist Mac.

In March 1943, with Dow Chemical handling operations for the new joint venture and a new plant in the planning stages, the Mellon pilot plant was discontinued, and shortly afterward John Goodwin joined the Navy, leaving three of us to carry on the research begun before incorporation. In the summer of 1943 we were joined by John Speier, who would add immeasurably to our understanding of silicone chemistry in the ensuing years.

Dr. McGregor.   Dr. McGregor studied sulfuric acid polymerization of dimethylsiloxanes, in a continuing attempt to generate high-molecular-weight materials. With this technique, polymerization would occur to some extent at room temperature, but the process was accelerated at elevated temperatures, between 212 and 482°F. A patent was issued covering this work.[8]

During the March 1943 joint research conference (Figure 2-6), Mac attempted to demonstrate this method of polymerizing cyclics. He added the sulfuric acid to what he was told was a beaker of cyclics and stirred while he continued his talk. When the cyclics did not increase in viscosity after some 20 minutes, he suspected someone had tampered with them.

No one ever admitted to adding a small amount of end blocker, hexamethyldisiloxane, to the cyclics. While the practical joke ruined Dr. McGregor's presentation, it did demonstrate, for all to see, how small amounts of end blocker could be used to control viscosity.[9]

Dr. McGregor's acid polymerization technique was further studied as a method of polymerizing the cyclic tetramer of dimethylsiloxane. This technique of polymerization became important in the plant processes for certain acidic-type polymers, including a defoaming product, DOW CORNING® Antifoam A compound, developed after the war.

---

[8]R. R. McGregor and E. L. Warrick, U.S. Patent 2,437,204, 1948.

[9]An end blocker is a material that prevents a molecule from polymerizing further; it controls the length of the molecule and thus the viscosity of the material.

Figure 2-6. The Dow Corning research team meets in Midland for one of the many research conferences held in the early days. *Front row (left to right):* Art Barry, Frank Hyde, Rob Roy McGregor, Pauline Hopfer, Mary Thayer, John Goodwin, Earl Warrick, Fred Knight. *Second row:* Paul Samsel, John Gilkey, Mel Hunter, Bill Daudt, Shailer Bass, Leigh Fowler, Olie Blessing. *Third row:* Jim McHard, Andy Kauppi, Hal White, Ken Bacon, Dick Clark, Dick Freeman, Bill Collings. *Fourth row:* Phil Servais, Earl Kropscot, Bill Pedersen, George Greminger, Chet Currie, Bill Kuhlman, Avery Stearns, Jim Fletcher. *Fifth row:* Luther Berhenke, Zeke Dennett.

Although Dr. McGregor and Helena Corsello conducted most of these polymerization experiments, the Mellon fellowship was so small that discussions and planning were quite regular among all the members. As a result, many of the early patents were issued jointly.

In addition to the work on sulfuric acid polymerization, McGregor and Corsello carried out lubrication studies on DOW CORNING 200® silicone fluid. The results of their research confirmed earlier findings that the fluids did not work well in this capacity.

Warrick.   During this wartime period, I studied a number of mono-tri resins with degrees of substitution (average number of organic groups per silicon atom) between 1.2 and 1.6. These resins were in the all-methyl system; I was studying them because a paper by Dr. Paul J.

Table 2-3. Temperature of Siloxane
Compounds for Equal Induction Periods*

Dimethylsiloxanes	392.0°F
Diethylsiloxanes	280.4
Dibutylsiloxanes	248.0
Diamylsiloxanes	235.4

*Temperature at which oxidation rates for all
compounds are equal.

Flory[10] had shown that such resins could be carried further toward the higher molecular weights we were seeking, without gelation.

During the course of my research I measured a number of physical properties of cyclic and linear polymers and incorporated this information into a report on the structure of methyl silicane polymers.[11] The research was intended to aid in correlating physical properties of these new compounds with their chemical components.

In addition, early in 1943 I made studies of the oxidation resistance of various dialkylsiloxanes—methyl-, ethyl-, butyl-, and amyl-. We knew from the cooperative study with Mine Safety Appliance Company that methyl compounds had high oxidation resistance; now we wanted to know how methyl compounds stood in relation to other silicones and to organic compounds.

The first studies were qualitative in nature, but soon I developed a reliable, quantitative comparison of oxidative resistance of the various alkylsiloxanes, measuring the temperature at which the compounds oxidized at the same rate (Table 2-3).

These results indicated that the dimethylsiloxane was the most thermally stable of the four types of siloxane compounds, and thus the most potentially useful. This was one of two bits of evidence which prompted the decision to build the Midland plant to produce methyl, in addition to ethyl, compounds. (The other motivating factor was the finding by Mel Hunter in November 1943 that methyl-based resins were much more thermally stable than ethyl-based resins).

Even though the dimethylsiloxanes proved to be more heat-resistant than the other types of compounds tested, their stability was limited by oxidation of the product at the high temperatures at which it would be

[10]Paul J. Flory, *J. Am. Chem. Soc.*, 63:3083 (1941).

[11]At this time we were using the term "silicane" instead of "silicone" in this new field. We hadn't yet adopted the standard nomenclature set forth in *Chemical Abstracts* and other journals.

used. It seemed logical, then, that stability could be improved by the use of inhibitors to block oxidation. An extensive study of various classes of inhibitors followed and did indeed result in a more thermally stable product. A series of patents covering these findings was awarded to Dr. McGregor and me.[12]

While continuing my research work, I began graduate studies at Carnegie Institute of Technology, not far from the Mellon Institute. Mellon permitted members of the fellowships to take time off to pursue courses at the nearby University of Pittsburgh or at Carnegie Institute, a few blocks away. As a result of this opportunity to pursue my academic studies while continuing my research work at Mellon, I completed my D.Sc. degree at Carnegie Institute of Technology in mid-1943, using research done at Carnegie, completely separate from my Mellon work, as material for my dissertation. (Later, John Speier would obtain his Ph.D. degree at the University of Pittsburgh on the basis of his organosilicon research for the Mellon fellowship.)

After Dow Corning was incorporated, I continued my research on silicone rubber. We had observed in the lab that batches of dimethylsiloxane fluids polymerized by sodium hydroxide (KOH) often "coasted" to a gel structure. This material was rubbery in nature and lacked only a method of vulcanizing at the appropriate times to transform it into a rubber.

A friend from one of the labs across the hall at Mellon told me that duPont was vulcanizing its saturated Paracon rubber with benzoyl peroxide.[13] I decided to try the same technique.

Soon I milled some of this rubbery dimethylsiloxane compound on a two-roll mill with some benzoyl peroxide, and on heating, the compound did indeed vulcanize. I reported this first silicone rubber on December 31, 1943; the research was covered by Dow Corning's first rubber patent.[14]

The early rubbers produced in our labs were weak; the samples I first showed to the researchers in Midland were quickly reduced to crumbly pieces. I spent much time experimenting with fillers and peroxides to improve the quality of the rubber.

Speier. John Speier joined the Mellon fellowship in August 1943 and soon took over the study of mono-tri resins. After several samples of the new resins were developed, they were shown to Andy Kauppi's

---

[12]R. R. McGregor and E. L. Warrick, U.S. Patents 2,389,802, 1945; 2,389,803, 1945; 2,389,804, 1945; 2,389,805, 1945; 2,389,806, 1945; 2,389,807, 1945.

[13]B. S. Biggs and C. S. Fuller, *Chem. Eng. News, 21:962 (1943).*

[14]E. L. Warrick, U.S. Patent 2,460,795, 1949.

Product Development group in Midland. Using the techniques and formulation developed at Mellon, the group converted our research into two laminating resins, DOW CORNING® 2101 and DOW CORNING® 2102.

John Speier, 1943.

As the Midland laboratories became more interested in these resins as laminating materials, Speier scaled up his production to a 22-liter flask and continued to study the nature of the materials. He showed that the activity of the resin, i.e., the rate of cure, was directly proportional to the amount of hydroxyl group retained during the initial polymerization process. This gave us a new understanding of how the resin could be modified and production controlled.

In his work on mono-tri resins, Speier also discovered that many agents would react with the siloxane bond (Si—O—Si) that forms the backbone of all silicones. For example, Speier found that water, ethanol, and hydrochloric acid molecules would readily react and insert themselves into the siloxane bond.

John Speier reported this surprising finding at the December 1944 research conference. Up to this time, it was a commonly held belief that the Si—O—Si backbone was too strong to be broken, because it was associated with a very rigid material, quartz, which is wholly composed of these bonds. Many at the research conference therefore expressed doubt about Speier's findings, but in the months that followed, additional experimentation confirmed his results.

While the results of this research were never published or patented by Dow Corning, they did aid us greatly in our understanding of the siloxane bond in silicones. We used this knowledge to generate a variety of new organosilicon compounds in the labs at Mellon, and eventually this discovery led to many new commercial applications.

The Rubber Program. In mid-1945, 1½ years after I reported on the first silicone rubber and shortly after the first commercial rubber had been developed in Bill Pedersen's lab at Dow Chemical, a detailed program of study of the field was developed for the fellowship at Mellon Institute. Under this rubber program, we conducted a variety of research projects aimed at improving the quality of the initial weak compounds.

We tried to understand the vulcanization process, testing new peroxides and studying their activity. We also tested other types of vulcanizing agents, but none proved quite as useful as the peroxides. Other polymers were prepared with the hope of increasing intermolecular forces within the rubber compound and thus making it stronger. In addition, we experimented with various fillers, but no outstanding effects were noted.

We also studied the properties of silicone rubber in its various forms. We developed foamed silicone rubbers and showed that silicone rubber could be vulcanized in steam so long as air was excluded. Studies aimed at improving compression set were also undertaken.[15] Throughout the war years and beyond, we continued such experiments to improve on the materials we'd developed. We strove to learn all we could about the nature of these early rubbers, in an ongoing effort to produce stronger and better versions.

Progress at Dow

Within the Cellulose Products Department at Dow, silicone research and product development efforts were fruitful during the war years. Dr. Bass continued to direct the research efforts, while Andy Kauppi was responsible for the product development groups.

The Analytical Group.   Early in 1943, around the time of incorporation, Jim McHard organized a small group within the Cellulose Products Department to concentrate exclusively on analytical work. This was in response to a request by Shailer Bass, who wanted McHard to develop methods for analyzing the new organosilicon compounds being produced in Dr. Britton's lab. Bass had an eye to the future and wanted to ensure that we would learn as much as possible about the new silicone compounds that were continually being developed.

Hal Clark and Phil Servais left Dr. Hunter's research group to become early members of the new analytical department. Later they were joined by Cliff Boomer, Harry Dingman, and several assistants. McHard's group was productive from the first, turning out more than 9000 analyses in 1943, the year of its formation. By May 1944, when the group moved to the new Dow Corning site, it had grown to about a dozen members. The data provided by the analytical group greatly aided the researchers in their quest to understand the makeup and activity of the new compounds they were developing.

Research under Dr. Barry.   Art Barry's research group during the war years included Lee DePree, Don Hook, and John Gilkey. Shortly after

---

[15]Compression set testing involves putting a rubber sample under a load which compresses the rubber. When the load is removed, the rubber "recovers" its original form, but only to a certain extent. For example, if it recovers 80 percent of its original thickness, the compression set is 20 percent.

incorporation, Barry got involved in resin research but became discouraged because of the lack of purity of the compounds with which he worked. Because distillation was imperfect and thus the compounds impure, each batch of resin varied slightly in composition and performance.

By the end of 1943, Dr. Barry had proposed three guidelines for future research, aimed at solving the problem of impurity and positioning the company for the day when the war would end:

1. Resins and other organosilicon compounds should be made only from carefully distilled grades of chlorosilanes.

2. For maximum thermal stability, only phenyl and methyl groups should be used.

3. In preparation for competition in the peacetime economy, products should not be based on a costly Grignard process. Direct methods of synthesizing phenyl- and methylchlorosilanes should be developed.

As pointed out in Chapter 1, Dr. Barry's group had worked on developing direct processes for synthesizing the intermediate products used in making resins, fluids, and compounds since the early days of Dow's silicone research. After incorporation, the group continued its focus on developing a direct process for silicone production, studying a number of direct reactions of methyl chloride with finely ground silicon in the search for a Grignard replacement.

The researchers learned in the course of their early experiments that better results were obtained with a metallurgical grade of silicon containing small amounts of iron and aluminum than with purer grades.

The principal product produced by this early direct process was methyltrichlorosilane, with some silicon tetrachloride and some trichlorosilane as by-products. While these first experiments were somewhat successful, they didn't yield the product the group was in need of, dimethyldichlorosilane.

The key to perfecting this direct process was unlocked in June 1945 at the Gibson Island High Polymer Conference, an annual event sponsored by the American Association for the Advancement of Science. The conference, held at a large house on Gibson Island in Chesapeake Bay, was attended by some of the most distinguished polymer chemists of the day, including Dr. Herman Mark, Dr. F. R. Mayo, Dr. C. C. Price, and Dr. C. S. Fuller. Dow Corning had been invited to send speakers to the conference, and Shailer Bass, Frank Hyde, and I made presentations to the group.

At this conference, Dr. Eugene Rochow of General Electric Company discussed the process he had developed for direct synthesis of methylchlorosilanes, the work that Dr. Barry's group had been trying so hard to perfect, with limited success. Dr. Rochow gave the audience a small demonstration of the process, which involved using methyl chloride from a cylinder passing over a hot tube of silicon, to which some copper catalyst had been added.

Figure 2-7 compares the conventional Grignard reaction with Rochow's new direct process for making silicones, using copper as a catalyst. The simplification of the beginning step of the procedure makes the direct process a great deal cheaper than the Grignard method. The direct process is also a safer method of producing silicones, as it eliminates the need for handling large volumes of volatile and combustible ether.

It was the copper catalyst that provided the missing link that Barry's group had been searching for in its direct-process experimentation. Enhanced by the information gleaned from the conference and an article on the subject written by Dr. Rochow,[16] the work on the direct process in Dr. Barry's group progressed rapidly. Soon, however, a patent interference put a temporary halt to the group's progress and brought the issue of cross-licensing into sharp focus.

In September 1944, the first signs of a patent interference with General Electric Company began to surface. The interference involved several patent applications pending by both General Electric and Dow Corning, covering similar areas of research. Because the field of silicones was so new and because the applications involved so much similar, often overlapping, research in many cases, it was difficult for the patent office to determine which company should be awarded priority on certain patents.

As the interference proceedings dragged on, it became apparent to all concerned that Dow Corning and General Electric each needed licenses under the other's patents in order to operate commercially; otherwise, patents of one company would block progress of the other at some point. For example, while Rochow held the rights to the direct process he'd developed, Corning held patents on the final products the process yielded, a situation preventing either company from coming to market with a commercial version of the product.

In order to solve this problem of competing processes and products, an agreement was signed on July 2, 1945, whereby Dow Corning exercised its right to sublicense Dow and Corning Glass patents and to license patents of its own to General Electric Company. General Electric in turn licensed Dow Corning under a number of its early patents. Both companies could now proceed unencumbered in their work.

---

[16]Eugene G. Rochow, *J. Am. Chem. Soc.*, *67:963 (1945)*.

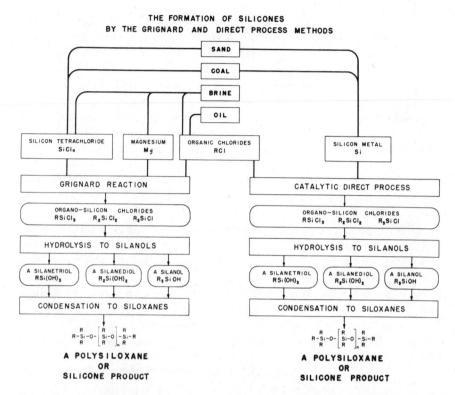

THE FORMATION OF SILICONES
BY THE GRIGNARD AND DIRECT PROCESS METHODS

Figure 2-7. The formation of silicones by the Grignard and direct-process methods.

Dr. Barry's group was responsible for the development of another process of some importance to Dow Corning. This was the rearrangement of trimethylchlorosilane $(CH_3)_3SiCl$, methyltrichlorosilane, CH_3SiCl_3, or silicon tetrachloride, $SiCl_4$, the unwanted by-products of the Rochow direct process, in the presence of aluminum chloride, at a temperature of 662°F, to generate high yields of the much needed intermediate dimethyldichlorosilane, $(CH_3)_2SiCl_2$. By repeated redistribution, it was possible to increase the yield of dimethyldichlorosilane produced by Rochow's direct process.

Initially the patent for this work was rejected on the basis that another researcher, George Calingert of Shell Oil, had earlier performed a similar rearrangement process. However, Barry's group produced yields of dimethyldichlorosilane that, from a statistical standpoint, far exceeded the probability established by Calingert in his research. As a result, the patent was approved.[17]

[17]A. J. Barry, U.S. Patent 2,647,912, 1953.

Another direct process was studied by Art Barry's group beginning in 1944. The group was trying to prepare the phenylchlorosilanes needed in resin production, by vapor phase reaction of benzene with trichlorosilane, $HSiCl_3$, at elevated pressures. The Barry group's work on developing this process was almost halted by Bill Collings, who felt strongly that all the group's effort should go into the development of resins for the Navy. He encouraged the group to forget about the direct process, reminding Dr. Barry of pressure from Hyman Rickover to intensify research and development of resins for motor insulation. In fact, Barry's group had already turned out a number of resins for this purpose, and more were in the works, but Collings was adamant in his demand that the direct-process work be stopped.

Around this time, Dr. Veazey, Dow Chemical's director of research, came into the Barry group's laboratory, and a bit of an altercation developed between him and Collings. Veazey felt the direct-process work was more important to the long-run prospects for the company than was the resin research. The argument continued. Finally Dr. Barry, caught in the middle, made peace between the two by promising to find time to carry out both research projects.

He kept his promise. With resin production continuing, by Christmas 1944 the Barry group succeeded in producing phenyltrichlorosilane via the direct process they'd developed, which was variously referred to inside the plant as the "pseudo-Friedel-Crafts (PFC) process," or the "Barry process." Many patents were issued covering this work.[18]

The group put a vial of the first batch of phenyltrichlorosilane produced by the PFC process in a piece of plastic and stapled it to a Christmas card, which was then sent to Dr. Bass. He received the card at the new Dow Corning plant and passed the good news along to Collings. While Collings was a man of strong opinions, he was equally willing to admit his errors of judgment. As soon as he got word of the success of the process, Collings hurried to the lab and saluted the group with a beaming "Congratulations!" Thereafter, the direct-process work proceeded smoothly, with Collings's blessing.

Another direct process studied by the Barry group as a replacement for the Grignard reaction was the addition of SiH-containing silanes to a variety of olefins (a class of hydrocarbons containing carbon-carbon double bonds, C=C) at temperatures between 284 and 572°F. Methylethyldichlorosilane was obtained by this method and was used in the production of hydraulic fluids. Octadecylmethyldichlorosilane was also prepared in this fashion and found use as an additive in car and furni-

[18] A. J. Barry, L. DePree, and D. E. Hook, U.S. Patents 2,510,853, 1950; 2,556,462, 1951. Other foreign equivalents of these patents were issued.

ture polishes. This technique was patented and a discussion of the process published a few years later in the *Journal of the American Chemical Society*.[19]

Much later, John Speier showed that such olefin additions could be catalyzed at low temperatures by a variety of platinum catalysts. This modified process became very important and much used, since it made possible the production of a variety of additional compounds that would have been destroyed by the 284 to 572°F temperatures used in the original procedure.

One early application of the Barry group's research was a water-repellent fluid. The researchers' work with Si—H bonding led them to produce methyldichlorosilane, CH_3HSiCl_2, from which fluid polymers were produced. In the course of their experimentation, the group applied dilute solutions of these fluids to filter paper. The dry paper disk looked unchanged, but it had become extremely water-repellent and would not adhere to Scotch tape (Figure 2-8). This finding led to additional work by Zeke Dennett that resulted in a new fluid, DOW CORNING® 1107, to be used for waterproofing textiles.

Dr. Hunter's Group.   Mel Hunter's group continued the basic research begun before incorporation and took on new projects as well. In an effort to find a cheaper method of making dimethylsiloxane fluids (200 series fluids), Hunter's group pursued a new project involving the reaction of a normal methyl Grignard reagent with diethoxydichlorosilane, $(C_2H_5O)_2SiCl_2$, and on $SiCl_4$.

Through use of the ethoxy compound in the Grignard process, distillation was far easier, as the boiling points of the resultant products are far apart. However, while this process proved to be more efficient, it was still no less expensive than the in situ Grignard process that had previously been used, and its use was limited.

Hunter's group also studied the effect of different end groups on the dimethylsiloxane polymer. These studies clearly demonstrated the need for high-purity dimethyldiethoxysilane in order to obtain high polymers upon hydrolysis.

Viscosity slopes and molecular weights were measured in the process of fully characterizing these low-molecular-weight fluids as well as the cyclics and linears. Basic properties of the DOW CORNING 200® silicone fluids, such as density, expansion coefficient, and freezing point, were measured.

In June 1943, Dr. Hunter began a series of tests with Owens Corning

---

[19]A. J. Barry, L. DePree, J. W. Gilkey, and D. E. Hook, "The Reaction of Olefins and Chlorohydrosilanes," *J. Am. Chem. Soc.*, 69:2916 (1947).

Figure 2-8. Volunteers demonstrate the effectiveness of Dow Corning's first water repellency treatment, DOW CORNING® 1107.

Fiberglas on various silicone materials which might be used as lubricants and binders for glass-fiber bundles, to prevent one fiber from damaging another and to hold the fibers in a yarn. Many materials were tested. One of the silicone resins developed proved to be a good "size" to replace the starch which had previously been used for this purpose. The resin was put into commercial production and given the name "DOW CORNING® 1210."

In the course of their research, Chet Currie and Mel Hunter prepared a series of diethyl fluids and studied the low polymers as well as the high polymers. Relying on Dr. Hyde's technique for recovering gelled resins, Fletcher and Hunter also showed that high polymers in the dimethyl system could be depolymerized with ethanol and sodium hydroxide to yield ethoxy-end-blocked, lower-molecular-weight fluids.

Fletcher and Hunter also prepared a series of acetoxymethyl silicones by interchanging ethoxyl groups with acetic anhydride. Much later, these acetoxy-ended polymers became the basic material in a curing system for a one-part sealant that was marketed many years later as a bathtub caulk.

Chet Currie and Mel Hunter investigated the fluids resulting from copolymers containing a mixture of phenylmethylsiloxanes, trimethylsiloxanes, and dimethylsiloxanes. These were the 700 series of diffusion-pump fluids.

After incorporation, the Hunter group became involved in studying the elements of DOW CORNING® 990A additive. The group studied volatile by-products of the phenylethylsiloxane (990A) system and isolated pure cyclics from these low polymers.

In addition, the researchers experimented with mixing phenyl and methyl compounds to produce a resin with greater thermal stability than DOW CORNING® 990A additive, and greater strength. By November 1943, Currie, Hal Clark, and Hunter reported the first such phenylmethylsiloxane resin and showed that it was outstanding in its resistance to crazing (cracking) at 482°F. Dr. Hunter showed that the phenylmethyl resins in general were 100 times more heat-resistant than phenylethylsiloxane resins.

By February 1944 the Hunter group was coupling phenyl and methyl Grignards simultaneously to produce these more heat-resistant resins. Later in the year, they produced phenylmethylsilanes by the in situ Grignard process. By December, Phil Servais and Mel Hunter showed that simultaneous Grignards of phenyl and methyl could be run on $SiCl_4$ to generate higher yields of phenylmethyldichlorosilane.

By February 1945, Earle Smith had joined the group and reported the effects of degree of substitution on the strength of the phenylmethylsiloxane resin. By this time the new compound had been put into commercial production and given the designation "DOW CORNING® 993."

Dr. Hunter's researchers were interested in studying the properties of pure compounds. They wanted to see what would happen if chlorine ends were attached to silicone molecules. The group showed that benzoyl chloride reacts with high polymers to produce chlorine-ended lower polymers. Also, benzoyl chloride reacted with ethoxy compounds, $(CH_3)_x Si(OC_2H_5)_{4-x}$ to produce the chlorinated derivatives.

Unlike the chlorine-containing mixtures, the ethoxy compounds produced pure dimethyldichlorosilane, which Delong had tried to get by distillation alone. Because the compounds were pure, their true boiling points could be established. These data were valuable in the calculations used in building the distillation column in the new plant.

During these war years, Currie and Hunter also studied the preparation of various greases and compounds. One important study initiated during this period came at the suggestion of Dr. Britton, director of Dow Chemical's organic lab, who had applied DOW CORNING 4® compound to his hunting boots in an effort to waterproof them. While the compound alone did not work well, this gave the researchers the idea to search for a way to waterproof leather.

Another incident spurred Dow Corning into beginning water repellency studies. Near the end of the war the government called on a professor at the University of Cincinnati, who was well known for his work on the chemistry of leather, and asked him to search for a solution to the problem of trench foot in soldiers, involving blisters and sores caused by repeated exposure to water and cold. The professor in turn approached Dow Corning for assistance, since he knew that silicones were water-repellent.

After this visit, Dow Corning began working in conjunction with the University of Cincinnati to produce a water-repellent treatment for leather. Studies were initiated in June 1945, and they continued over the next several years.

Translating the Research: Product Development

Andy Kauppi, manager of product engineering for the new company, headed up three groups within Dow Chemical that focused on transforming the findings of the research groups into viable commercial products.

Kolderman and Kin: Submarine Insulation. One group, headed by Roger Kolderman and Mike Kin, was primarily interested in developing materials to insulate the Navy's submarine drive motors. The group concentrated on evaluating DOW CORNING® 990A additive, DOW CORNING® 993, and subsequent resins produced in Britton's lab and at the new Dow Corning plant for possible use as electrical insulating materials.

Grant: Motor Test Laboratory. The Motor Test laboratory (Figure 2-9), headed by George Grant, was involved in evaluating the performance of silicone resin–insulated electric motors. In this group, full-sized electric motors, prepared by Westinghouse using DOW CORNING® 990A additive and subsequent resins, were tested by running them continuously at 392, 428, and 464F° to determine the time-temperature life curve for silicone insulation.

Pedersen: Resins, Fluids, Greases, and Rubber. The third group was supervised by Bill Pedersen. This group worked on laminating resins to produce slot sticks needed in motor manufacture as well as greases for motor ball bearings. In addition, the group became a catchall for a number of products, including phenylmethyl fluids and paints to coat hot motors.

The group was responsible for commercializing the DOW CORNING®

2101 and DOW CORNING® 2102 laminating resins developed at Mellon Institute. These resins were applied to glass cloth, partially cured, and cut into pieces for laminating under pressure at 302°F. The DOW CORNING® 2101 and DOW CORNING® 2102 laminates were then used in producing slot sticks for motors.

Following production of these early samples of laminating resins, a joint development program was begun between Mellon Institute and the researchers at Dow, to search for better versions of the resin. The groups focused on resins containing a combination of monomethyl-, trimethyl-, and monophenylsilanes, in varying proportions.

The most promising of the laminating resins developed by Larry Rauner was given the name "DOW CORNING® 2103." The product was widely used, since it met military specifications. Molding compounds also were prepared from these resins, proving far more successful in this application than the molding resins prepared in the early days at Mellon, when we still knew so little about the underlying characteristics of the compounds we were producing.

Hyman Rickover's request for protective paint for the Navy's high-temperature electric motors was fulfilled in Pedersen's lab. Westinghouse was also interested in such a paint product. Pedersen's group worked in the laboratory to produce heat-resistant enamels from blends of typical paint pigments, catalyst, and DOW CORNING® 990A additive.

Early formulations worked but were impractical because they had to be baked on the surface of the product for several hours at high temperatures in order to obtain any abrasion resistance at room temperature. After this problem was solved by development of a new resin catalyst system, a workable product, given the name "DOW CORNING® 801 Paint Resin," was produced. The bulk of it was sold to paint companies for aluminum finishes that were used on metal smokestacks (Figure 2-10).

Pedersen's group also worked on a program to develop silicone-based greases for ball bearings, evaluating the compounds developed by the research groups for their effectiveness as lubricants and for their thermal stability, relative volatility versus viscosity, and compatibility with thickening agents. From this work, several fluids and greases were produced for commercial application.

The results of testing in Pedersen's lab showed that fluid products which contained 10, 50, and 100 percent phenylmethylsiloxane units were suitable for commercial use and should be offered as products. These were named "DOW CORNING 510®," "DOW CORNING 550®," and "DOW CORNING 710®" fluids.

Of all the soap-type thickeners that had been developed for greases, lithium stearate offered the most promise in silicone greases, but it was difficult to incorporate and did not produce much thickening effect. In addition, these silicone fluids offered little corrosion protection to ferrous metals.

An additive was sought to solve both of these problems. After much testing, 1 percent phenyl stearate was shown to be effective. Through combination of DOW CORNING 550® fluid with lithium stearate and phenyl stearate, an effective high-temperature grease was produced and given the name "DOW CORNING 44® grease." The group also combined DOW CORNING 510® fluid with the two stearates to make DOW CORNING 33® grease, primarily for use in low-temperature applications.

Bill Pedersen.

Pedersen's group responded to another Navy request, this one from the Naval Research Laboratory, which had been using DOW CORNING 4®

Figure 2-9. The Motor Test laboratory, where silicone-insulated motors were run continuously to evaluate their life span and ability to withstand high temperatures.

Figure 2-10. Two smokestacks, painted at the same time. The stack on the left was painted with a silicone formulation, preventing it from rusting, unlike the stack on the right, which is rusting.

compound and DOW CORNING 33® grease for dynamic lubrication between organic O-rings and metal cylinders in pneumatic systems. However, they experienced shrinkage of the organic O-rings when using either of these silicone greases. Pedersen's group produced a modification of DOW CORNING 33® in which 8 percent of the silicone fluid was replaced with octyl sebacate. The substitution of the octyl sebacate eliminated this O-ring shrinkage and led to complete acceptance of this formulation in pneumatic systems. The formulation eventually became known as "DOW CORNING® 55M pneumatic grease."

All these soap-type greases could be used up to 302°F, but at higher temperatures their life was limited because of the degeneration of the stearate thickener. Work was undertaken in 1944 to find other means of thickening fluids to acceptable greaselike consistency. Formulations using the silica found in DOW CORNING 4® compound were not successful because of extreme bleeding of the fluid from the grease at high temperatures or with agitation. After much experimentation, a nonvolatile carbon black (a very finely divided carbon) was milled into DOW CORNING 710® fluid with the phenyl stearate, and produced a grease with excellent heat stability, useful in many high-temperature applications in relatively slow-moving bearings. In 1945 this grease found its way into some of the automobile foundries in the Michigan area, where it was used to lubricate chains that drew automobile parts through high-temperature ovens. The product was given the name "DOW CORNING® 41 grease."

In mid-1944, shortly after I developed the first silicone rubber, Bill Pedersen visited Mellon Institute to learn more about our rubber work. Upon returning to Dow, he and his researchers began developing silicone rubbers for commercial use.

The first successful commercial rubber formulations were developed in Pedersen's lab early in 1945. A number of different formulations were prepared, using a variety of fillers. These rubbers were marketed under the trade name "SILASTIC®." The first commercial data on SILASTIC® was issued on March 12, 1945, announcing SR stocks for compression molding or extrusion and SC stocks for knife coating on fabrics or for manufacture of SILASTIC® products reinforced with metal, glass, fabric, and asbestos products.

Because of the relatively poor properties of the initial silicone rubbers, it was decided to limit distribution to a single fabricating company of modest size. Shailer Bass was acquainted with one of the executives of Connecticut Hard Rubber Company in New Haven, Connecticut. The company was selected as the sole distributor of SILASTIC®, and it also agreed to participate in joint studies to improve the quality of the rubber.

Around the time SILASTIC® was introduced, General Electric held a press conference in New York City, heralding the introduction of its own version of silicone rubber. Late in 1944, GE had published a booklet promoting its new rubber, and the December 10, 1944, issue of *Chemical and Engineering News* had shown a photograph of searchlight gaskets made of the new product.

News of General Electric's success prompted us to hasten distribution of SILASTIC®. At the same time, we accelerated the pace of the joint study with Connecticut Hard Rubber to develop stronger and better versions of the product.

In order to increase production and distribution of silicone rubber, another building, 305, was added to the new Dow Corning plant. This building was devoted to production of SILASTIC®, and an adjoining laboratory was set up as a product development and technical service laboratory for SILASTIC®. Over a relatively short period of time other additions to building 305 were made to accommodate the increased

production of various SILASTIC® compounds as well as DOW CORNING 4®
compound and related compounds, plus silicone greases DOW
CORNING 33®, DOW CORNING® 41, and DOW CORNING 44®.

On May 5, 1945, shortly after Dow Corning introduced SILASTIC® to
the marketplace, the Allies won the war in Europe. Three months later,
on August 14, the Japanese surrendered, and World War II finally
came to an end.

Almost immediately after the war ended, Dow Corning began receiving Telexes from around the country, canceling all orders. With peace
at hand, the company was left with a substantial inventory of products
developed to meet the requirements of the war effort. After 2½ years
of steadily building the business, Dow Corning suddenly found itself
without a base of customers to serve. Virtually overnight, the million-
dollar company saw its sales plummet to zero.

3
The Postwar Years: New Products, New Markets

*Man, unlike any other thing organic or
inorganic in the universe, grows beyond his
work, walks up the stairs of his concepts,
emerges ahead of his accomplishments.*
        JOHN E. STEINBECK
        THE GRAPES OF WRATH

The cancellation of wartime orders dealt quite a blow to the struggling
young company, not yet 3 years old. As canceled orders poured in, Bill
Collings called his key people together to discuss how they were going
to deal with the grim situation facing them. There was no choice but to
find new uses for the silicones quickly, if the company were to survive.

Wartime products had been developed in response to clearly defined
needs of the military. Unfortunately, no such clear-cut civilian needs for
silicones were evident. Collings's message to the assembled group was
simple and succinct: "Find something people will buy!"

Although 300 employees were dependent on the young Dow Corning
for their livelihood, morale was high even as the wartime business came
to an end, according to Bill Caldwell (manager of engineering at the
time). While there was anxiety about what the future would bring, the

employees realized they were in the struggle together, and would either sink or swim together. A solid spirit of cooperation prevailed.

The problem facing Dow Corning as it entered the postwar period was not so much the selling of products as it was the selling of concepts. Silicones were unfamiliar to the private marketplace. These new compounds had properties not seen in other materials, and potential buyers were cautious and skeptical. Repeated demonstrations had to be made to convince people that these unusual hybrids performed functions no other materials could match, and that their superior performance justified the higher cost of silicones versus organic materials.

During the war, Dow Corning had been in a favored position, producing a unique set of products to meet the ongoing demands of the military. But the end had come, and in August 1945, as Collings addressed his staff, the very future of the company was at stake. In the months and years ahead, Dow Corning would have to grow beyond its wartime work, to create and unearth new uses for its products, to develop new markets and attract civilian customers where now there were none.

The war had ended, but for Dow Corning, the real battle was just beginning.

First Postwar Products

Tire-Mold Release: DOW CORNING® 35 Emulsion

There were some natural transitions from military to civilian applications. In addition, some research findings made during the war years were useful as springboards to postwar product developments. One such finding led to the development of Dow Corning's first civilian product.

During the war, workers in the Cellulose Products Department in Dow Chemical had used DOW CORNING 200® silicone fluid as a release agent for molds used in their operations. The fluids worked well in this capacity and did not react with the various plastics used in the molds, nor did they build up in the molds, a problem with existing release agents.

On the basis of this experience, in the fall of 1945 Charlie Sanford (Figure 3-1), who worked under Olie Blessing in the sales department, took a sample of DOW CORNING 200® silicone fluid in a solvent solution to U.S. Rubber Company in Detroit. With the end of the war, synthetic rubber had become available for use in civilian tires. There was a considerable backlog of demand, as civilian tires had been scarce for some time. Sanford knew there would be strong demand for the 200 fluid if it would work, as he believed it would, as a release agent in tire molds.

Tire-mold release agents at that time were combinations of waxes

Figure 3-1. Charlie Sanford testing DOW CORNING 4® compound on his outboard motor ignition.

which tended to build up in the molds. Rejected tires, or "seconds" were commonplace and were accepted as part of the business. In addition, molds had to be continually cleaned to eliminate wax buildup problems.

Sanford's pitch to U.S. Rubber, promising an end to tire rejects and wax buildup, was attractive, and the company agreed to test the new material. On the first trials using DOW CORNING 200® silicone fluid, defective tires were still produced. It was standard practice to throw out the last release agent tried when defective tires came out of the mold, so the production workers at U.S. Rubber were ready to escort Sanford and his product to the front door.

Fortunately, Sanford was a persuasive man, and he convinced the group that DOW CORNING 200® silicone fluid could not possibly have been responsible for the defective tires. As a result, he got another chance, and the fluid was successful in this second trial. Subsequent tests confirmed Sanford's claim; the tires from the first trial were proved to be defective for other reasons.

While the test results impressed U. S. Rubber, the company could not use DOW CORNING 200® silicone fluid in the solvent Sanford brought because its high flammability posed a fire hazard. It would use the fluid, Sanford was told, only if he could bring it back in a water-dilutable emulsion.

The problem was solved by Chet Currie's group in the laboratories of Dow Corning. The group members had no experience with the emulsification of fluids, and they quickly had to become "experts" on the subject in order to develop a solution. This was a typical situation in the early days of the company; lab engineers regularly had to become proficient in new technologies and industries in order to solve the problems brought to their attention.

Despite their lack of experience, Currie's lab workers came up with a solution within a relatively short period of time. Morpholine oleate proved to be a suitable emulsifier, and the new formulation was sent to U.S. Rubber.

The tire maker was quite pleased with the new formula. When DOW CORNING® 35 emulsion was used in tire molds, the rejects, which were formerly considered a routine part of the business, literally dropped to zero. Furthermore, tire molds no longer had to be taken out of service periodically for removal of wax buildup (Figure 3-2).

Soon U.S. Rubber was using DOW CORNING® 35 emulsion in its daily operations. In fact, the company liked the new product so well that it tried to buy Dow Corning's total output. Olie Blessing, however, wisely insisted on holding back some product for testing at other rubber companies. William Wiard was hired from U. S. Rubber to help in promoting DOW CORNING® 35 emulsion to all the major tire manufacturers. These companies were equally pleased with the product, and before long most tire manufacturers around the country were using DOW CORNING® 35 emulsion.

So successful was the first product of the postwar era that for a time, Dow Corning could not produce DOW CORNING® 35 emulsion fast enough to meet the mushrooming demand. The transition to the civilian marketplace had been a smooth one. With the success of the tire-mold release, the immediate future of the company was ensured—and 300 employees breathed a sigh of relief.

Rescuing the Bakeries: Pan Glaze

Dow Corning's second postwar product was also a release material. Its development came about in an incidental fashion. Late in 1945, Bill

Figure 3-2. Rejects became a thing of the past once DOW CORNING® 35 emulsion mold release was introduced to tire manufacturers.

Collings gave a general presentation on silicones to the Saginaw Valley Torch Club. One member of the audience was from the Baker Perkins Company of Saginaw, a supplier of machines to the baking industry. After the speech, this man pointed out to Collings that the baking industry needed a better product to release bread from baking pans.

The release agent then used in bakeries was lard, which was applied by hand to the pans before each bake. As the bread baked, the excess lard burned, smoking up the ovens and the entire bakery. Another problem with lard was that, after a number of uses, each pan required cleaning or replacement.

This information was passed along to the product labs at Dow Corning. Lab trials of DOW CORNING 200® silicone fluid as a replacement for lard successfully released baked bread, but the effect lasted for only a few bakes. When a resin solution was sprayed on the pans, however, the coating was successful for many bakes.

The laboratories then conducted extensive field testing with the Rainbow Bakery in Saginaw and the Harvest Bakery in Midland. The resin coating proved quite effective and was easy to apply in a bakery setting.

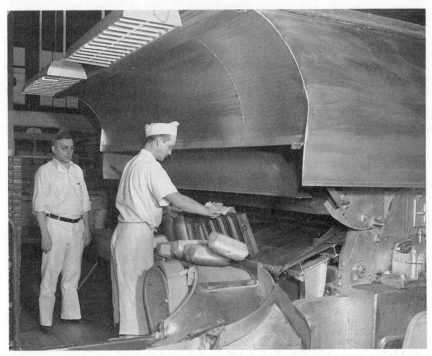

Figure 3-3. *Left:* Pan Glaze transformed the bakery from a smoke-filled factory to a pleasant, efficient workplace. *Right:* Early advertisement for the popular product.

Baking pans were normally fastened together in groups of four or more. These pan units were sprayed with the resin and allowed to air-dry. A short bake at temperatures achieved in the bakery ovens completed the curing process, and the pans were ready for use.

The testing at the two bakeries was presumably confidential, so the Midland sales office employees were surprised to receive calls from bakeries around the country shortly thereafter, asking for the "new Dow Corning Pan Glaze"—a designation which was quickly adopted as the product trade name. The calls stemmed from the word of an enterprising yeast salesman who had seen the pans at Harvest Bakery and had spread the news at a national bakery convention.

Early experience with Pan Glaze varied, but between 100 and 150 bakes were generally achieved before it was necessary to recoat the pans. Bakers loved Pan Glaze, and its use spread rapidly, for it transformed the bakery from a smoky, smelly factory to a pleasant workplace. Sales of Pan Glaze quickly grew to 10,000 gallons per month (Figure 3-3).

After a few months of successful sales, however, a problem arose. One day Joseph Lubbehusen, a baking expert, and John Tyner, a Dow

Figure 3-3. (*Continued*)

Corning sales representative, were visiting customers in the Cleveland area. They were told that after pans were recoated 16 to 18 times, the pan units would stick together, requiring that the silicone coating be removed. No one, including Lubbehusen, knew how to remove the coating.

Lubbehusen put in a call to Mike Kin's Technical Resin Service laboratory back in Midland. Kin suggested several cleaning compounds and various solvents the bakers might try. Nothing worked. Finally, Lubbehusen reluctantly suggested the bakers go back to using lard until a solution could be found.

Back at the Dow Corning laboratories, word of the problem with Pan Glaze spread quickly, and every chemist who had any idea about a possible solution was put to work on developing one. A partial solution was quickly discovered. Laboratory experiments showed that removing the resin coating was easily accomplished using alkali in water. Unfortunately, this also removed the tin plating on the pans. Bakers needed this tin to prevent rusting in the high humidity of the "proof boxes" where bread was placed for rising.

At this point the problem was turned over to Leo Stebleton, who quickly abandoned water solutions in favor of alcoholic alkali, which served to remove the Pan Glaze while leaving the tin intact. To make the solution less flammable, Stebleton combined the alkali with a Dow Chemical solvent. Stebleton was issued a patent[1] covering this removal technique.

Stebleton's technique involved the use of tanks and rinsing and drying equipment not found in the bakeries. As a result, with encouragement and assistance from Dow Corning, several enterprising businesspeople started up service operations around the country to coat and clean pans for bakeries. Once these cleaning and coating services were in place, most commercial bakeries adopted Pan Glaze, and its popularity steadily grew.

First Consumer Product:
SIGHT SAVERS®

After two successes in the industrial marketplace, Dow Corning turned its attention to consumers. Shortly after the war ended, and the young company was facing the prospect of starting all over, two board members from Corning Glass Works, Dr. Sullivan and Charles LaFollette (who was then director of sales for Corning) suggested that the new

---

[1]Leo Stebleton, U.S. Patent 2,710,843, 1955.

company enter the consumer marketplace. This was familiar territory to Corning, which targeted most of its products to consumers.

While Collings mulled over the idea, Corning Glass researchers pursued development of a silicone product that Dow Corning could sell to consumers. The group soon discovered that DOW CORNING 200® silicone fluid was an effective glass cleaner. After initial tests in the labs, a few optometrists in the Corning, New York, area were given small bottles of the DOW CORNING 200® fluid in a solvent mixture, for cleaning and polishing eyeglasses.

This cleaner-polish worked well, but no one liked carrying the bottles of solvent. The researchers solved that problem by impregnating tissue paper with the silicone solution.

Corning Glass did some preliminary market research and concluded that the new product would best be distributed through drugstores. Sullivan and LaFollette encouraged Collings to produce the eyeglass cleaner for the consumer marketplace.

Collings agreed to manufacture the new product, which consisted of several small tear-out tissues in a folder similar to a large match folder. It was to be called "SIGHT SAVERS®." Collings managed a team brought together to design and build a machine to make the folders. He brought in Harold Brown, a machinery maker who had worked closely with Dow Chemical in the past, to work on the project. Arthur Weirauch and Owen Cookingham converted Brown's design ideas to paper, and together the team designed a SIGHT SAVERS® machine that cut and folded the paper and bound it into a folder with a plastic cover.

The product was popular from the start, and to this day SIGHT SAVERS® sell well in drugstores around the country (Figure 3-4). The consumer marketplace represented an entirely new base of customers for Dow Corning, and the success of SIGHT SAVERS® made the company optimistic about additional consumer product possibilities.

Market Research. In addition to encouraging Collings to enter the consumer marketplace, Sullivan and LaFollette had suggested that Dow Corning form a market research department. Corning Glass had an active market research group focusing on its consumer products business, and Corning management credited the group with providing substantial support for marketing and strategic business decisions. Since the experience with SIGHT SAVERS® made it apparent that the consumer marketplace held considerable promise for silicone products, Collings agreed to establish a market research function within Dow Corning. This was early in 1948, when M.B.A. degrees were not common, but the general feeling among Corning and Dow Corning management was that the market research director should have one. Collings asked A..W.

Figure 3-4. SIGHT SAVERS®, Dow Corning's first consumer product, were distributed through drugstores around the country. They were an instant success.

("Dusty") Rhodes , at the time a sales trainee for Dow Chemical, to head up the new department. Rhodes, with an M.B.A. as well as an engineering degree, was well-qualified for the job.

Since Dow Corning had traditionally served industrial markets, market research was an unfamiliar area to most employees. The salespeople didn't feel the need for such research, and Collings initiated most of the department's projects.

One of the primary functions of market research is to predict the likelihood of success of a potential new product. This was a difficult task in the case of silicones. Because these materials had unusual properties that would allow their use in a host of unique applications, it was impossible to predict how the market would react to many silicone products.

Instead of concentrating on new applications, Rhodes focused his efforts on markets for products which silicones could readily replace, estimating the participation level that Dow Corning was likely to achieve in those markets. Such estimates guided product development efforts in the early years of the company.

In addition to providing this general research into markets for silicone products, Rhodes's department worked to make existing products more successful. One of the group's early efforts was to enhance sales of SIGHT SAVERS®. This was done primarily through outside research studies aimed at determining sales trends and the impact of such things as packaging and pricing on store sales. In addition, SIGHT SAVERS® tissue cleaning stations were introduced to industrial concerns as a way to expand the market. The effort was successful, and SIGHT SAVERS® are still found in many industrial plants today.

A. W. ("Dusty") Rhodes, *Manager of Market Research.*

Rhodes's department also provided valuable information to the salespeople in these early days, through the production of the monthly "Technical Bulletin" which provided the most up-to-date information (gleaned from mandatory "trip reports" submitted by everyone in the company who had any customer contact) about who was using silicone products, for what purposes, in what quantities, under what conditions, etc. This information was critical to the sales effort in those days, when new product applications were being developed almost weekly.

Electrical Products

While new products—DOW CORNING® 35 emulsion, Pan Glaze, SIGHT SAVERS®—were being developed for civilian markets, a group of wartime products was being resurrected for civilian use. After the war, Dow Corning launched a program to begin selling impregnating resins for electric motor insulation. These resins were the principal products for which the plant had been built during the war. Now Dow Corning would try to sell them to civilian customers uneducated in the electrical uses of the silicones.

Electrical Resin Sales. In September 1946, Bill Collings (now known as "Dr. Collings")[2] and Olie Blessing hired Clayton Doremire to promote

---

[2]In mid-1946, W. R. Collings was granted an honorary degree of doctor of science (D.Sc.) by his alma mater, Case Institute of Applied Science (now Case Western Reserve University), in recognition of his years of work within Dow Chemical Company and his pioneering efforts in bringing silicones to the marketplace. From that point on, he was addressed as "Dr. Collings," or in more familiar references, "Dr. C."

Clayt Doremire, *Manager of Electrical Product Sales.*

and manage sales of electrical resins. Doremire had the perfect background for the position. While working in the Electrical Maintenance Department of Dow during the war, Doremire had been asked by Collings to accept an appointment in the Navy Bureau of Ships, working for Hyman Rickover. His Navy experience involved supervising research projects to develop silicone insulation and made him a perfect choice to head up sales of electrical products to civilians.

In his new position, Doremire found that manufacturers of motors, generators, transformers, and other electrical equipment were somewhat interested in the idea of silicone resin insulation, but were also a bit skeptical. The introduction of silicones represented a major transition in electrical equipment manufacturing, and manufacturers were reluctant to plunge into the unknown.

Perhaps more importantly, they worried that with longer-lasting silicone insulation in their motors, they would lose a certain amount of repeat buying. Because of this reluctance on the part of manufacturers, Doremire decided to pursue another avenue.

Selling the Rewind Shops.   After the manufacturers had ignored his advances, Doremire tried to persuade rewind shops to use silicone resin insulation on the failed equipment that was rewound in their shops. Unfortunately, this approach wasn't very successful either, since the rewind shops, like the manufacturers, worried about the potential loss of repeat business. However, little by little the rewind shops started experimenting with silicone-insulated electrical wires. They bought in small quantities, just enough for two or three motors at a time. Sales were sluggish, since electrical distributors were not eager to stock items that had such low turnover. Although the war had ended, copper for electrical wires was still under allocation and distributors and manufacturers did not want to tie up their allocations in silicone-insulated wire. To further add to their concern about these risky new products, the silicone-insulation coating on the wire was weak and had to be handled with care.

The best Doremire could do at this point was to convince two or three electrical distributors to carry silicone resins, greases, and other products for use in electrical equipment, but none of them was willing to stock a complete line. This posed another problem. Because customers couldn't buy a complete line of silicone-insulated materials, they might repair their equipment using class A or class B insulation along with the class H silicone insulation, which operated at far higher temperatures than A or B. This would inevitably lead to equipment failure, as the lower-class insulation broke down at high temperatures, while silicone insulation continued to function.

Dow Corning as Distributor. Doremire relayed these problems to Dr. Collings, who responded, "If distributors won't stock a complete line of products, Dow Corning will." This decision took courage, for the young company was just beginning to come into its own after the war. Dow Corning sales were not yet robust, and the future was by no means certain. But Dr. Collings, like Dr. Sullivan, was a man of vision. The utility of silicones in electrical applications had been amply demonstrated during the war. Collings knew that the potential for silicones in the electrical industry was strong, and he was determined to translate that potential into sales.

Doremire told distributors of Dow Corning's decision to stock a complete line of electrical products. He explained that the intention was not to compete with the distributors; since they were not interested in carrying a full line of products, Dow Corning had no choice but to do so. Fortunately, Doremire managed to relay this message to the distributors without alienating them.

Once Dr. Collings made the decision that Dow Corning would become a distributor of electrical products, Clayt Doremire's most difficult task was to convince Anaconda Wire and Cable, one of the largest wire manufacturers in the country, to coat and then sell to Dow Corning a stock of silicone insulated magnet wire, even though Dow Corning did not have the copper allocation needed to purchase the wire. Doremire succeeded by convincing Anaconda that the product would be resold to Dow Corning customers who would have the required allocations.

Anaconda agreed to sell the wire, and when the full line of electrical parts was in place, Dow Corning started selling silicone-insulated wire, impregnating resins, and glass-laminate slot sticks to rewind shops. The shops then were able to rewind equipment using only silicone insulation.

This backdoor entry into the electrical business was expensive for Dow Corning, but highly successful. Once users of rewound motors witnessed the impressive results of silicone resin insulation, they began pressuring manufacturers of electrical equipment to make new equipment insulated with silicones.

Major Electrical Industry Sales. Once word of the new silicone-insulated motors began to spread, manufacturers of special equipment began to take notice and come calling on Dow Corning. This resulted in major sales of silicone resin for use in large-scale applications. The first such sale was to Automatic Transportation Company, which made an electrically driven lift truck. Customers were experiencing problems with their motors' continually "burning out" because they ignored the load and grade limits set by the company. Use of silicone insulation solved the problem of burnout.

General Motors was the next to take advantage of silicone insulation. The Electromotive Division of GM, which manufactured diesel electric railroad locomotives, was continually receiving requests for more powerful locomotives. The electric motors for these locomotives were mounted underneath the engines next to the axle shafts; there were severe space and exposure problems. To redesign the cars to accommodate a larger, more powerful motor would entail the building of new jigs, dies, and tools—a prohibitively expensive proposition.

The use of silicone insulation solved the locomotive problem. A new silicone-insulated motor was built for GM, using existing jigs, dies, and tools. While it was the same size as the previous motor, because it was insulated with silicones, it could be operated at higher power, over a far longer life, than the previous motor the company had been using (Figure 3-5).

Since GM was so pleased with the silicone insulation used in the armature of its traction motors that it requested a better insulation for the field coils, which were subject to vibrations. Dow Corning's electrical laboratory, under John Dexter's supervision, developed a SILASTIC®-coated glass tape, which worked beautifully.

Doremire could not convince any insulation manufacturer to make the silicone rubber insulating tape, so once again Dow Corning took matters into its own hands, modifying an old piece of equipment and manufacturing the "R tape," as it was named, for General Motors and others.

Soon Allis Chalmers, a supplier of electrical control equipment, heard of Electromotive's success with the SILASTIC®-coated glass tape and set out to develop a complete motor insulated with the tape, with the help of Dow Corning's electrical laboratory.

Once these hard-earned successes with the rewind shops and motor manufacturers were achieved, Clayt Doremire was finally able to convince distributors to carry a full line of silicone insulation stocks. Less than a year after it had gone into the distribution business, Dow Corning withdrew, having secured for itself a solid position in the electrical industry.

Figure 3-5. Coil being wound with silicone rubber tape.

Expansion

The success of Dow Corning's first postwar products could not have been realized without a substantial expansion in the sales force. Olie Blessing had added Charlie Sanford and Roger Kolderman to his staff near the end of the war. Once the war ended and experienced personnel from companies in the area became available, Collings and Blessing began to recruit them for the sales effort. A group from the Willow Run Ford Motor Company bomber plant outside Detroit had been training Air Force personnel. Five of these trainees—Don Francisco, Del Youngs, Max Leavenworth, Rome Minard, and Irvin Schneider—were hired by Dow Corning. Tony Woods was recruited from Defoe Shipyards in nearby Bay City.

These new employees were the first people outside Dow Chemical or Corning Glass Works to be hired by the company. All of them had been schoolteachers before their war assignments. Collings favored this background, reasoning that industry needed to be taught about silicones.

Branching Out: New York, Chicago, Cleveland

In the summer of 1945, with sales volume growing, Olie Blessing began to establish sales offices outside of Midland. The first to be established was in New York City. Mel Langford, an electrical engineer from Detroit Edison, was hired to head up this branch. Harry Boulton, an engineer from the Cellulose Products Department in Dow, moved to New York to become Langford's assistant.

The first office was rented on the seventy-seventh floor of the Empire State Building. The opening of the branch was delayed because of a rather unusual accident. On July 28, a B25 bomber struck the building at the seventy-eighth and seventy-ninth floors, and scaffolding for repairs occupied the seventy-seventh floor office the Dow Corning sales personnel were to occupy.

Chicago and Cleveland branches soon followed. Early in 1946, Roger Kolderman opened the Chicago office, with Irvin Schneider as his assistant. Shortly thereafter, Harry Boulton transferred from the New York office to replace Schneider when he left Dow Corning. Around the same time, Bill Pedersen moved from TS&D to sales, establishing a new office in Cleveland with the assistance of Tony Woods.

Earle Smith and Ira Hutchison also left their posts in TS&D to contribute to the New York sales effort, alternately commuting to the east coast from Midland for 2 weeks at a time. In the meantime, Don Francisco and Max Leavenworth, who had been recruited from the Ford Motor bomber plant, began servicing the state of Michigan out of Midland.

As the sales force fanned out across the country, they faced the formidable task of instructing prospects, over and over again, in the unique characteristics and benefits of silicone materials. In some ways, the fact that silicones were still a relatively unknown quantity in 1946 aided the salespeople in their efforts. As Don Francisco recalls, "Even though we were neophytes, we were looked upon as experts, especially by R&D people." He and Leavenworth jokingly referred to the sales presentation they repeatedly gave in their territory as the "silicone magic show."

More Sales Offices: Los Angeles, Dallas, Atlanta, Washington

The sales force continued to expand in 1947. Early in the year, an office was opened in Los Angeles, with Harry Boulton continuing his westward migration and taking over as branch manager. John Thomas left TS&D to replace Boulton in Chicago.

In early 1948, Max Leavenworth moved from Michigan to head up a new sales office in Dallas. Around the same time, R. B. ("Dutch") Ehlers opened an office in Atlanta. John Tyner took over for Harry Boulton in Los Angeles in 1948.

As a result of the Korean conflict and the new opportunities for silicones it presented, a Washington, D.C., sales office was added to the list of branches in 1950. Earle Smith moved from New York to head up the new D.C. branch.

Changes in the branch offices were many as personnel moved to other responsibilities within the growing company. Earle Smith moved back to New York as manager in 1953. Gordon McIntyre became the manager of the Washington office following Smith. The Boston office was first established as a subbranch of the New York office in 1952 with Jim Duane as manager, and later became a separate branch.

Despite the significant expense involved, the addition of several branch sales offices during the early postwar years proved profitable for Dow Corning, in more than one way. The presence of local sales offices helped to bolster sales volume in major cities. Perhaps more importantly, because of increased contact with the users of silicones, salespeople were able to learn more about customers' problems and suggest ways in which silicones could be applied to solving them. By the same token, customers offered numerous suggestions for new applications of the silicones that the sales force and Dow Corning management back in Michigan probably would not have generated on their own.

By the end of 1953, Olie Blessing noted that Dow Corning had roughly 12,000 customers served by 68 salespeople in the branch offices and 37 salespeople in Midland. The first formal sales training program had also been developed by this time.

International Beginnings

Shortly after the war ended, Dow Corning took its first steps toward becoming a multinational company. Silicones had been developed and used under a veil of secrecy during the war. When the war ended, few people in the United States or abroad knew much about the new materials. The British government, however, was quite familiar with the silicones, as it had been involved in joint efforts with the U.S. Navy to solve the problem of high-altitude ignition loss in jet aircraft, the problem that was solved by DOW CORNING 4® compound. After the war, the British were interested in learning more about these novel materials.

Dr. Sullivan was acquainted with Clifford Paterson, director of the

General Electric Company, United Kingdom (no connection with the American company). Because of this association, Shailer Bass was invited to accompany three other scientists who were to visit England in October 1945 at the expense of the British government, to work on improving the radio and radar equipment England had developed during the war. Dr. Bass was invited to educate British industry and government leaders in the application of silicones.

There were no commercial jetliners in those days, so the group made the trip overseas on a British military aircraft, leaving from Baltimore and arriving in England 29 hours later. The return trip was aboard the *SS Queen Elizabeth* passenger line, filled with U.S. troops headed home. Bass was well prepared to spread the word about silicones; he had loaded his luggage with three large boxes of samples and display materials and had another large box of catalogs and reprints shipped via the *Queen Elizabeth.*

Shailer Bass spent 2 months in England, giving speeches to British companies, government agencies, and universities, extolling the virtues of silicones. He was excited by the enthusiastic response to his lectures, and about the business opportunities he saw in England. Just 2 weeks after arriving in England, he wrote to Dr. Collings recommending that "we should not hesitate to set up the strongest organization here we can, and as soon as we ·can, or we will miss out on the opportunity that is here for a considerable amount of business."

Dr. Bass's enthusiasm was not shared by the board of directors back in Midland. Funds for expansion overseas were not readily available. As Collings pointed out, the domestic market for silicones was rapidly expanding and there was more than enough business to be had at home. Collings recognized the importance of becoming involved in the international arena at some point, but he felt it was premature for the 2-year-old company to make the move too quickly.

The First Foreign Distributor.   Among the companies Shailer Bass visited during his 2-month stay in England was Albright and Wilson Ltd., a large producer of phosphorus, silicon tetrachloride, and ethyl silicate. The company was also branching out into organic chemicals and had begun some research into silicones at the time of the visit. During this trip, Bass laid the groundwork for a distribution arrangement with the British company.

While Dow Corning's directors were not entirely sold on the proposition of going international, they were willing to support a limited involvement in overseas markets. As a result, on his second European trip in 1946, Bass appointed Albright and Wilson Ltd. as Dow Corning's first overseas distributor.

The French Connection: St. Gobain. During this second trip, a distributor relationship was also set up with a French company, St. Gobain, Chauny et Cirey. St. Gobain was a manufacturer of specialty glass (the company is famous for having produced the glass for the Hall of Mirrors in Versailles), chemicals, and plastic products. St. Gobain was familiar to Dow Corning because it was cross-licensing patents with Corning Glass.

SISS. In 1948, Dow Corning went beyond the 1946 distributor agreement with St. Gobain and established its first European joint venture with the French company. The 50-50 joint venture was named "Societe Industrielle Des Silicones et des Produits Chimiques Du Silicium (SISS)." At the outset, SISS was set up to manufacture silicone products, with St. Gobain retaining distribution rights; eventually SISS took over the distribution as well. The SISS plant was built in St. Fons, a suburb of Lyons.

Midsil. In 1950, a second joint venture was formed in Europe, this one with Albright and Wilson, the first European distributor. Under the agreement, Dow Corning formed a wholly owned subsidiary, Dow Corning Limited (DCL); this subsidiary then formed a 50-50 joint venture with Albright and Wilson, to be known as "Midland Silicones Limited (Midsil)."[3] Under this arrangement, Midsil was licensed to sell silicone products covered by all of Dow Corning's British patents. Originally, Midsil was set up strictly to sell silicones, with the British parent company, Albright and Wilson, responsible for manufacturing. After a while, however, a plant was built for Midsil, and the joint venture took over the manufacturing process as well.

The site chosen for Midsil's silicone plant was in Barry, south Wales. On the site was a plant that had been built by the British government during World War II. The plant was to manufacture metallic magnesium by taking inflow from the magnesium-rich Bristol Channel. However, the plan did not work out, and the plant had never been put into operation. Albright and Wilson had subsequently purchased the site, and when the Midsil joint venture was formed, the plant was converted to accommodate the manufacture of silicone products.

On to Germany: Wacker-Chemie. In all, Shailer Bass made four trips to Europe between 1945 and 1950. During his final trip in 1950,

---

[3]"Midland" in the name had nothing to do with the Dow Corning location in Michigan. It was used because the location of Albright and Wilson's corporate headquarters and major plant was in Birmingham, England, in an area known as the "Midlands."

Wacker-Chemie GmbH, a German chemical manufacturer, was licensed to manufacture silicones under Dow Corning's German patents. The agreement further allowed Dow Corning to use Wacker-Chemie's patent department to file for German patents and allowed the German company to file U.S. patents through Dow Corning's patent department.

A Visit to the Father of Silicones.   During one of his trips, Shailer Bass paid a weekend visit to Frederick Stanley Kipping (Figure 3-6), the father of silicone chemistry, at his oceanside resort in north Wales. Dr. Bass presented Kipping with a beautifully bound volume of the collection of papers that had laid the groundwork for the Corning group's silicone research. Kipping was touched by the gift, as he had lost all the original papers in a wartime bombing raid.

Professor Kipping, now retired from his post at University College, Nottingham, asked Shailer Bass for the latest news in silicon chemistry. He knew vaguely of the work we were doing but had not kept up with the literature. When Bass spoke of the silicone polymers, Kipping was disappointed. Time had not changed his opinion of the materials he had once referred to as "uninviting glues."

Dr. Collings in Europe.   Once Bass discovered the great potential for international business and had established working relationships in key countries, he encouraged Bill Collings to make a trip abroad. On March 1, 1951, Collings and his wife set sail from New York on the *Vulcania* of the Italian Line, bound for Europe and a visit to our overseas associates. On the second day out, a storm developed, which lasted 2 full days. Passengers were confined to their cabins. The storm wrecked the dining room and lounge furniture and broke some portholes 60 feet above the waterline. No one was seriously hurt, but the ship was 2 days late in docking in Lisbon.

During the storm, Collings wrote the first of a series of letters from Europe to Dow Corning employees, describing his experiences. He continued writing letters throughout his trip, forwarding photographs and postcards from the many places of interest he visited: Gibraltar, Palermo, Naples, Cannes, Milan, Basle, Munich, Rheinfelden, Frankfort, Paris, London, Barry in Wales, and finally Southampton, where he and his wife boarded the *Queen Mary* for the trip home. Because of the warm response to these travel letters, beginning in July 1951 Collings initiated a series of "Me to You" letters to employees that would continue over the next 11 years.

Dr. Collings's European excursion gave him a better understanding of the extent of opportunities overseas. Like Bass, he realized that the

Figure 3-6. Dr. Shailer Bass with Dr. Frederick Stanley Kipping, the "father of silicones."

potential for silicones in the international marketplace was great, and he knew that to realize that potential, a substantial commitment of people, effort, and money would be required.

As a beginning step, shortly after his return from Europe, Collings called Ira Hutchison back from the New York sales office and appointed him manager of foreign technical service, responsible for providing technical assistance to overseas customers and associates.

Hutchison joked that for the first 2 years he was not only the manager but also the entire staff (with a great deal of support from the tech-

Ira Hutchison, *Manager of the International Department.*

nical service, engineering, and manufacturing departments in Midland).

Dr. Bass Visits Japan. With a firm foundation laid in Europe, Shailer Bass headed to Japan late in 1951, with the intent of establishing joint venture arrangements in that country. In Tokyo he met with Eric Crane, the manager of A. R. Brown McFarlane & Co. Ltd., a distributor that had become heavily involved in working with the Japanese government after the war had ended and Japan was opening its doors to foreign business. Brown McFarlane started out as an old Scottish trading company that operated in Japan as far back as the late nineteenth century. During his trip, Dr. Bass discovered that the Japanese had learned about silicones during the war, by studying downed American airplanes that were utilizing silicones in their ignition systems. By the early 1950s, a few Japanese companies had made significant headway in their study of silicones. Eric Crane arranged for Bass to meet with some of these companies. He toured a pilot plant of Japan Silicones Ltd. and visited Shin-Etsu Chemical Company, which was using the direct process for producing silicones and was also manufacturing its own silicon.

In addition to visiting silicone manufacturers, Bass spoke before 25 members of the Ministry of Science and Industry and lectured to the Sumitomo Group in Osaka, one of the largest networks of industrial companies in Japan. In addition, Brown McFarlane arranged a silicone exhibit in Osaka for 1000 guests from industry and government who had an interest in silicones. Two of Japan's foremost scientists lectured on the Japanese silicone industry, and Bass spoke about developments in the United States.

No business commitments were made during this initial visit; the Japanese were still wary of outside competition. However, the trip was successful nevertheless, as it laid the groundwork for future negotiations with the Japanese.

Canada. Closer to home, a Canadian company was incorporated in 1953 as Dow Corning Silicones Ltd., a wholly owned subsidiary. While the market for silicones was not extensive in Canada, it was easily accessible and it was felt that Dow Corning should take advantage of whatever opportunities were available for dealing with our neighbors to the north.

International Department. The steady growth of overseas sales and the growing demand for manufacturing and production support for Dow Corning's foreign affiliates made Dr. Collings recognize the need to establish a separate organization to focus exclusively on international business. As a result, the International Department was formed in 1953, under the direction of Ira Hutchison.

Several employees moved over from the export sales group to staff the newly formed department. Bob Kroeger, who had joined Dow Corning in 1947 as its first export sales employee, was appointed sales manager of the department. Bruce Smith, who had joined the group in 1951, was named technical service manager. Other members of export sales who transferred to the International Department included Joe Closs and Tom Nehil in Midland and Jim McSorley in New York.

Hutchison's department focused on three goals: assisting Dow Corning's joint ventures in England and France; developing new markets in other areas of the world, including Japan, Latin America, and Australia; and providing technical support to all foreign distributors of Dow Corning products.

To help realize these goals, experienced manufacturing and engineering employees in Midland made many trips overseas along with International Department staff, calling on joint venture partners, distributors, and customers. Often the visits by product engineering people were coordinated with invitations to present papers on silicones at European technical meetings. This helped to spread the word about silicones throughout Europe and to expand Dow Corning's overseas sales. Providing basic manufacturing and production engineering service to our associates in England and France was a big job. Engineers from each of our joint venture partners came to Midland to learn more about silicone production. Robert Gay of St. Gobain's Chemical and Plastics Department spent 6 weeks in Midland after St. Gobain was appointed a distributor. Also remembered is the 7-week visit by Freddie de Vaissiere, an engineer from St. Gobain. James Bottomley and Ray Gregory, a delightful and hardworking team, came from Albright and Wilson.

Each of these visitors from overseas produced enormous reports to be used in designing silicone manufacturing plants in their countries. Both the English and the French had begun large-scale production using intermediate products from our Midland, Michigan, plant. It was a happy day for each group when they began producing chlorosilanes on their own. Andre Hernette, plant manager of SISS, summed up the sense of accomplishment the groups felt when they took over the production process, in a three-word telegram to Hutchison in Midland: "Victory, dear Ira."

Selling Dow Corning products abroad presented many problems. Price was one stumbling block. Customers resisted the higher prices they had to pay for silicones versus organic products. This pricing problem was exacerbated by the fact that governmental trade barriers, import duties, and, in many countries, other taxes and "deposits" were added to the basic cost of silicone products to compensate for exchange shortages.

Outside England and France, Dow Corning sales were made through distributors who carried many other product lines, and this posed another problem. Sales personnel were in many cases inadequately trained in silicones. Too often they concentrated on other products which were much easier to sell.

The language barrier was another obstacle. While English was spoken and read by many of the management and technical people in European manufacturing industries, it was necessary to provide translations of technical data sheets for most of Dow Corning's products sold overseas.

Traveling from Midland to Europe was quite an undertaking in the early 1950s. When Shailer Bass and Ira Hutchison visited Japan and Europe late in 1953, all their flights were made on Pan Am Clippers and DC6 four-engine planes. The flight from Tokyo to Frankfurt, Germany, took 40 hours. With such long traveling hours, trips abroad had to be lengthy in order to be worthwhile. Ira Hutchison recalls that in the early years of the International Department, he and others made many 13-week trips to Europe—quite a strain on those involved, as well as on the families left behind.

Finally, despite the newness of silicone technology, the pace of competition overseas was quickening. In some cases the competition came from Dow Corning's own joint venture partners. Once European silicone manufacturers (including Dow Corning's associates in England and France and patent licensees in Germany and, later, in Japan) began producing in their own plants, competition increased sharply.

In countries where there were no local producers, potential users had quite an array of foreign silicone products and distributors from which to choose. Astute buyers had many opportunities to better the price they could obtain by playing one supplier against the other.

Dow Corning recognized, of course, that granting patent licenses to manufacturing companies overseas would stimulate competition. However, the expectation was that the market would be enlarged and Dow Corning's participation in that market would be enhanced in the process. Licensing also provided a needed cash flow to finance total foreign operations.

Despite these obstacles, sales of Dow Corning silicone products grew steadily overseas, primarily because quality and technical service were highly important to potential customers, and Dow Corning had an excellent reputation in both these areas. By the mid-1950s, Dow Corning had a firm foothold in all the major European markets.

On to Latin America. Early in 1954, Ira Hutchison and Robert Kroeger visited a number of countries in South America with the objective of establishing distribution agreements. However, the obstacles to conducting business in South America were great at that time, and it was not until many years later that such distributor relationships were established.

Personnel Expansion

With the growth of Dow Corning's domestic and foreign markets in the postwar years and a steady increase in the number of employees, more formal personnel systems were established, most of them patterned after Dow Chemical's. Personnel screening tests were adopted in an attempt to build a quality work force. Job ratings were gradually developed.

In addition, many new personnel functions were established. Howard Christensen was hired from Dow in early 1947 to manage labor relations and the hiring of the hourly work force. Bob Bott, who was trained in both personnel and vocational training, was hired in 1948 to provide the technical training needed to upgrade hourly workers from Dow to journeyman status at Dow Corning.

Leo Johnson, a Dow veteran, was brought in to manage the fire and plant protection activities, as well as the Service Department, both under Personnel. He is best remembered for a management decision he made as head of the Service Department. A former lumberjack, Leo chuckled when it was suggested that an outside vendor be hired to remove a tree from a parking lot that interfered with its expansion. He scoffed when one of the workers felt the cars nearby should be moved in the event the tree didn't fall where his lumberjack's eye calculated. After the tree was expertly notched and the saw cut completed at the precise angle, this lonely tree began to topple. But, alas, it spun around as only a few trees do and fell directly on top of one of the parked cars. Leo took it in stride, quietly instructing his staff to "cut up the tree, haul it away, and get the car fixed."

Mary Dawson, who managed the Personnel Department, supervised the transfer of many Dow employees to Dow Corning in the early postwar years. However, in late 1947 Dow notified Dow Corning that there would be no more employee transfers. With the business growing, the parent felt it was time for Dow Corning to begin standing on its own. At this point, Howard Christensen and Mary Dawson took to the road and began an ongoing recruiting program.

In 1950 Mike Stinton was hired to head up Plant Protection Administration; safety and security functions were added to round out his job. In 1951, Bill Sheeran transferred from consumer sales to manage hourly employment. Ray Harris, who had been Dr. Collings's personal driver, joined the Plant Protection group. Jim King was hired from Purdue to supervise Trades Training and Job Evaluation when Bob Bott was recalled to active duty in the Navy during the Korean war. The department moved to new quarters in the 205 building in late 1952 and was joined there by Bob Bott who returned from Korean war duty and continued the work he'd begun before the war. By this time employment stood at about 800 and sales per month were roughly $600,000. Howard Christensen was named manager of the Personnel Department. Jim King moved to labor relations, and George Momony came into the department from the pilot plant to supervise trades training. Bill Hargreaves, who had been in the Analytical Department since 1946, joined the Personnel Department in 1953 to head up Personnel Recruitment. Reporting to Hargreaves were Howard Christensen, who handled Midland personnel functions; Mike Stinton, head of Safety and Security; and Jack Ludington, manager of Professional Personnel.

Supervisory Training

Dr. Collings was concerned about personnel problems a proposed plant expansion might create. To address this concern, in his July 1951 "Me to You" letter, Collings announced the formation of the Auxiliary Management Committee, composed of middle management employees, to study problems associated with the proposed expansion and plans for the future. The committee included eight members from all areas of the company. The group focused on addressing personnel issues that grew out of the expansion, for example, developing new job rating systems and altering personnel policy as the company grew.

The Auxiliary Management Committee made a study within the company, and from this they recommended establishing a supervisory training program. Dr. Collings instructed Bob Bott to develop the program internally, telling him, "Don't do this with outsiders; we know how to manage, the trick is to get our experienced managers to share their knowledge with others."

Bott based his course on a knowledge of group dynamics taught at that time by the National Training Laboratories of Group Development. Seven groups of 15 supervisors and managers were formed from experienced people as well as new employees. These groups met and discussed various topics such as motivation, job efficiency, discipline, and sick leave. In some instances experts from within the company would appear with each group to provide information as well as answer questions. The experiences with this program were published in an article in *The American Society of Training and Development* magazine.

Another recommendation of the Auxiliary Management Committee was that a consistent personnel policy be developed. Collings appointed the Personnel Policy Committee made up of Burl Huber, treasurer; Andy Kauppi, director of development; and Bill Caldwell, general plant manager, with Bob Bott as executive secretary (Figure 3-7).

The Auxiliary Management Committee also recommended an employee counseling program to guide employees to their goals and discuss their performance. Under the Personnel Department, two evening courses were developed for employees. A course on silicone chemistry and production was taught by research, product development, and production managers. The second was called "Know Your Dow Corning" and was meant to introduce employees to the variety of career opportunities available within the firm.

Spreading the Word: Advertising and Publicity

Advertising

In order to promote the sale of silicones to civilian markets after the war ended, the Advertising Department expanded, adding Maurie Hommel

Figure 3-7. The Personnel Policy Committee (*left to right*): Bob Bott, Bill Caldwell, Burl Huber, and Andy Kauppi.

and Bob Argyle in the summer of 1945. The expansion meant that more space was needed. Unfortunately, by this time space was at a premium at the Dow Corning plant site (Figure 3-8), and the department was moved to a corridor outside the pilot plant, which it shared with some members of the sales department.

Some products, for example, DOW CORNING® 35 emulsion, were sold primarily by word of mouth. Others, such as SILASTIC® and Pan Glaze, needed a boost from print and other forms of advertising. The Advertising Department began producing a series of brochures, known as "Silastic Facts," to educate customers about the types, properties, and applications of silicone rubber.

The group also began to make use of direct mail to promote its products. Direct mail could be aimed at smaller, more "targeted" segments of the market than could be reached by journal advertising. Niles Foss headed the direct-mail effort, which succeeded in building a large and continually expanding list of prospects for the salespeople to approach as new silicone products became available.

Dr. Collings had a great interest in educating prospects about sili-

Figure 3-8. Dow Corning quickly outgrew its office facilities as the silicones business expanded in the late 1940s. Office space was at such a premium that one sales representative reportedly had to set up his desk in a janitor's closet.

cones as a way of promoting their sales. With the opening of the Washington, D.C., sales office in 1950, Collings gathered a group together to discuss how to best advertise silicones to people in government agencies. A display of silicone products and their capabilities was suggested. The Don Wagnitz Advertising Agency in Midland was commissioned to design the show. Technical people contributed to the effort, and with the help of Clayt Doremire and Lou Putnam, the agency developed a major display in six sections covering the various beneficial aspects of the silicones.

In the durability section of the exhibit, a "Ferris wheel" transported samples of bearings from an ice-cold bath to a hot bath. Repeated exposure of an organic-lubricated bearing soon froze the bearing, while the silicone-lubricated bearing continued to turn. In the electrical section, a silicone-insulated motor was repeatedly dunked in a large tank of water, and continued to run. In the water repellency section, a multistage washing, drying, and testing machine demonstrated the durability of cloth treated with water-repellent silicone fluid. A number of other animated exhibits demonstrated the advantages of silicones over their organic counterparts.

Two showings of the exhibit were planned initially, one at an open house in Midland in the week of the American Institute of Chemical Engineers meeting in October 1951, and a second in Washington, D. C., shortly afterward. Potential customers were invited to attend.

Because of the positive response to the Midland showing, and before the visit to Washington, Dr. Collings decided the show should be taken to other major cities where Dow Corning had potential customers. He asked Wayne ("Sandy") Sanderson, who had worked on the design stages, to supervise the traveling show, with assistance from George Webster (Figure 3-9).

The exhibit received the attention of some prominent businesspeople. At the Detroit show in 1951, a distinguished gentleman visited the exhibit a few minutes after normal closing hours and commented about the quality of the show. Later it was found out that he was K. T. Keller, the president of Chrysler Motors. Keller was involved in a government committee that was working on military problems he felt silicones might solve, and he requested that the show be brought to Washington a second time, even offering to have Chrysler foot the bill (Dow Corning declined on that point). As a result, a second Washington show was scheduled in February 1952 and was attended by many high-ranking government officials, at the personal request of Keller.

So popular was the traveling display that it was actively exhibited for nearly 3 years. From Montreal to Winston-Salem, North Carolina, from Los Angeles to Chicago to Boston and New York, 32 showings were held in 25 cities throughout the United States and Canada, and a sig-

Figure 3-9. *Above:* A section of the traveling exhibit of Dow Corning products, which toured the country for 3 years in the early 1950s, helping to educate customers and prospects about the benefits of silicones. *Left:* Sandy Sanderson supervised the popular exhibit.

nificant amount of business was generated as a result. The traveling show was deemed a solid success despite its rather high cost. Perhaps more than any other advertising vehicle in the early postwar years, the traveling display effectively educated prospects about the broad range of problems for which silicones, and Dow Corning, could provide solutions.

Publicizing Silicones

After the war ended, Bill Collings encouraged Dow Corning management and scientists to take advantage of every opportunity to tell the world about silicones. As a result, several articles by Dow Corning employees began appearing in a number of professional and trade journals in the immediate postwar years.

Collings took his own message to heart, reporting on the production of silicones at the new Dow Corning plant for *Chemical Engineering News;*[4] Andy Kauppi (along with G. L. Moses of Westinghouse) discussed silicone resins in electrical insulation for an engineering trade journal;[5] Kauppi and Shailer Bass wrote about silicones in the radio industry for an electrical engineering journal[6] and published a general article on silicones in the journal *Plastics;*[7] Roger Kolderman spread the word to the north with an article for a Canadian chemical journal;[8] and Drs. Bass, Hyde, Britton, and McGregor discussed silicone resins in *Plastics Catalog.*[9] In May 1947, *Fortune* magazine published an article, "The Silicones, Cornerstone of a New Industry."[10] The article, which told the basic story of silicones and described the progress being made by the two major producers of silicone, Dow Corning and General Electric, generated a good deal of publicity. The author concluded that "within a decade the silicones will be among the most important industrial plastics and synthetics." This helped to reinforce the optimism Dow Corning employees had long felt about the potential of the curious compounds Dr. Hyde had introduced.

-

[4]W. R. Collings, *Chem. Eng. News,* 23:1616 (1945).

[5]T. A. Kauppi and G. L. Moses, *IEEE Trans. Ind. Appl,* 64:90 (1945).

[6]S. L. Bass and T. A. Kauppi, *Proc. IEEE,* 33:44 (1945).

[7]S. L. Bass and T. A. Kauppi, *Plastics,* Chicago (1945).

[8]R. Kolderman, *Can. Chem. Process,* 29:147 (1945).

[9]S. L. Bass, J. F. Hyde, E. C. Britton, and R. R. McGregor, *Plastics Catalog,* 190 (1945).

[10]*Fortune, May 1947,* p. 104.

More New Products...

As Dr. Bass became more involved with overseas sales and joint ventures after the war, his role in the United States was expanded and he was named assistant general manager in 1946. For a time, Bass continued to head up the research groups as well. In 1947, Mel Hunter, who had served as assistant director of research since 1945, replaced Bass as director of research.

With these management changes came a shift in the orientation of the company, from an emphasis on research to a new focus on product development. To accelerate the development effort, a number of specialized laboratories were formed under the umbrella of Product Engineering, headed by Andy Kauppi.

Under this new arrangement, a series of additional products began to emerge, as it was discovered that many industrial and consumer problems could be solved by silicones. Soon Dow Corning began to introduce silicones in a host of new applications, from antifoaming products to car polishes and shoe treatments.

Product Engineering Labs

Fluids Section

Diffusion-Pump Fluids: DOW CORNING 702® and DOW CORNING® 703.   Chet Currie (Figure 3-10) managed the Fluids Section of the Product Engineering group, which was housed in new quarters in the 105 building. Included in this group were a number of chemists and engineers who later moved on to greater responsibilities, including Bill Ragborg, Dick Gergle, Joe Keil, Bob Vidal, Charlie Todd, and Bill May.

Currie worked on developing diffusion-pump fluids, a new avenue of exploration for the company. No one in Dow Corning knew anything about diffusion-pump fluids, how they worked and what characteristics they should have. As a result, Currie had to start from scratch and learn all he could about the technical requirements of the users of diffusion pumps.

Currie prepared many different fluids with phenyl and methyl groups, finally producing two successful commercial products, DOW CORNING 702® and DOW CORNING® 703. These fluids were superior to organic diffusion-pump fluids in that they could be exposed to air while hot without oxidizing and gelling. This was important, as many diffusion-pump applications required that the system be opened to the air periodically without allowing time for the fluid to cool down.

DOW CORNING 4® Compound.   When World War II ended, many new civilian applications for DOW CORNING 4® compound were developed.

Figure 3-10. Chet Currie, manager, Fluids Section of the early
Product Engineering labs.

Each user seemed to require different specifications for his or her particular application of the compound. It would have been impossible for Dow Corning to meet all the varied specifications submitted. Instead, Currie's group worked with these users to simplify their requirements to reasonable levels, so that the labs could concentrate on a limited number of DOW CORNING 4® compound variations.

Paper Coatings. Currie assigned Joe Keil to work on a coating for paper—one that would prevent various materials from sticking to the paper. Zeke Dennett's Water Repellency laboratory had developed the first samples of such a paper coating, but in many instances the coating transferred to the material which was being released.

After some experimentation, Keil came up with an effective product and began running field trials with several interested companies. Tom Hildebrand, in the Dallas sales office, located a box manufacturer who made containers for tar. The containers would be filled with molten tar and shipped; upon arrival, the cardboard would be peeled off and the tar remelted. However, it was almost impossible to remove all the paper from the tar.

Hildebrand proposed that the box manufacturer consider silicones as a possible solution for his sticky problem. He made arrangements for a paper treater to coat the cardboard with a silicone treatment before it was made into containers for tar. He also convinced a manufacturer to make boxes from the silicone-treated paper and arranged for a tar producer to fill the boxes.

The product was a resounding success. Such cooperative efforts between Sales and Product Engineering were responsible for many new product introductions in the early postwar years.

Car Polish. The Fluids Section also became involved with the development of silicone car polish. Many Dow Corning employees had used DOW CORNING 200® silicone fluid as a car polish in the early days of the company, as it gave a sparkle to the finish, imparted water repellency, and, perhaps most importantly, was easy to apply (all previous car polishes were wax-based, and as anyone who polished cars with these early car waxes can attest, they required intense labor to buff to a high gloss). Chet Currie improved on the basic formulation by adding a mild abrasive and solvent to the fluid, in a water emulsion, and developed an effective car polish.

Once the polish was patented, Currie and others approached Simonize, S. C. Johnson, and other polish manufacturers, and much to their chagrin they encountered considerable resistance to the use of silicones in car polish. The feedback from these visits was that the 1 or 2 percent of silicone used in the polish would cost more than all the other ingredients, plus the container. The polish manufacturers felt that such a high-priced product would not be marketable.

Rebuffed by the big manufacturers, Dow Corning gave consideration to marketing its own brand of car polish. SIGHT SAVERS® were already on the market, and many within Dow Corning felt a car polish would be a good consumer product addition. However, the Market Research Department concurred with the assessment of the polish manufacturers, that the product would be too expensive to be a success.

Meanwhile, Tone Corporation, a small furniture company in Grand Rapids, Michigan, requested silicone fluid samples from Dow Corning. Don Francisco, sales representative for the Michigan territory, visited the company shortly after the samples were delivered and found it was experimenting with silicones in furniture polish, and getting such exciting results that it had decided to market a silicone-based furniture polish.

The silicone furniture polish was well accepted locally, and when Tone heard about Dow Corning's experimentation with car polish, it decided to expand its line to include a silicone car polish under the Tone trade name.

Before long, the new Tone car polish, containing the DOW CORNING 200® silicone fluid, was developed and sent out for test marketing in three medium-sized cities, for a price three times the going rate for car polish. Much to everyone's surprise, the product became the predominant choice almost overnight.

At this point the major polish manufacturers took note and soon introduced their own silicone polishes. Unfortunately, Tone did not survive once the large companies entered the picture. Dow Corning decided it would be too risky to compete with the big manufacturers at this late date and turned its attention instead to other more promising consumer products.

DOW CORNING® Antifoam A Compound.   A number of new products were developed in response to customer problems brought to the attention of the sales representatives in the field. One of the fastest growing and most profitable of these products came in response to a duPont inquiry. The company had found that the stopcock grease developed as an extension of DOW CORNING 4® compound was an effective defoamer, and the company was using it in the production of latex-dipped gloves. DuPont ordered more, but claimed that the new lot was not effective.

Chet Currie made many permutations of the stopcock grease in attempts to match the earlier performance. Currie was handicapped in his efforts because he did not know how duPont was testing antifoam effectiveness, a procedure they deemed secret. Though he sent many samples back to duPont, all failed.

Finally, frustrated by his repeated attempts to reproduce the grease and skeptical of duPont's claim that the new formulations did not work, Currie sent a sample from the original lot, but with a new number. DuPont immediately informed him that this material was also effective. Clearly there was something unique about the original batch of stopcock grease.

Finally, duPont relented and gave Currie its secret test procedure, and he was finally able to duplicate the original material. The new product, named "DOW CORNING® Antifoam A compound," became a substantial success.

Shortly after perfecting the new product, Dow Corning learned that many industries had foaming problems and began advertising DOW CORNING® Antifoam A compound as a general solution, primarily through direct mail and ads in trade magazines. The ads simply stated: "If you have a foam problem, write to Dow Corning for a sample." DOW CORNING® Antifoam A compound was so universally effective that these samples alone sold the customer.

Shailer Bass felt that DOW CORNING® Antifoam A compound might have uses in food and other products consumed by humans, so he arranged for feeding tests and other tests of the toxicity of the defoamer. Ultimately, Dow Corning was able to establish the biosafety of Antifoam A. This led to the introduction of DOW CORNING® Antifoam A com-

"What's the opposite of 'Eureka!'?"

pound into many food and drug products, including one popular antacid.

Sales growth of DOW CORNING® Antifoam A compound used in various applications grew steadily and rapidly. It was several years before significant competition developed from other silicone producers, and by the time it did, Dow Corning had established a dominant place in the market.

Resin Laboratories.   While Currie's group was working on fluid products, resin research and development was being carried on in several laboratories. Involved in the research were Jim Lyons, Earle Smith, Mike Kin, John Thomas, Wayne Barrett, Larry Rauner, Don Kime, Del

Youngs, J. G. Bachand, Bob Hedlund, Joe Francis, John Goodwin, Charlie Kohl, Sue Gordon, Larry Brown, Bill McLean, Ken Moorhead, Merritt Koster, and Joe Keil.

The new DOW CORNING® 993 resin was produced in the labs as a replacement for DOW CORNING® 990A additive. A great deal of effort was also spent on the development of a magnet wire enamel, a resin that could be used as the only insulation on copper for winding small coils, such as those found in the ¼-horsepower motors of household appliances.

The DOW CORNING® 993 resin continued to be a successful product, but the work on the magnet wire enamel was never completely successful despite many trials. Generally the resin was too soft to resist penetration by a neighboring wire. If the resin was made harder, the resin coating the wire would crack when the wire was wound.

A compromise solution was finally developed. When the wire was passed through a small glass sleeve and then coated with resin, the problem of hardness was solved and most of the magnet wire specifications were met.

In addition to the work on DOW CORNING® 993 and the magnet wire enamel, new resin catalysts were explored in a search for faster cures. The resin labs also worked on finding new applications for the laminating resins first developed at Mellon Institute. In addition, they developed two new and very successful intermediate products, silicone additions for organic (alkyd) resins. These products, Sylkyd 50 and Sylkyd 60, were sold directly to paint companies for use as additives to various heat-stable paint formulations.

Motor Test Laboratory. The Motor Test laboratory, headed by George Grant, stayed in operation until the early 1950s. Over the years, the lab continued its life tests of silicone-insulated motors. In addition, the group studied the effect of silicone insulation on the life of carbon brushes used in some motors and found that silicones seemed to accelerate the wear of the brushes.

SILASTIC® Laboratory. Phil Servais, who had been to Mellon Institute to learn the details of the early silicone rubber, was named manager of the SILASTIC® laboratory. He was joined in the research and development effort over the next few years by Bob Selfridge, George Konkle, Jim Davidson, Floyd Dryzga, B. T. Miska, Al Chipman, Hugo Schmidt, Ray Maneri, Keith Polmanteer, and Silas Braley.

Many of the early studies of SILASTIC® were aimed at determining the silicone rubber's properties, for example, the effects of greases and solvents on the rubber. The lab also measured the basic electrical characteristics of the rubber, testing it for dielectric breakdown and power losses. Aging characteristics at various temperatures for the different stocks were determined and were important in suggesting potential uses. A conductive SILASTIC® stock was developed and used in automotive ignition systems. New ways of compounding the rubber were explored and a variety of mixing machines tried. The group also found a way to lower the freezing point of silicone rubber, by the addition of small amounts of diphenylsiloxy units or methylphenylsiloxy units.

One crucial problem had to be resolved shortly after SILASTIC® 250, the first high-strength rubber, was introduced in 1949. Two or three months after the first orders for SILASTIC® 250 were shipped, several batches were returned to Dow Corning. Customers found that the 250 stock which had been on the shelf for a few weeks hardened, as if it already had a light vulcanization. Remilling to soften the stock prior to molding or extruding took an exceptionally long time. This phenomenon became known as "crepe hardening."[11] It had not been identified in the laboratories because samples were molded quite soon after formulating and milling the stock.

Servais's lab spent a great deal of time trying to solve this problem. Keith Polmanteer developed an interim solution, a plasticizer known as "PA fluid." This fluid was used for months, until a better (but more expensive) solution was found in the form of special silica fillers, which not only eliminated crepe hardening but resulted in even higher-strength SILASTIC® as well. Once the crepe hardening problem was solved, sales of SILASTIC® 250 grew steadily.

Within Phil Servais's SILASTIC® laboratory was the Rubber Formulation lab, under the direction of Del Youngs. Paul Skalnican, Bud Smith, and Bob Witman worked in the lab, developing methods of fabricating silicone rubber. Such processes and products as hot-air vulcanization, sponge extrusion, and specially shaped electrical tape were developed in the Rubber Formulation lab.

Textile Treatment Laboratory. As pointed out in Chapter 2, Dr. Barry's group early on had been working on the problem of waterproofing textiles and had developed a fluid, DOW CORNING® 1107, that proved to be an effective water repellent. When Dr. Barry became heavily involved in the direct-process experiments, the water repellency work was shifted to Dr. Hunter's group.

Zeke Dennett joined Hunter's research group in the fall of 1945 and continued the waterproofing experiments Dr. Barry's group had begun. In 1947, Dennett transferred from Hunter's group to Andy

---

[11]The term "crepe hardening" was used because crepe rubber has a look similar to crepe paper; it appears to be "crumbly" but is not.

Kauppi's Product Engineering group and headed up a new Textile Treatment laboratory, where he continued the waterproofing experiments. He was joined in the new lab by Mary Thayer Sprague and Clarence ("Hoot") Gibson.

Up to this point, fabrics were made water-repellent by treatment with waxes that had to be reapplied after each dry cleaning. The goal was to find a water-repellent treatment that would be permanent.

Bill Collings, who was quite interested in the water repellency studies, volunteered several of his hats for testing with these early treatments. Dr. Collings was well known for his

Zeke Dennett, *Manager of the Textile laboratory.*

love of hats; he had a wide variety of high-grade, expensive fur and felt hats. The hats Collings turned over to Dennett and Mary Thayer Sprague were beautiful, but he neglected to tell them he planned to wear them again; they assumed the hats were of no further use to him.

As Dennett tells it:

> We proceeded to treat them as experimental material for one week. The treatment included a heating cycle in an oven to develop water repellency. To be truthful, we didn't know what effect this heating would have on the hats. The application of the water repellency treatment did not change the appearance, and we duly demonstrated the water repellency to Dr. Collings on his next visit to the laboratory.
>
> After expressing pleasure with the results, Dr. Collings tried on one of his new water-repellent hats. We could see immediately that it did not fit quite right, but he said nothing, nor did we. He tried a second and a third in quick succession, with the same results. He then put on the hat he was wearing, pulled it over his forehead (a well-known signal of his displeasure) and muttered, "You shrank them!" and immediately left the laboratory.[12]

Dennett worried for the next few days that he would find a pink dismissal card in his time-card rack. No such card appeared, but no further hat treatments were tried.

The Textile Treatment laboratory improved on the basic DOW CORNING® 1107 fluid Dr. Barry's group had developed and tested its new formulation with a number of companies. The field trials were suc-

[12]Dorothy L. Yates, *William R. Collings: Dow Corning's Pioneer Leader,* Kay Press, Midland, Mich., 1985.

cessful, and the commercial formulation was given the name "Decetex 104." Dr. Bass was invited to demonstrate Decetex 104 on an ABC television program (Figure 3-11), and the publicity helped to boost sales of this first successful fabric treatment.

While not a separate area of product sales management, textile treatment sales were handled by Charlie Sanford. In the fall of 1953, a group headed by Sanford recommended that Dow Corning set standards of performance for the treatment of textiles with silicones and permit those who complied with these standards to use Dow Corning hangtags on their garments. To make the hangtag of value, the concept had to be aggressively advertised and promoted. Such a promotion had to be nationwide in scope to gain acceptance by the garment makers.

It was at this point that the program *Home*, hosted by Arlene Francis on NBC, was selected to tell the story to an estimated 3 million viewers. One of the demonstrations involved a small piece of treated open-mesh cloth which supported water drops but clearly allowed smoke to go through.

Paper Treatments.   In addition to making fabrics water-repellent, Zeke Dennett had worked on water-repellent treatments for paper, again starting with DOW CORNING® 1107 fluid. The interest in paper treatment was sparked by Johnson & Johnson Products Company, which wanted to improve the release characteristics of the paper backing on its Band-Aids. A suitable treatment was developed, resulting in a substantial business of 30 tons per month of treated paper.

Leather Treatment Laboratory.   Dennett was responsible for all the work on water repellency, and this included managing the Leather Treatment laboratory in Product Engineering, which continued the work on waterproofing of leather that had begun during the war. Charles Dudley, from the University of Cincinnati, had joined the group shortly after the war, and soon afterward Murrel Brown, a production worker from a tannery in Alpena, Michigan, joined Dudley and Dennett.

SHOE SAVER®.   It was not until after the war ended that an effective waterproofing treatment for leather was developed in Zeke Dennett's laboratory. The treatment, which was given the name "SHOE SAVER®" (Figure 3-12), enjoyed considerable success in the civilian market, particularly among people who wore hunting boots, but for some reason which was not quite understood, it was never adopted by the Army, which had originally requested it.

Sylflex.   With the SHOE SAVER® product successfully launched, Charles Dudley worked with Dennett's group on waterproofing leather during the tanning process, before it was made into shoes or boots. Together the group developed an effective, air-drying, water-repellent formulation to be applied to leather during the tanning process and named it "DC 1109."

Figure 3-11. Shailer Bass demonstrating the effectiveness of Dow Corning's silicone water repellency formula on national television.

One of the first trials of the new product was made at a tannery in Rockford, Michigan, on leather prepared from pigskin and used in shoes sold as "Hush Puppies®." It took a long while to convince tanneries to try the new waterproofing treatment, for they were reluctant to alter their production process to accommodate it. Dennett's group persisted, however, and trial runs were made at virtually every tannery in the eastern and midwestern states, and Ontario.

The trials went well, and the DC 1109 treatment was given the commercial name "Sylflex." Dennett promoted the new product by presenting a pair of Sylflex-treated boots to Mort Neff in Detroit on his television show *Michigan Outdoors*. The group's aggressive efforts to promote Sylflex to tanneries and to the general public paid off in substantial sales of the new leather treatment (Figure 3-13).

Specialty Products

The success of SIGHT SAVERS®, which were distributed primarily through drugstores, made Dr. Collings realize that many potential new

Figure 3-12. Early advertisement for SHOE SAVER®.

Figure 3-13. Charles Dudley developed a special flexing machine to show how leather treated with DC 1109 repelled water but allowed for transmission of water vapor, keeping feet dry and comfortable.

products could not be sold through Dow Corning's direct-sales organization. He therefore established a separate Specialty Products Division to handle such products. Dusty Rhodes was named manager of the new division, and at that point Bob Springmier took over as head of market research.

The new division tested a variety of products over the next few years, including a high-vacuum grease, stopcock grease, Slipicone (a silicone spray used on food counters and work surfaces to prevent food from sticking to them), and a variety of materials for use in laboratories and as process aids.

Gripmitt.   One specialty product that held great promise for the consumer marketplace was Gripmitt (Figure 3-14), a pet project of Dr. Collings. Gripmitt was a slightly foamed pad of SILASTIC®, used for handling hot dishes. The pad withstood all baking temperatures and was easily cleaned with soap and water. It had an unusual attraction for glass or metal, making it virtually impossible to accidentally drop a glass or metal article without dropping the pad along with it. This feature sparked the suggestion for the product name "Gripmitt."

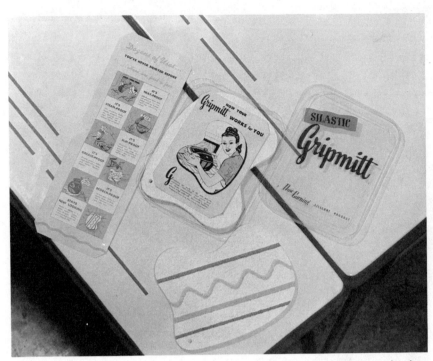

Figure 3-14. Gripmitt was one of Dow Corning's first entries into the consumer marketplace.

Dr. Collings took a significant part in the development of this product, working with Harold Browne once more to develop a machine to make Gripmitt. Stove Toppers and other larger hot pads were prepared and marketed as part of the Gripmitt line. Market testing was conducted at a number of major department stores, including Marshall Field in Chicago. Unfortunately, the relatively high cost of SILASTIC® made these products too high priced (e.g., $3.95 for a pair of Gripmitts) to have mass-market appeal. The Gripmitt line of products was dropped after some months of test marketing.

Product Management

With a string of successes in the industrial and consumer marketplaces and a growing list of product offerings, Dow Corning management decided that market penetration could be increased by establishing a more specialized marketing approach. Thus, near the end of the decade, the position of "product manager" was established to boost sales by concentrating on specific markets. Four product areas were designated initially. Clayt Doremire, who had been so successful in resurrecting the silicone resin effort, was given responsibility for all electrical industry products. Don Francisco moved over from sales to take charge of managing mold release fluids. Ray Naegele took over all SILASTIC® products. George Marx was named manager of consumer products.

By the early 1950s, after a decade of operations, Dow Corning could point to a long list of accomplishments. It had survived the cancellation of its wartime contracts and developed a thriving civilian business in many new markets. Thanks to the introduction of innovative new products such as DOW CORNING® 35 emulsion and expansion into consumer markets with SIGHT SAVERS® and other products, sales had grown steadily in the early postwar years, surpassing $6 million by 1950.

At the same time, the seeds of a thriving international business had been sown. Thanks to the farsighted efforts of Dr. Bass, by 1950 the company that had been addressing questions of survival just a few years earlier already had a strong toehold in the international marketplace. All the while, Dow Corning was building the internal systems needed to make it grow and thrive as a self-sufficient business. Personnel functions were established. An effective product development structure had been put in place and a means of increasing sales through better product management established.

The early postwar products could not have been produced without the benefit of advances made by the research groups. After the war ended, the ongoing efforts of the Dow Corning researchers to expand on silicone technology provided the raw material for Andy Kauppi's Product Development labs. Chapter 4 focuses on the manufacturing and chemistry of the postwar years, the expansion of research and production efforts that helped Dow Corning to survive the transition to a peacetime economy and thrive in the first postwar decade.

4

Chemistry and Production in the Postwar Years

A travelor through a dusty road strewed
acorns on the lea, and one took root and
sprouted up, and grew into a tree.
CHARLES MACKAY

With the blossoming of the postwar marketplace came a growing need for raw materials consumed in new product development. As a result, during the postwar years, new and better processes for producing silicones were continually introduced and refined at the Dow Corning plant. One of the greatest demands in the early postwar years was for a method of producing larger quantities of dimethyldichlorosilane needed to make DOW CORNING 200® silicone fluid, the basic ingredient in DOW CORNING® 35, the popular tire-mold release.

Production Advances

Grignard Production

During the war, dimethyldichlorosilane had been produced by the normal Grignard process in 301 building. After the war ended, the production group continued to search for a more economical process. Gordon

Brown, Howard Fenn's assistant, tried to produce dimethyldichloro-silane by means of a continuous methyl Grignard in a packed bed, without success; the methyl Grignard in ether was quite reactive and formed a variety of unwanted compounds.

Meanwhile, production of dimethyldiethoxysilane by the more efficient in situ Grignard process, using ethyl silicate, continued within Dow Chemical. In 1947, the two 600-gallon, nickel-clad reactors that were used in this work at Dow were purchased by Dow Corning and installed in 303 building at the new plant.

When the less expensive methyl Grignard process using chlorides was perfected, the in situ process was discontinued. Once this conversion was made, production of DOW CORNING 200® silicone fluid expanded rapidly. In spite of increased output, however, there were times when the fluid was being made by both the in situ and the normal Grignard processes to meet demand due to the popularity of the tire-mold release.

Direct Process

Because of the cross-licensing agreement with General Electric, after the war Dow Corning was able to use the more economical Rochow direct process as an adjunct to the Grignard production of dimethyldichlorosilane. It took some time to perfect the process in the new plant. The first reactions were carried out in two gas-fired rotary tumblers, 18 by 18 inches, which were located in 304 building, the former site of $SiCl_4$ production. The direct process yields a variety of chlorosilanes, and the two tumblers primarily produced methyltrichlorosilane, with only a small amount of the desired dimethyldichlorosilane. Nevertheless, the limited output of the tumbler significantly increased production of dimethyl until a better method could be found.

Big Bertha.   Dr. Collings came up with an unorthodox idea for further increasing production of dimethyldichlorosilane. He proposed to convert a used tubular lime dryer purchased from a St. Louis, Missouri, company into a rotary reactor for the production of chlorosilanes.

The engineering staff could not believe this wild idea. Sandy Sanderson and Bill Cunningham were given the task of designing the reactor. Collings was interested only in the shell of the dryer, with its sliding rings, and the drive and rolls which would rotate the shell while it was slightly inclined. Inside the shell would be a reactor which could be heated and cooled and which would "rain" ground silicon as the reactor rotated, with connections for feeding a stream of gas in one end to react with the silicon, and connections at the other end for releasing the products of the reaction. The reactor would be about 6 feet in diameter and about 40 feet long.

Cunningham said, "I believe Dr. Collings could 'see' just how this reactor would work. He also believed it was a scheme which had nothing but some engineering problems for which we had the technology to build it while work continued on alternate schemes. He wanted something 'now'."

Sanderson's reaction to the proposed reactor, affectionately referred to as "Big Bertha,"[1] was one of skepticism. But as he pointed out, "can't" wasn't in Dr. Collings's vocabulary. Still, no one in Sanderson's engineering group gave the project a ghost of a chance.

There were many reasons why the monstrosity shouldn't work. It would have to be operated under pressure and high temperature; it would have to rotate about its long axis; and it would lie at only a slight angle to the horizontal. That was just for starters. The fact that its dead weight plus the weight of the process chemicals came to many tons didn't help matters any. Despite all odds, with the support and encouragement of Dr. Collings, Big Bertha was a success. The reactor unit was mounted in the outer dryer shell by a fabricating shop in Clare, Michigan. The completed unit was equipped with an exterior ball-gear drive mechanism and was mounted at a slight angle on massive concrete piers. Heat was supplied by hot air circulating between the inner and outer walls of the unit. The reactor was trucked down the road 30 miles from Clare to Midland in March 1948. Big Bertha was so heavy that the trip had to be made before the ground thawed and Michigan highway weight restrictions went into effect. To accommodate Big Bertha, a 60-by 70-foot addition was made to the south end of 304 building, along with several other plant additions, including a new continuous bubble cap distillation column, which was erected in 302 building.

Out of Dr. Collings's incredible idea came a chlorosilane reactor that remained in production for many years and dramatically increased the volume of dimethyldichlorosilane in the immediate postwar years.

Rearrangement. The combined output of Big Bertha and the Grignard operations at the plant yielded an excess of the by-product methyltrichlorosilane; a considerable amount of trimethylchlorosilane was also produced, far more than was needed to end-block fluids, its primary usage. The laboratories had shown that redistribution or "rearrangement" of these two materials over aluminum trichloride would

---

[1]Taken from Dorothy L. Yates, *William R. Collings: Dow Corning's Pioneer Leader*, McKay Press, Midland, Mich., 1985.

produce additional amounts of the desired dimethyldichlorosilane. For this process, a coil unit was built and installed outside at the east end of 30A building. This rearrangement process further expanded dimethyl production. An additional batch still was installed in the 302 building to handle the increased output.

Polymer Production

The next step in the production process was the hydrolysis to produce DOW CORNING 200® silicone fluid. The first hydrolysis at the new plant, in August 1945, was done on a small scale, in a 200-gallon Pfaudler kettle in 303, the Polymer Finishing building. A year later, hydrolysis was being carried out in a 750-gallon Pfaudler kettle. By January 1947 a continuous hydrolysis system was established in 303. The Polymer Finishing group was responsible for preparing resins and fluids developed in the laboratory for shipment to customers. The group worked closely with the laboratory people, adjusting formulations to meet varying customer specifications.

Around this time there was much shifting of personnel. By October 1945 Zeke Dennett, who had been supervisor for the 303 building, transferred to Andy Kauppi's Product Development group, and Jim Fletcher, his assistant, took over the pilot-plant operation from Dr. Moyle. Bill Kuhlman became the new superintendent of 303, Polymer Finishing, and in 1946 Dick Clark transferred from Dr. Hunter's research group to become assistant superintendent.

Because of the increased production of fluids and resins made possible by Big Bertha, the 303 building was doubled in size in the years 1948 and 1949. By this time, a variety of fluid products were being commercially produced, including dimethylsilicone fluids (the 200 series) in a number of viscosities, emulsions of the fluids, and phenyl-containing fluids DOW CORNING 510®, DOW CORNING 550®, and DOW CORNING 710®. Resin products included coating resins DOW CORNING® 801, DOW CORNING® 802, DOW CORNING® 803, and DOW CORNING®804, Pan Glaze, DOW CORNING® 2103 laminating resin, and the electrical insulating resins DOW CORNING® 993 and DOW CORNING® 996. The Polymer Finishing group also produced an intermediate product, a mixture of cyclic dimethylsiloxanes used in producing SILASTIC®.

Fluid Bed Techniques

The continuing growth of civilian markets and the beginnings of international operations put continual strains on plant capacity in the postwar years. Although the direct process helped increase the volume of chlorosilanes produced, new production techniques were needed in order to meet continually increasing demand.

After Big Bertha was installed, a more efficient, continuous technique for making chlorosilanes in a fluid bed was developed. Bob Rownd and two other chemical engineers, Tom Vukovich and Don Gilson, along with Don Vallender, a laboratory technician, established a small group to study fluid bed techniques for producing dimethyldichlorosilane in two experimental 6-inch-diameter beds in an extension of the 304 building.

After much experimentation, a 2-foot-diameter fluid bed was designed and installed in 304 building and began operation in June 1951. A larger, 4-foot fluid bed reactor began operation in December 1951, in 309 building, south of 304. These new fluid beds greatly increased the capacity and efficiency of dimethyldichlorosilane production. With the ample volume of material produced by the 4-foot bed, Big Bertha was converted to producing trichlorosilane for the Barry process.

As the business continued to grow, two additional fluid beds were installed east of the original bed, in 317 building. A new hydrolysis and polymerization building, 501, was built for the exclusive production of methyl silicone–containing products.

When the 501 building began operation, the equipment in 303, which had been used for methyl silicone production, was gradually converted to the production of silicone resins and phenyl-containing fluids. The supervisory personnel for the two operations, under the direction of Bill Kuhlman, were Dick Holm, Joe Francis, Wayne Barrett, William ("Red") Strack, and Dick Clark.

At the same time 501 was built, a new distillation facility, 502, was installed for the continuous separation of the various products of the direct-process fluid beds. Tom Kelly transferred from the Design Engineering Department to manage the new facility.

Water-Repellent Products

One of the by-products of the fluid bed direct process was methyldichlorosilane, a raw material used in manufacturing the water-repellent fluid DOW CORNING® 1107. Since the anticipated demand for DOW CORNING® 1107 and related products was great, it was necessary to study the means for producing this raw material on a fairly large scale. As a result, included in 501 building was a unit for producing DOW CORNING® 1107.

To produce greater quantities of methyldichlorosilane from the direct process in a fluid bed required some experimentation. The 2-foot-diameter bed installed in the 304 building addition was used for this purpose. Later, several small, glass, fluidized beds heated by an oil bath were installed to evaluate various lots of elemental silicon and copper catalysts. The experimental program showed that by varying conditions in the fluid bed, the direct process could be altered to reduce production of dimethyl and increase production of methyldichlorosilane needed for DOW CORNING® 1107.

Advances

About this time, the production process received a boost in two important areas. First, the Analytical Laboratory began using infrared spectrometers to analyze chlorosilanes. Up to this point, the distillation process was used as a means of analyzing the composition of the products of the direct process. The distillation process required a day or more, and production was held up until the analysis was completed. With the use of infrared spectrometers, the same analysis could be performed in just a few hours, and this greatly increased the efficiency of production.

Second, Dr. Collings formed the Chlorosilane Committee to study in detail the production of chlorosilanes in the fluid beds, in an attempt to improve the process and increase the yield of dimethyldichlorosilane. Through this committee, a strong cooperative effort developed between the plant, the analytical group, and the researchers. The committee was active over the next 10 years, with continual interaction between Bob Rownd's development group and Bud Lankton's manufacturing employees. This close cooperation led to many advances in production techniques during that time.

Trichlorosilane and the Barry Process

While advances were being made in the production of methyl-containing products, processes for improving the production of phenyl-based compounds were being developed. Laboratory work had shown that gaseous hydrogen chloride reacted with elemental silicon at elevated temperatures to produce trichlorosilane in good yield, with only small amounts of silicon tetrachloride as a by-product. It had also been shown that phenyltrichlorosilane, the raw material in phenyl resins and in phenylmethyl rubber, was produced in high yield when a reaction was formed between benzene and trichlorosilane in the presence of boron trichloride (the PFC, or Barry, process described in Chapter 2). This was a much less expensive and more efficient way of producing phenyltrichlorosilane than was the previous phenyl Grignard reaction with silicon tetrachloride, which involved the use of expensive magnesium and produced a variety of unwanted by-products.

After the war, efforts were made to increase the production of phenyltrichlorosilane by the Barry process. To carry out the Barry process on a larger scale, a coil reactor heated by hot air was erected east of 304 building. The coil volume of the new reactor was roughly four times that of the previous one. To provide distillation capacity for these new developments, an addition to 308 building was constructed on the east side of the 302 building tower, and three batch stills were installed in this new location. Gradually, over a period of time, the Barry process replaced the phenyl Grignard reaction for phenyltrichlorosilane, and the messy silicon tetrachloride plant was shut down. Other plant additions were made to accommodate the increased production of phenyl compounds made possible by the new coil reactor.

Around this time additional machinery was installed in 305, the silicone rubber production building. Among the equipment was an 84-inch, two-roll mill for the production of SILASTIC® rubber, plus a 75-gallon Baker Perkins mixer for the production of two silicone greases, DOW CORNING® 33 and DOW CORNING 44®. A further expansion of 305 building provided an isolated area for the production of carbon-black-containing high-temperature DOW CORNING® 41 grease.

Plant Expansion

With silicone products gaining popularity in the civilian marketplace and business steadily growing, Dow Corning quickly outgrew its original plant capacity (Figure 4-1). In order to accommodate increased production, additions to the existing plant would be required, and new plants would have to be constructed.

In January 1952, Dow Corning received a government clearance to proceed with a $10 million expansion of its basic plant in Midland. Bill Caldwell, Howard Fenn, and Gordon Brown supervised the design of the plant additions, which would accommodate increased production of fluids and resins.

One of the areas that needed expanding was that of steam and electricity. Earl Newkirk of Dow Chemical helped locate a 90,000-pounds-per-hour steam boiler with a superheater and stokers, a secondhand piece of equipment for sale by a paper mill. The boiler was without tubes. Although the original price was $80,000, Newkirk closed the deal for $70,000.

Bill Caldwell called Dr. Collings, who was in New York attending a

Figure 4-1. By 1952, Dow Corning had already outgrown its original plant, and a $10 million expansion was added. In the background is the original water tower, purchased from the Bureau of Ships excess property list.

board of directors meeting, to tell him of the purchase. Collings told him there was no hurry, as the board had just turned down the authorization to purchase. At the next board meeting, when Collings reported the purchase, there was a proposal to sell the boiler, but Collings persuaded the board to authorize the purchase. Caldwell was reluctant to mention that the boiler needed $26,000 worth of new tubes. To avoid another confrontation with the board, Collings suggested that Caldwell buy the tubes out of the materials and supply budget and book them as normal inventory. This caused a few raised eyebrows when Haskins and Sells came later that year to conduct its annual audit.

First Plant Outside Midland

As the textile markets for silicones began developing in the early postwar years, Bill Collings decided that a separate facility should be set up to service the textile industry. A site search was conducted by Collings,

Olie Blessing, and Howard Fenn, with the help of Dutch Ehlers, sales manager of the Atlanta office.

Since many textile companies were located in the southern states, Greensboro, North Carolina, was selected as the site for a small finishing plant to prepare silicone emulsions for water-repellent fabric treatments and to stock other items used by the textile trade. Ed Sprague, who had joined Dow Corning earlier in SILASTIC® rubber production, was assigned to manage the Greensboro location. Eventually facilities for the production of consumer products, beginning with SIGHT SAVERS®, were added to the site.

New Plants

As business continued to expand, plant additions were needed to increase production capacity. In his first "Me to You" letter in July 1951, Dr. Collings announced the board's approval to build three new plants: a building for the manufacture of SILASTIC® rubber; a silicon plant to produce silicon for the direct process; and a plant for the production of methyl chloride.

Up to this point, SILASTIC® was being produced in 305. Further expansion of that building was impractical because of space limitations and operating inefficiency. A totally new building was needed in order to increase rubber production.

The major goal in building an elemental silicon plant was to free Dow Corning from its reliance on a single supplier of silicon, Union Carbide Corporation, which also happened to be a major competitor, the third-largest silicone manufacturer in the United States. The plant would serve another important purpose: by producing its own silicon, Dow Corning could control the purity of the product and thus improve the direct-process production. For these reasons, the silicon plant was promoted despite the facts that raw materials were far from the Midland, Michigan, plant location and that power cost, a principal expense in silicon production, would be high.

The third plant, for the production of methyl chloride, would reduce costs by utilizing by-product hydrochloric acid from plant operations. Another goal of the methyl chloride plant was the recovery of chloride ion from Dow Corning's waste stream. Most important, such a plant would make Dow Corning self-sufficient in the production of the starting material for both the direct process and the Grignard reaction.

Dow Chemical had been Dow Corning's first supplier of methyl chloride. Shortly after the new plant was built, Dow informed Dow Corning that it had firm commitments for its total output of methyl chloride and could no longer supply Dow Corning. When Dow Chemical cut off its supply, Dow Corning initiated a long-term contract with Ansul Chemical Company of Marinette, Wisconsin. While this would suffice in the short run, Dow Corning management realized at this point the importance of being able to produce its own raw materials.

With the onset of the Korean war in 1950, the need for a methyl chloride plant became more pressing. The total capacity for methyl chloride for civilian uses became severely restricted, since much of the material was being diverted to military use. In fact, so urgent was the need for methyl chloride at the time the new plant was proposed that Dow Corning found it necessary to construct a temporary plant to produce the material until a permanent facility could be built.

While the temporary methyl chloride plant was in operation, authorizations were approved for a plant to produce 500,000 pounds per month of SILASTIC® rubber compounds, a plant to produce 500,000 pounds per month of 98 percent pure elemental silicon, and a plant to produce 1 million pounds per month of methyl chloride.

SILASTIC® Plant. The new SILASTIC® plant 207 was built just north of the materials warehouse and shipping building. By April 1953 most SILASTIC® production had been moved to the new facility. Bob Jackson was in charge of the two SILASTIC® buildings, the old 305 building and the new plant in 207. Others associated with the operation were Bob Selfridge, Bill Heckrodt, Mark Day, Jim Henry, Floyd Dryzga, Ernest Quehl, and later Dick Przybyla. Shift leaders for the 207 operation were Austin Schmidt, Howard Wing, and Jack Mason.

A Banbury mixer was installed in the 207 building along with the usual 84-inch, two-roll mills and Baker Perkins mixers. These were an improvement over the earlier equipment, as all the compounding was done internally, with no loss of the dustlike filler added to the rubber.

A unit for the production of Degussa silica, a flame-produced silica[2] purchased in Germany, was installed at the same time as the SILASTIC® plant, in a new building, 311, north of the methyl chloride plant. Supervision of the silica production was assigned to Howard D. Fashbaugh.

Silicon Plant. The production of elemental silicon was a totally new venture for Dow Corning. The concept was actively supported by Ralph Hunter, director of electrochemical operations for The Dow Chemical

[2]"Flame-produced" silicas are manufactured by the burning of a silicon compound in a hydrogen flame.

Company. Hunter knew a lot about the use of electricity in producing chemicals, and his advice was greatly valued in this new endeavor.

The process involved extracting silicon from quartz by heating quartz rock, charcoal, and coke in an electric arc furnace (Figure 4-2). Hunter suggested Pittsburgh Electro-Melt as a company to build the furnace and later to consult on its operation. George Grant, the electrical engineer who had been running the Motor Test laboratory, was chosen to manage the operation.

The silicon building, 312, was located in the southeastern section of the plant near an extension of the railroad line. Near this building was 319, a facility for the crushing and grinding equipment to prepare elemental silicon for the fluid bed operation.

Raw materials for the production of silicon were stored outside the 312 building in silos which were fed by a series of mechanical conveyors. Quartzite rock came from Manitoulin Island, in Lake Huron, and was transported by ship to the Weirt stone dock on the Saginaw River in Bay City, then hauled from the dock by truck to the Midland site. Later,

Figure 4-2. Dr. Collings (*right*) observes technician George Grant operating an electric arc furnace, where silicon is extracted from quartz at a temperature in excess of 3632°F.

quartz rock from North Carolina came to the plant by rail. Charcoal from the upper peninsula of Michigan also came to the plant by rail.

The silicon plant began operating in late 1954. Dow Corning hired Clare Carlson, who had operated a ferrosilicon plant in Kentucky, to work closely with George Grant, former manager of the Motor Test laboratory, to manage the silicon operation.

Methyl Chloride Plant. Don Beshgetoor was assigned the task over the Christmas holidays in 1950 of developing the process for the new methyl chloride plant. He was to design the plant as quickly as possible because of the threatened shortage of methyl chloride at the time of the Korean war. Development work, design, and construction went on almost simultaneously.

The plant was completed in January 1951, with subzero temperatures and bitter winds slowing construction. The urgency was so great that normal equipment delivery schedules were inadequate. As a result, much of the equipment came from Dow Chemical Company's salvage department.

The equipment was made from Haveg, a composite with a corrosion-resistant lining. The scaleup was from a 1-liter glass flask to a 3000-gallon Haveg reactor. The Haveg was old and fragile and subject to many breakages of the piping. Shop people became proficient in patching the reactor at all hours of the day and night.

At one point it was necessary to shut down the plant and replace the cover of a reactor with a plastic-lined steel cover. This reactor also had a temporary steel dip pipe which lasted only one shift because of the corrosive environment. The success of the plastic-lined cover led to reconstruction of the whole plant with lined steel vessels and Saran-lined pipe.

Initially the plan had been to feed the methyl chloride directly to the direct-process reactors, but the material was not pure enough to do so. Instead, a system was added to compress the gaseous methyl chloride, condense it, and then distill it to remove any impurities. This also allowed for storage of the product, since it was now in liquid form.

Bud Lankton operated the plant, and Clayt Davidson assisted him. Four operators oversaw the production process: Matt Penney, Roy Darwin, John Lyon, and Austin Sullivan.

Advances in Silicone Chemistry

While better manufacturing processes were being developed and plants built and expanded, the research that made it all possible continued and accelerated. The time from the end of World War II to the early 1950s was one of the most productive periods of silicone research.

Pioneers of Progress

During the first 10 years of its existence, Dow Corning had gained widespread recognition for its contributions to the technology of silicones. In 1953, the company was honored by *Chemical Processing* magazine, which carried a series of articles on people from eight companies in the chemical industry they considered "pioneers of progress." Fourteen employees of Dow Chemical, Corning Glass Works, and Dow Corning—Bill Collings, E. C. Britton, Glen Cole, Willard Dow, Howard Fenn, Mel Hunter, Frank Hyde, Eugene Sullivan, Bill Veazey, Ken Johannson, Rob Roy McGregor, Andy Kauppi, Shailer Bass, and I—were honored in the August issue of the magazine, for contributing to the founding and growth of Dow Corning Corporation.

Bill Blackburn.

Patents

After World War II ended, the patent process resumed its normal course and a number of patents pending from the war were finally issued. The important postwar patents based on wartime research in Corning were concerned with the methylchlorosilanes, some of the cyclics of the dimethylsiloxane system, alkali polymerization, alkali cracking to produce cyclics, and methods of resinification.[3]

Postwar patents from early work at Mellon Institute covered a molding compound, dimethyldiethoxysilane and the etherless Grignard method of making it, and a method of preparing liquid polymeric dimethylsiloxane and pure trimethylchlorosilane prepared from trimethylethoxysilane.[4] These all involved the methyl system of producing silicones.

William C. Blackburn managed the patent effort in the postwar years.

---

[3]W. Daudt, U. S. Patent 2,397,727, 1946; J. F. Hyde, U.S. Patents 2,371,050, 1945; 2,377,689, 1945; 2,386,466, 1945; 2,386,467, 1945; 2,410,346, 1946; 2,413,049, 1946; 2,413,050, 1946; O. K. Johannson, U. S. Patent 2,429,883, 1947.

[4]R. R. McGregor and E. L. Warrick, U.S. Patents 2,375,998, 1945; 2,380,057, 1945; 2,384,384, 1945; 2,386,488, 1945.

He had joined Corning Glass Works in May 1945. Fred Knight, Corning's general counsel, had hired Blackburn to review the silicone patent situation and to join Dow Corning in Midland in 6 months as a replacement for Dr. Leigh Fowler, who had accepted a new position outside Dow Corning.

After his arrival in Midland, Blackburn worked closely with Shailer Bass, not only because Bass was director of research but also because Dr. Collings was uncomfortable with attorneys. On one occasion, lunching with the Basses and another guest, Blackburn was asked by the guest what his job was at the plant. Before he could reply, Bass said, "Bill is the only one at Dow Corning who makes everyone's business his business and can get away with it."

Bill Blackburn did make the researchers' business his own, as he worked aggressively to expand Dow Corning's patent effort. The summary of patents Blackburn gave to Bass in the fall of 1945 indicated a poor position for the company. Blackburn suggested a more structured, aggressive approach to patenting be adopted. Among other things, this meant filing for patents as early as possible, before all data were available. These initial applications often contained guesses (which irritated the opposition), but as a result, Dow Corning began to win interferences and to strengthen its patent position.

Bill Blackburn had a sharp eye for information that could be patented, and he worked closely with the researchers to make certain they were patenting everything possible. Many good patents were issued as a result of Blackburn's incisive probing of patent ideas. I remember how closely Blackburn worked with our group at Mellon, helping us to see broader concepts and more patentable information in the data we were accumulating. In fact, Bill was so effective in determining what to patent that he was actually responsible for more patents than were the researchers.

Blackburn also worked closely with Blessing's salespeople, making sure they were not giving away any proprietary information. The sales staff regularly compiled data sheets for customers, and Blackburn carefully reviewed those sheets to be certain they didn't contain any information that a competitor might use in applying for a patent.

For a while, Blackburn was solely responsible for the patent effort. In 1948, Bob Fleming from the Corning research group joined him. Over the next several years, the two greatly added to the list of patents issued to Dow Corning, both in the United States and abroad.

Bill Blackburn brought to the international business the same aggressive approach that quickly improved Dow Corning's patent position in the United States. Shortly after joining the company, when negotiations were proceeding with Wacker-Chemie, Blackburn spent several weeks in Munich finalizing the licensing agreement and filing applications for

German patents. During World War II it had not been possible to file patents in Germany or Japan, and now it was necessary to file for extensions for patent applications dating back to the war years. During his trip to Munich, Blackburn applied for extensions for the German patents, which were approved in the winter of 1949–1950. This led to the issuance of many German patents that were back-dated to the original U.S. filing date and led to a solid patent position in Germany.

Filing foreign patent applications was an expensive process, involving firms which acted as agents for Dow Corning in each foreign country. As a result, patent filing was limited to certain important markets, primarily in Canada, the United Kingdom, France, and Germany. Shortly after returning from Germany in 1951, Dr. Collings asked Blackburn to become Dow Corning's general counsel in addition to managing the patent effort. Blackburn's extensive patent experience in overseas markets enabled him to deal successfully with the legal aspects of foreign operations. This ability was clearly demonstrated in the early 1950s, when Canadian customs charged Dow Corning with "dumping" silicone fluids on the Canadian market and proposed duties and penalties totaling more than $2 million.

Canadian attorneys advised Dow Corning that it could not possibly win the case. Blackburn argued that no products were produced in Canada with the same combination of properties shown by the fluids, resins, and compounds manufactured in the United States. His argument was persuasive, and these materials were ruled exempt. However, Canadian customs still claimed that Dow Corning was unfairly competing by "dumping" SHOE SAVER®, which customs considered to be a shoe polish, in Canada. Blackburn countered that this was not a shoe polish but rather a shoe treatment. On this point, customs won, but the duties and penalties assessed amounted to a mere $6000. As a result of Bill Blackburn's effective handling of the case, Dow Corning was saved nearly $2 million.

Midland Groups: Research and Analysis

Dr. Hunter's Group. After Mel Hunter (Figure 4-3) became director of research in 1947, two subgroups within his department began pursuing more specialized areas of research. One of these subgroups was headed by Hal Clark, who focused on preparing polysilanes, polymers with carbon groups linked through silicon atoms alone (Si—Si—Si), without the oxygen that is a part of the basic siloxane backbone (Si—O—Si) in silicones. These polymers could then be "cured," or cross-linked, by oxidation to form a siloxane linkage.

As part of this work, Clark created a new series of polymers

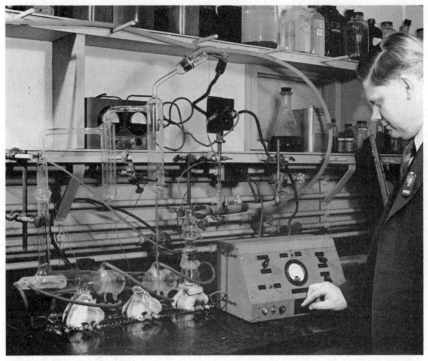

Figure 4-3. Dr. Melvin J. Hunter checks a vapor pump in Dow Corning's fluids research laboratory.

with phenyl groups linking the silicon atoms. These materials looked promising because of their good thermal stability, and in fact, later they were used in making heat-shrink rubber. However, they were quite expensive to prepare, so their use was limited.

Clark was assisted over the next few years by Art Gordon, Rome Minard, Lee Teichthesen, and John Thomas. In addition to the work on polysilanes, the group studied methyl alcohol reactions with many chlorosilanes in an attempt to produce methoxysilanes; these compounds were desired because they are easier to handle, less corrosive, and less damaging to the lungs than chlorosilanes. The work was successful, and many of the subsequent intermediate products developed in the labs, such as Sylkyd 50 and 60, contained methoxy groups.

Clark also developed a process, which was quickly adopted in the plant, for the continuous hydrolysis of chlorosilanes. This process was more efficient than the batch method previously used and could be carried out in much smaller equipment.

In addition to developing new compounds, Clark's group got involved in a variety of other research projects. The group studied the by-products of the rearrangement of chlorosilanes using aluminum trichloride, AlCl$_3$, catalyst, separated and identified the products of the direct-process residue, and studied laminating resins, their preparation and electrical properties, as well as pursuing better resin catalysts.

Dr. Leslie J. Tyler headed up another of the subgroups within the research department. Tyler had joined Dow Corning in 1948 as a Ph.D. graduate of Pennsylvania State University. His work in Hunter's group focused on the preparation of better fillers for rubber. SILASTIC® 250 had just been developed, and we were trying to solve the problem of crepe hardening caused by the use of flame-produced silica filler. PA fluid was providing a temporary solution, but Tyler sought a permanent solution in the form of a superior filler.

Les Tyler succeeded in developing silica fillers that were reinforcing without producing crepe hardening. He joined forces with Bill Daudt in treating silica sols[5] with chlorosilanes and came up with much the same result.[6] These two treatments produced silicas which were more reinforcing than flame-produced silica. However, the high cost of these special silicas prohibited their use except in special circumstances. The treatments did yield one successful by-product, the development of a soluble resin which found use as an additive in many other resin systems and elastomers.

Dr. Barry's Group. Dr. Arthur J. Barry's group in the early postwar years consisted of Don Hook, Elwyn Merrill, Bob Witman, John Gilkey, Sue Gordon, Duane Pugh, Bob Hedlund, Loren Haluska, and Bob Murch. During those years, the group carried out a number of basic research studies that greatly expanded the base of knowledge of organosilicon chemistry.

The researchers studied the distribution of molecule sizes in various high polymers used for SILASTIC®, in an effort to produce silicone rubber with a higher molecular weight. They studied residues from the aluminum chloride rearrangement process. The development of better fillers for rubber was pursued, and flame-produced silica was treated with organochlorosilanes to decrease the tendency to cause crepe hardening.

Fluid studies covered methylhydrogen siloxanes and ethylmethylsiloxanes and their fractionation into groups of narrow molecular weights. They attempted to prepare fluids with an acid group on a

---

[5]Sodium silicate can be neutralized to form a soluble silica sol. It soon begins to condense and polymerize. When it polymerizes far enough, it becomes insoluble. Before it reaches the insoluble state, it is in the form of a sol, a semigel.

[6]L. J. Tyler and W. Daudt, U.S. Patent 2,676,182, 1954.

phenyl group. Studies were made of the hydrolysis conditions to achieve the formation of anhydrous hydrochloric acid (a water-free gas). This would eliminate the by-product aqueous HCl in the production process, which posed a disposal problem. Related to this was a study aimed at forming methyl chloride from hydrochloric acid. In addition, physical data were obtained for a number of different materials and systems.

Analytical Laboratory. The Analytical Laboratory in the period 1945 to 1953 was staffed by Hal Clark (who returned to Mel Hunter's research group after a time), A. R. McNeill, Leon Van Volkinburg, Bill Hargreaves, Frances Henson, Paul Brown, Arnold Kolb, Bob Winger, Bob Horner, Larry Brown, Durelle Thomson, Jil Vandeusen, and Dr. A. Lee Smith. The lab was managed by Jim McHard.

McHard's group developed many new analytical tools after the war ended and expanded on the inventions of others. With the arrival of Dr. A. Lee Smith in the early 1950s, infrared spectrometer analyses of intermediates and products developed rapidly.[7] As noted earlier, this was a tremendous aid to the production process, as it allowed for the analysis of compounds in a few hours rather than the days previously required when distillation was the method of analysis.

In addition, the group performed a number of basic studies of materials and processes. The researchers showed that ferric chloride catalyzed reactions between ethoxyl groups to form siloxane bonds. They measured oxidation rates on various silicones as well as the rate of gas diffusion through SILASTIC® films. They studied ways of refining the distillation process and assisted the plant in separating compounds. They measured the explosive characteristics of many of the silane raw materials to assure safe handling in plant operations. The group made basic studies of silica fillers for high-strength rubber. Their work in studying the reactions occurring in the fluid bed direct process assisted in controlling and improving plant operations.

Each new product development brought with it another set of analytical problems that had to be solved in order to improve the efficiency of the production process. More than a simple support group, the Analytical Department was an essential partner in making the manufacturing process run smoothly in the plant.

[7]A. Lee Smith, "The Infra Red Spectra of Methylchlorosilanes," *J. Chem. Phys.*, 21:(11) 1997 (1953).

Pilot Plant. The pilot plant was primarily responsible for testing production processes on a small scale before they were adopted in the plant on a large-scale basis. For a number of years after the war ended, the pilot plant was a part of Dr. Hunter's research area and was headed by Jim Fletcher. During this period, Fletcher was joined in his efforts by Harry Dingman, John Ostahowski, Art Webb, Wayne Barrett, Ed Sprague, Don Van Winkle, Don Beshgetoor, Ken Moorhead, Jim Lyons, Earl Beck, and Glen Albert.

In addition to testing production processes, the pilot plant manufactured and sold small-volume products, such as DOW CORNING® Antifoam A compound and Sylkyd 50 and 60, that were not suitable for production in the main plant. The group also worked on improving products already on the markets, for example, undertaking a project to improve the lubricity of DOW CORNING 200® silicone fluid.

Fletcher's group was involved in a smorgasbord of projects that aided the plant in the development of fluids, resins, and rubber products in large volume. They showed how to convert cyclic dimethylsiloxanes to fluids and high-viscosity polymers for rubber and studied the cracking of hydrolysates, a method of producing cyclic silicones with few or no unwanted by-products. The group developed methods of continuous hydrolysis of the chlorosilanes and found better ways to distill the complex mixtures generated in the production process.

When the Korean war held out the threat of a methyl chloride shortage, the pilot plant studied alternative hydrolysis techniques as well as means of producing methyl chloride. All the work carried out in the pilot plant ensured that the larger plant would operate as efficiently as possible.

Dow Chemical: Toxicology Studies. From the time he became director of research, Shailer Bass was quite concerned about the toxicological effects of various silicones. As mentioned in Chapter 3, when DOW CORNING® Antifoam A compound was developed, Bass thought it might be useful in food products. He asked Dow Chemical Company's Toxicological Laboratory to conduct toxicological tests of the new product. This spurred an entire series of toxicological studies on a wide variety of products over the next few years.

The first report on the lab's findings on the toxicological effects of silicones was published in 1948.[8] The lab had found that chlorosilanes

[8]V. K. Rowe, H. C. Spencer, S. L. Bass, "Toxicological Studies on Certain Commercial Silicones," *J. of Ind. Hygiene and Toxicology*, 30:337–352 (1948).

were highly corrosive by vapor inhalation and by skin and eye contact. The ethoxysilanes varied in toxicity. Silicone fluids were shown to be low in toxicity, and early biosafety studies of resins showed them to be relatively inert. Early biosafety studies of DOW CORNING® Antifoam A compound also established its reasonable safety and laid the groundwork for approval of the new product in food and drug use.

These toxicity studies led to a better understanding of the effects of silicones in the workplace. As a result, procedures were established for more careful handling of corrosive silicone products in the plant, and in some cases the development of less corrosive intermediate materials.

Pennsylvania State University

While a great deal of silicone research was being carried out at Dow Corning after the war, the company also benefited from a growing volume of academic research being conducted at Pennsylvania State University. Dean Frank Whitmore, a professor at Penn State, became interested in organosilicon research in 1940 and instituted an ongoing program of study in the field. The first student in Whitmore's organosilicon research program was Leo Somer; by 1945 there were 10 full-time graduate students in the Whitmore group. On Dean Whitmore's death in 1947, Dr. Somer became manager of the program.

Not since the Kipping papers had any serious academic work on the subject of silicones been published. The first organosilicon research papers from Penn State were written during World War II, but their publication was delayed because of wartime secrecy. When they were finally published in 1946, these papers attracted the attention of Dow Corning. Dr. Bass and Dr. Hunter visited the university in 1947 to learn more about the work Dr. Somer's group was doing, and soon Dow Corning sponsored a research program under Somer's leadership.

This program lasted for 15 years and provided Dow Corning a wealth of information in the field of organosilicon chemistry. As a result of the sponsorship arrangement, many graduate students from the Penn State research group came to work for Dow Corning, and Dow Corning sent many employees through Penn State's Ph.D. programs over the years. Dr. Tyler was one of the early graduate students to join Dow Corning. Keith Michael, Marty Musolf, and Bob Leitheiser all joined Dow Corning with Ph.D.s from Penn State. Don Weyenberg, Cecil Frye, and Forrest Stark were three of the first Dow Corning employees sent to Penn for their doctorate degrees.

When Leo Somer moved to the University of California at Davis, the research sponsorship was discontinued because of the distance and the difficulty of recruiting graduate students from the west coast program.

By that time, however, organosilicon research had caught on in a number of major universities around the world, and Dow Corning was able to attract students from a long list of college campuses.

Corning Group

The Corning research group in the early postwar period consisted of Drs. Hyde, Daudt, and Johannson, Mary Purcell Roche, Harry Laudenslager, Joe Domicone, and Bob Fleming, who had returned from his wartime service. The group worked on a broad range of basic research, studying the use of siloxane salts in the polymerization process and learning more about the mechanism of polymerization, developing emulsion polymerization, experimenting with waterproofing processes for ceramics and textiles, developing the first room-temperature vulcanizing (RTV) silicone rubbers, and studying the reaction of vinyl groups with hydrosilanes.

Polymerization Studies. Ken Johannson and Harry Laudenslager did fundamental work on the mechanism and rates of polymerization, to better understand the relative effectiveness of various catalysts. The group demonstrated that potassium hydroxide was 500 times as fast as sodium hydroxide in polymerizing cyclic siloxanes. Hyde found that acetonitrile solvent and other polar solvents greatly accelerated the polymerization process. These studies were carried out over a number of years and became the basis of polymerization processes used in the plant, for producing high polymers for rubber and intermediate hydroxy-ended polymers for use in textile and paper treatments.

The studies of the alkali salts, their characterization and utility, involved most members of the Corning group during these postwar years. In 1953, Hyde and his coworkers published a paper covering the preparation and use of sodium salts of triorganosilanols.[9] Reactions of these salts with chlorosilanes formed special polymers, and they also were used to form waterproof coatings on ceramics, concrete, and fabrics.

First RTV Rubber. During the late 1940s, in the course of their experimentation, the Corning researchers discovered that phosphorus pentoxide, P_2O_5, could be used as a catalyst to form high polymers. These polymers would accept carbon-black fillers, and cross-linking, or vulcanization, would occur at room temperature when ethyl silicate was

---

[9]J. F. Hyde, W. Daudt, R. Fleming, H. Laudenslager, and M. Roche, "Sodium and Potassium Salts of Triorganosilanols," *J. Am. Chem. Soc.*, 75:5615 (1953).

used as the vulcanizing agent.[10] From this research came the development of the first room-temperature vulcanizing silicone rubber.

Basic Research Group. In the fall of 1951, Drs. Hyde, Daudt, and Johannson moved to the Midland plant from Corning, New York, and formed the Basic Research laboratory in newly constructed facilities. By this time, Bob Fleming had joined Bill Blackburn in the Patent Department. The others of the Corning group remained in New York.

The Basic Research group continued its studies in its new Midland location. The group found that hydrochloric acid (HCl) would depolymerize high polymers of dimethylsiloxanes. This helped them to better understand and control the polymerization process and eventually led to the development of a variety of new chlorine-ended compounds of different lengths. Out of this came studies of the reactivity of hydroxyl-ended polymers, and these in turn led to development of a number of different RTV systems.

The group worked to develop improved fillers for rubber, studying a variety of techniques, including a treatment by concentrated aqueous ammonia (which was not entirely successful). J. W. Curry joined the group and developed a copolymerizing mechanism which was used later as a new vulcanizing mechanism. Emulsion polymerization of cyclic dimethylsiloxanes was developed. This was a useful method of processing and formulating products that eliminated the need for solvents and solved the problem of recovering them.

Mellon Group

The Mellon group during the last half of the 1940s included Dr. McGregor, Helena Corsello, John Goodwin (returning from war service), John Speier, Ruth Zimmerman, Charlie Kohl, Joe Francis, Silas Braley, Jim Church, Jack Noll, Leonard Shorr, and me, along with a few others who joined the group for short periods and then left the Institute (Figure 4-4).

During these years, the group began a major effort in developing organofunctional silicones, i.e., silicones that were reactive rather than inert. A new silicone backbone also was developed, with one or more carbon atoms replacing the oxygen atom between silicons in the siloxane bridge (Si—C—Si versus the Si—O—Si backbone). Polymers with these backbones had the advantage that they were not subject to

---

[10]J. F. Hyde, U.S. Patent 2,571,039, 1951.

Figure 4-4. Early photograph of the Mellon researchers (*left to right*): Dr. McGregor, John Speier, Earl Warrick, Ruth Zimmerman, Helena Corsello, and Charlie Kohl.

depolymerization in HCl; however, they were fairly expensive to produce, so not much use was made of them.

We continued to improve upon SILASTIC® and carried out a variety of basic research studies that contributed a wealth of fundamental information about the chemistry of silicones during the years following the end of the war.

Dr. McGregor.   In this postwar period, Dr. Rob Roy McGregor left the laboratory and became a full-time administrator of the Mellon fellowship. As silicones became more widely publicized in industry journals and popular magazines, letters came to Mellon Institute regularly from prospective customers wanting to know how silicones might solve their particular problems.

Mac answered all these letters and traveled around the country, responding to invitations to visit manufacturing plants and demonstrating the use of silicones in various applications. He even appeared on a short televised program from a Pittsburgh department store, demonstrating some of the characteristics of DOW CORNING 200® silicone fluid.

At the same time, he continued to promote silicones to other fellows at Mellon Institute. Mac was responsible for Westinghouse's becoming involved in an extensive cooperative program of motor preparation and testing through his connection with the Westinghouse fellows at Mellon. Gulf Oil's discovery of the antifoaming and favorable viscosity properties of silicones also came about thanks to Mac's introduction of silicones to the Gulf fellowship at Mellon.

In addition to carrying out his responsibilities as an administrator and research manager during this period, McGregor garnered more publicity for silicones by writing journal articles[11] as well as a book[12] about the chemistry and uses of these new materials.

Dr. Speier.   As discussed in Chapter 2, a broad-ranging program for the study of silicone rubber was developed for the Mellon researchers in January 1945. John Speier's portion of the program was to discover new ways to "cure" silicone rubber by reactions that did not involve siloxane bonds.

At this time, silicone rubber was being cured by peroxides. Speier looked at most of the agents used to cure organic rubbers and found them to have no effect on silicone rubber. He examined other compounds, and some of them, such as various organometallics (e.g., tetraethyl lead), were partially effective; but nothing was found to be a better curing agent than benzoyl peroxide.

Speier then shifted his focus away from the rubber program and began working on developing silicone compounds with organic functionality. This proved to be the beginning of a major field of chemical research.

John Speier began work on developing functionality in the silicone molecule largely because he was an organic chemist who saw the great potential of products that would be different from the simple hydrocarbonlike silicone polymers which had been produced up to this time. He wanted to make silicone compounds with functional (reactive) organic groups on them. The silicones we'd been developing made use of a tiny subset of the vast range of organic compounds; Speier wanted to tap the potential of the entire range.

---

[11]R. R. McGregor, "Silicon—Cinderella of the Elements," *Duquesne Sci. Couns.*, 16:1 (1953); R. R. McGregor, "Silicones in Pharmacy," *Pharm. Int.*, 7:24 (1953); R. R. McGregor, "Applications of Silicones—Structure and Properties," *Chemtech*, 46:2323 (1954).

[12]R. R. McGregor, *Silicones and Their Uses*, McGraw-Hill, New York, 1954.

Specifically, Speier wanted to know how the reactivity of a functional organic group (one with a hydroxyl, OH, ending, such as alcohol) would be affected by being on a carbon attached to silicon. Would an alcohol, a highly reactive group, behave differently? Would an acid be stronger or weaker? Could those functionalities be used for something, to create new polymers with unknown reactivity?

In 1946, Speier made arrangements with Dr. Bernard Daubert of the University of Pittsburgh to develop a doctoral thesis on a portion of a study of organofunctional compounds. McGregor and Bass approved the concept of carrying out the study on a full-time basis at Mellon, so long as time was allowed to patent any discoveries before publication of the results.

Starting with dimethyldichlorosilane, $(CH_3)_2SiCl_2$, Speier sought to attach to the methyl, CH_3, in the compound one of four organic groups: alcohol, amine, aldehyde, and acid. These would make the resultant compound "functional," or reactive.

To accomplish this, Speier first added chlorine to the methyl group. This chlorine replaced one hydrogen in the group and produced chloromethyl, CH_2Cl. He then sought to replace the chlorine in the chloromethyl with one of the functional organic groups described above, by reacting this chlorine with compounds containing one of the functional groups. The end result was a silicone compound in which a reactive group was now on the carbon attached to silicon.

This was not always a straightforward process and often yielded surprises. In many cases, Speier had to form reactions between chlorine and several compounds in order to get the functional groups onto the compound. Sometimes the functional groups had to be placed further away from the silicon to prevent them from knocking off the methyl group to which the functional group was attached.

As a part of this work, Speier designed and built a continuous countercurrent photochlorinator to prepare the chloroalkylsilanes he needed in large quantity. This method of chlorination was covered by two U.S. patents.[13]

In his attempt to add functional groups to any organic group already attached to silicon, Speier first focused on replacing the chlorines on silicon with alcohols. He found that the simplest of these alcohols, hydroxymethylsilyl-, was in general more active than the simple one-carbon alcohol methanol. When one of the bonds to silicon was siloxane (Si—O—Si), the alcohol reacted with the siloxane bond to give a rearranged molecule.

---

[13]John Speier, U.S. Patents 2,510,148, 1950; 2,510,149, 1950.

Once the alcohol group was attached, Speier studied its reaction. Dehydrogenation of the alcohol proceeded, and Speier expected that this would produce an aldehyde, but the intended aldehyde decomposed. He then tried to convert the chloromethyl group to carboxylic acids, but this failed because water cleaved the organic group from the silicon; acid groups had to be placed farther from the silicon. Speier was unsuccessful in placing aldehyde groups on organic groups attached to silicon, and while he did manage to attach acid groups, the focus of his work at this time was primarily on alcohols.

In June 1947, John Speier received his Ph.D. from the University of Pittsburgh. The thesis that grew out of his work led to seven U.S. patents[14] and three publications.[15]

Ruth Zimmerman joined Dr. Speier in the fall of 1947 and greatly accelerated the organofunctional work. She soon became adept at analytical distillations, material balances, and physical property studies. She in turn went on a part-time basis to the University of Pittsburgh and ultimately received her bachelor's degree in chemistry.

For 3½ years Dr. Speier continued his study of chloroalkyl groups on silicon. Out of this work came a patent covering the preparation of bromo compounds (used in place of chlorine as a reactive agent)[16] and several publications, including two papers[17] on the results of these chlorination studies.

As an extension of the work on organofunctional silicones, Dr. Speier studied a method of "protecting" active hydroxyl, mercapto (a sulfur alcohol), or amino groups with trimethylchlorosilane, which prevented the groups from reacting while other synthetic steps were taken on another part of the molecule. Once these steps were taken, the trimethylchlorosilane "blocker" could then be removed to yield a product containing the original active group.

This was a crucial finding, with important potential applications. The development of drugs in many cases involves complicated molecules with more than one reactive group. Often chemists wish to work on one of those groups without affecting the others; the discovery of a protective mechanism made this possible.

---

[14]John Speier, U.S. Patents 2,510,148, 1950; 2,510,149, 1950; 2,527,590, 1950; 2,527,591, 1950; 2,550,205, 1951; 2,572,402, 1951; 2,576,428, 1951.

[15]J. Speier, *J. Am. Chem. Soc.*, 71:273 (1949); J. Speier and B. Daubert, *J. Am. Chem. Soc.*, 70:1400 (1948); J. Speier, B. Daubert, and R. R. McGregor, *J. Am. Chem. Soc.*, 70:1117 (1948).

[16]John Speier, U.S. Patent 2,640,064, 1953.

[17]John Speier, *J. Am. Chem. Soc.*, 71:273 (1949); John Speier, *J. Am. Chem. Soc.*, 73:825 (1951).

Dr. Speier's technique was presented in the *Journal of the American Chemical Society*,[18] and 14 U.S. patents[19] were issued to cover many types of previously unobtainable silyl-substituted[20] alcohols and phenols.

John Noll joined Dr. Speier in the fall of 1949, and together they began a systematic investigation of the synthesis of silyl-substituted amines (—NH$_2$). This was not a straightforward process. One successful route made use of a Grignard method, starting with the chloroalkyl group, followed by reaction with an alkoxy amine. Another route involved the reaction of certain alkyl amines with the chloroalkyl group to form a hydrochloride. This hydrochloride, on reaction with alkali, yielded the silyl amine.

In the spring of 1950 Jim Webster joined Dr. Speier and began to build an "amine machine" under the front steps at Mellon Institute. The interest was in forming reactions of volatile amines, especially liquid ammonia, under pressure to make aminoalkylsiloxane derivatives in quantities large enough to permit their evaluation for commercial applications.

Webster was very adept at these preparations and succeeded in making liter quantities of many compounds. However, no interest was shown in Midland, where these compounds were regarded as "chemicals," not silicones, and their utility has never been explored.

In January 1951 the amine machine was converted to make silazanes, compounds with a Si—NH—Si backbone, which are formed on the reaction of chlorosilanes with ammonia. A few such compounds had been made before this work, but no detailed study had been carried out.

Silazanes reacted with alcohols, phenols, mercaptans, and HCN to produce alkoxysilanes, silthianes, —Si—S—Si—, and cyanosilanes, —Si—CN. One use of this reactivity was to treat silanol, —Si—OH, structures on the surface of flame-produced silica. A patent[21] covered this process, which was used to prepare fillers known at Dow Corning as "J fillers," which prevented crepe hardening and yielded higher-strength SILASTIC®.

One important application of silazanes was as a protective mecha-

---

[18]John Speier, *J. Am. Chem. Soc.*, 74:1003 (1952).

[19]John Speier, U.S. Patents 2,584,751, 1952; 2,584,752, 1952; 2,611,776, 1952; 2,611,777, 1952; 2,611,778, 1952; 2,611,779, 1952; 2,611,780, 1952; 2,611,781, 1952; 2,626,272, 1953; 2,626,727, 1953; 2,628,245, 1953; 2,629,725, 1953; 2,645,630, 1953; 2,649,067, 1953.

[20]A "silyl" compound is one with the general formula R$_3$Si—, where "R" is an organic group; silyl substitution refers to replacing a hydrogen atom with a silyl group.

[21]John Speier, U.S. Patent 2,676,163, 1954.

nism. Just as trimethylchlorosilane acted to block hydroxyl endings on molecules and prevent further reacting, hexamethyldisilazane could accomplish the same end, with the advantage that it was easier to use, less toxic, and less corrosive than trimethylchlorosilane. Silazanes made it possible to protect any reactive group in a molecule by the reaction of that group with a mixture of trimethylchlorosilane, $(CH_3)_3SiCl$, and hexamethyldisilazane, $[(CH3)_3Si]_2NH$. The process was patented[22] and is now widely used among analytical and synthetic chemists.

Dr. Speier's work on organofunctional compounds represented a tremendous breakthrough in the field of organosilicon chemistry. Essentially, Speier made it possible to prepare almost any organic compound in the vast list of organic compounds (possibly as large as 1 million) with the inclusion of one or more silicon atoms in the compound. In one field alone, that of biologically active organic compounds, the number of useful compounds may be in the tens of thousands. By adding silicon to these compounds, that list may be greatly enlarged, with exciting potential for discovering as yet unknown activities that could lead to many useful new drugs.

Eli Lilly and Company. On December 15, 1951, Speier and McGregor went to Indianapolis to talk with the research staff of Eli Lilly and Company. Speier lectured to several groups within the company on the synthesis of organofunctional silanes.

Before Mac and Speier left Eli Lilly that day, general agreement was reached on plans for a broad cooperative research effort to study the effect of silicon on the biological activity of organic molecules. This would be another venture into the unknown. During the previous 7 years Speier and his group had made hundreds of organofunctional compounds, but to their knowledge, none of these had been studied for the purpose of assessing their biological activity.

Eli Lilly was eager to begin the research, and Dr. Speier gave the company 24 compounds to study—alcohols, phenols, and amines, or derivatives of these. Experts at Eli Lilly were to test these compounds for activity in any way they chose and communicate to Speier, through regular meetings, the results of their efforts.

The joint program with Eli Lilly lasted 3 years. During that time, Speier supplied the company with 94 pure compounds. A few of the products held out the promise of commercial success, but the program was halted under the early years of Dr. Collings's administration, and none of the compounds was commercialized by Eli Lilly.

---

[22]John Speier, U.S. Patent 2,746,956, 1956.

"*Fourteen months ago, I started with H_2O.
I just ended with H_2O.*"

Dr. Goodwin. John Goodwin returned to Mellon from his wartime service to begin major work in a new field. Early in 1946 he began to study the reaction with sodium of the chloromethylsilanes that Dr. Speier was making. Sodium is an active metal and will readily remove chlorine from a compound. Goodwin wanted to remove chlorine from the chloromethyl group, then form a reaction between the methyl sodium group, —CH_2Na, and the chlorine on silicon, to insert a methylene group between two silicons. He soon succeeded in preparing the first silmethylene with a backbone of alternating silicon and carbon atoms, —Si—CH_2—Si—.

These compounds differed from siloxanes in that they were not subject to rearrangement in acid or alkali. The higher polymers were also stable in the presence of steam, whereas siloxanes would react with steam under pressure and degrade to a lower-molecular-weight polymer.

Goodwin's work resulted in the issuance of five patents[23] covering these new polymers. While these polymers were later used in developing heat-shrink rubber, the high cost of producing the polymers severely limited other applications. Continuing his studies, Goodwin prepared polymers with both siloxane bonds and silmethylene bonds in the backbone, e.g., —Si—O—Si—O—Si—O—Si—CH_2—Si—O—Si—. Joe Francis joined Goodwin to assist him in this effort in 1947.

John Goodwin earned his Ph.D. degree at the University of Pittsburgh for this research on silmethylenes. In 1948, he moved to Midland and took a position in the Dow Corning research department.

Kohl. Charlie Kohl had joined the Mellon group in January 1945. His first project was to continue the work John Speier began on developing peroxides which might have a better vulcanizing effect on silicone rubber than did benzoyl peroxide. Kohl developed a variety of new peroxides, but despite his extensive efforts, nothing better than commercially available products was found.

Kohl's next project in the rubber program was to study the possibility of fluorinating alkyl or aryl substituents on silicon. By that time, we knew that fluorine on carbon would give a solvent-resistant material; this had been shown in the form of Teflon® products which were now on the market. We were looking for a solvent-resistant rubber, one that wouldn't swell, and thought that fluorine might hold the key.

The fluorination process was a difficult one. Some thought was given

[23]J. T. Goodwin, British Patents GB 624551, 1949; GB 624814, 1949; GB 632563, 1949; U.S. Patents 2,511,056, 1950; 2,592,682, 1952.

to direct fluorination using F_2 gas over cobalt fluoride, but this met with no success. Later, trifluorotoluene and hexafluoroxylene compounds became available. With a chlorine directly on the tolyl or xylyl ring it was possible to prepare Grignards and add groups to $SiCl_4$. These Grignards proved to be quite sensitive, and transferring a completed Grignard often caused a fire. It became necessary to stand by and blanket the pouring operation with CO_2 from a fire extinguisher. Once the fluorine-containing groups were on silicon and the products separated and hydrolyzed, the siloxane polymer, resins, or fluids that were produced proved to be quite stable. They were so stable that tests were made at the Bureau of Mines facility outside Pittsburgh in the presence of 90 percent hydrogen peroxide, which reacts with carbon compounds in an explosive manner. The trifluorotolyl and hexafluoroxylyl silicones were better than dimethylpolysiloxanes (the basic ingredient in DOW CORNING 200® silicone fluid), although they were still somewhat explosive. Although the work on fluorination was fairly successful, these new materials were never exploited because of the hazards involved in their preparation and the high costs associated with the production process.

Dr. Warrick.　My part in the overall plan of the rubber program was to work on several different aspects of silicone rubber, along with a few separate projects. Assisting me through the early 1950s were Helena Corsello, George Cmorik, Silas Braley, Jim Church, Charles Brooks, and Frank Fekete.

I continued the work Mac had begun, studying the sulfuric acid polymerization of cyclic dimethylsiloxanes to develop a quicker polymerization process. After much experimentation, I succeeded in developing a process whereby a cyclic compound would polymerize to a nonflowing high polymer in just 1 minute. Once the process was perfected, I demonstrated it at one of our research conferences in Midland (unlike Dr. McGregor, I brought all my raw materials with me from Mellon Institute, to ward off any would-be practical jokers).

High polymers were desired for silicone rubber, and a great deal of research went into developing suitable ones. For a time, K gel was the best that could be obtained. It was a relatively high polymer, but it was already cross-linked, and we were searching for simple long-chain polymers that would cross-link only upon vulcanization.

In his studies of mechanisms and rates of alkali polymerization, Ken Johannson greatly improved on K gel by forming a soluble high polymer, which became the polymer of choice in preparing higher-strength silicone rubbers. Acid polymerization also produced soluble high polymers, but neutralizing the small amount of acid catalyst used in the process proved quite difficult. Consequently acid polymers were not used commercially for rubber.

We tested all the new peroxides developed by Kohl and free radical generators from Speier as vulcanizing agents for silicone rubber, but nothing proved to be more effective than commercially available peroxides. We then turned our attention to the study of rubber fillers.

We soon noted that the benzoyl peroxide used to vulcanize silicone rubber would not tolerate the carbon-black fillers used in organic rubbers to develop high strength. The carbon black tended to react with the benzoyl peroxide and break it down. Later, we found special peroxides that would not be destroyed by carbon blacks, but carbon-black fillers never played a major role in silicone rubber. For the next few years, inorganic fillers—titanium dioxide, iron oxide, zinc oxide, aluminum oxide, calcium carbonate, and a few diatomaceous silicas—were used in the production of silicone rubbers.

In late summer of 1948 another fellowship at Mellon requested a sample of a thin film of silicone rubber. They proposed to use the film to separate gases, for it was known by this time that silicone rubber was more permeable to gases than were plastic films.

Silas Braley, assisting me, took a high polymer and attempted to prepare a thin film of unfilled silicone rubber, but the sheet proved to be too weak for any use. I suggested that he try adding a small amount of a new silica filler, Linde A. We'd just received a sample of the filler the previous week from Linde Air Products Company.

The new filler was added and the film pressed and cured without edge confinement, allowing the rubber to run. Braley was excited when he discovered how strong the resulting thin film was. Next, he made up the same formulation in a normal thickness and discovered we had made the first really strong silicone rubber. Adding more silica filler produced a silicone rubber with a tensile strength over 1000 pounds per square inch and elongation of more than 400 percent. I reported this finding on September 11, 1948.

The Midland development people moved quickly once they learned of the new high-strength rubber and brought out the commercial product, SILASTIC® 250, within a few months. In May 1949 a preliminary data sheet was issued describing SILASTIC® 250. Table 4-1 compares the characteristics of the new high-strength rubber with those of earlier versions of SILASTIC®.

While the high tensile strength of SILASTIC® 250 was not by itself unusual, and while some rubbers had elongation characteristics that approached those of SILASTIC® 250, it was a major breakthrough to find

Table 4-1. Properties of SILASTIC® Stocks

Stock	Early SILASTIC® stocks*				
	150	160	167	180	250†
Tensile strength, pounds per square inch	400	600	600	700	600–700
Longation percent	300	200	110	75	300–400
Shore hardness	45–55	55–65	55–65	75–85	45

*Cured 48 hours at 392°F.
†Cured 24 hours at 482°F.

this combination of high strength and elongation in the same sample of silicone rubber.

We knew that the silica filler we'd used was responsible for the high strength of our new rubber, but we didn't know why. We spent a great deal of time characterizing various fillers, to see what it was about Linde A that made the difference. This included making many measurements of particle size; these measurements ultimately led us to conclude it was the small particle size of Linde A that was the key. A patent was issued covering the techniques we used to differentiate various fillers.[24] Next, we searched for other small-particle fillers and came across Degussa silica, a flame-produced silica which was the best small-particle filler commercially available (Linde A was available only in limited quantities at this point). The silica was manufactured in Rheinfelden, West Germany, and we soon began using it in the commercial manufacturing process.

Soon after SILASTIC® 250 was distributed, the problem of crepe hardening developed and customers began returning product to us. As noted earlier, the problem was solved first by a plasticizer, PA fluid, suggested by Keith Polmanteer. Later a number of other solutions to the problem were found, including a host of new special silicas.

During this period I carried out one other study in connection with the development of high-strength silicone rubber. One of the raw materials used in preparing high-strength rubber was a high-molecular-weight silicone polymer. I studied the use of cesium hydroxide as a catalyst in polymerizing cyclics to achieve this high polymer and found it to be a faster-acting catalyst than potassium hydroxide.

[24]E. L. Warrick, U.S. Patent 2,541,137, 1951.

Another part of my work during the final years of Dr. Sullivan's presidency involved the development of a system of bond refractions[25] which was used to confirm the identity of new simple chemicals or polymers. This system allowed us to confirm the structure of new compounds developed in the labs by means of their optical properties. I also developed a technique for the reaction of polydimethylsiloxanes with water under pressure to yield hydroxy-ended smaller molecules, which turned out to be similar to the PA fluid used in solving the problem of crepe hardening.

Around the time I graduated from Carnegie in mid-1943, I had begun working on chlorination of dimethylsiloxanes to see what compounds such experimentation would yield. I found that by adding 50 percent or more of chlorine by weight to dimethylsiloxanes, it was possible to produce a waxlike solid.

In the fall of 1948 I'd just completed building my home in the Pittsburgh suburbs. The aluminum windows in the house began to lose their putty quite soon after installation, and I thought the solid silicone compound I'd developed might make a good putty substitute. I made a putty using a high polymer and one of the nonreinforcing (large-particle) silica fillers. This inert putty remained soft for a number of years.

Later I developed a better formulation that cured on the surface but remained soft underneath. I caulked another window with this formulation, which was made of one of Dr. Speier's chloromethyl compounds. I painted the surface with amine and solvent, and the chloromethyl reacted with the amine so that the putty cured on the surface but remained soft underneath. While this particular caulk was never brought to market, it was a forerunner of Dow Corning's commercial bathtub caulk.

Beginning in 1948, some of the Mellon group moved to Dow Corning in Midland. John Goodwin was first to make the move, and he was followed by Joe Francis, Charles Kohl, and Silas Braley. Personnel came to Mellon from Midland as well. Dolf Bass, son of Shailer Bass, joined us in 1951 and was later joined by his brother, Arlen. Still later, Forrest Stark and Gary Haberland came to Mellon.

Dow Corning Corporation had come a long way in its first decade. By the time Dr. Sullivan relinquished the presidency in December 1954, the company had made great strides, surviving the cancellation of military orders and firmly establishing itself in the civilian markets for silicones. It had grown from a fledgling joint venture with sales of $1 million in its first complete fiscal year, 1944, to a steadily growing, increasingly self-sufficient company with nearly $18 million in sales in 1953 (Table 4-2).

Table 4-2. Dow Corning Revenues and Profits, 1943–1953

Year	Sales, $1,000s	Profit (loss)
1943	$ 75	$ (9)
1944	1,015	24
1945	1,376	(60)
1946	1,057	(181)
1947	2,582	184
1948	4,210	454
1949	5,108	489
1950	6,387	676
1951	12,875	2,033
1952	15,013	1,381
1953*	17,805	1,678

*Calendar year (fiscal year was changed to calendar year in 1953).

The young company had a strong profit picture by the end of Dr. Sullivan's tenure, despite enormous disruptions caused by the growth of domestic and international markets, the addition of new plant and equipment, and continual refinements of production processes.

As Dr. Collings readied himself to assume his new role as president of Dow Corning, he had a solid base from which to expand the business. Overseas operations were firmly in place, thanks to the efforts of Dr. Bass. An enormous amount of basic research done in the first decade would continue to guide the product development effort for years to come. The company had taken major steps in becoming self-sufficient in basic raw materials and had seen substantial improvements in the efficiency and cost-effectiveness of production processes.

Although Dr. Sullivan had been president of Dow Corning during this first decade, he remained in Corning, New York, and turned over the responsibility for daily operations to Dr. Collings. During that time, Collings had established himself as a strong personal leader who knew how to inspire and encourage the best from his workers, even under the most trying of circumstances. Those qualities would serve Collings well in his new role as president of Dow Corning, as the company entered its second decade of growth.

5

The Collings Era: Personal Leadership

You're our envoy; lead the way, and we'll precede. RICHARD B. SHERIDAN
The Rivals

Dr. William R. Collings: The Man

Long before Dr. William R. Collings was named the second president of Dow Corning on December 16, 1954, he had established a loyal following among the employees of the young company. Collings was a true leader, one who could inspire and encourage his workers to produce their best efforts, one who could maintain a healthy optimism even in the face of the most trying circumstances. "Impossible" was not a word in Dr. Collings's vocabulary. His consistently positive outlook had helped to ensure the survival of the company during the first critical decade of operations. That same positive attitude would help it to thrive in the second.

Bill Collings was a man of action; in his view there was only one time to get things done: *now.* His ability to move decisively and take risks had served the company well thus far. It was Collings who pulled the troops together when business fell flat after the war ended, and Collings who guided the successful transition from manufacturing products for the war to serving the needs of a civilian marketplace.

Dr. William R. Collings.

Even after Dow Corning was on solid footing in the postwar years, Bill Collings maintained his involvement in every aspect of company operations. He was no figurehead leader. Collings personally made many of the critical decisions about plant and equipment, regularly paid visits to the laboratories to hear about the latest developments, and saw to it that employee morale remained high.

Dr. Collings was sensitive to the people around him and often took a personal interest in their problems. There was not a single person working in the company during these early years who did not feel the impact, on either a personal or a professional level, of the Collings touch.

The Collings era really began the day Willard Dow selected the manager of the Cellulose Products Department to take charge of the new silicones project at Dow Chemical. It continued after formation of the joint venture, when Dr. Sullivan assigned to Collings responsibility for the daily operations of the newly formed company. By the time he was named president, Bill Collings had already established himself as the driving force behind Dow Corning's growth and direction.

Collings's style of management was of a highly personal nature. He was a great communicator; this is epitomized in the many "Me to You" letters he wrote to employees over the years. He organized a variety of recreational activities to bring all the employees together as a family— softball and golfing events; an elaborate picnic 100 miles away on Lake Michigan (during which he acted as official photographer); bowling tournaments, in which he frequently participated (Figure 5-1)—to name just a few.

Dr. Collings loved to participate in professional affairs and never missed a chance to tell the story of silicones and of Dow Corning. For example, in his keynote address, "How Research Built an Industry," to the December 1951 American Chemical Society scientific meeting in Midland, he told the story of Dow Corning's beginnings. And in 1953, with facilities expanding, he arranged for a tenth-anniversary open house, inviting editors, suppliers, and customers to Dow Corning in an effort to sell the increased production made possible by the expansion.

Each employee saw Collings in a different light. Some knew him as the man of action, firmly rooted in the day-to-day operations of the plant. Others saw him as a visionary, carefully guiding the company into the future. Still others viewed him as a father figure, guiding and nurturing the joint venture through its formative years. Shailer Bass wrote of Collings, "It was so exciting in those early days! Dr. Collings' dedica-

Figure 5-1. Bowling tournaments were just one of the many activities Dr. Collings promoted to instill a feeling of family within Dow Corning.

tion to training, his dedication to science and chemical engineering and the research that had to go along with it—always an interest in the customer—he wrapped up a lot of qualities in one energetic man, getting the young company off to a good start."[1]

Ray Maneri remembered Collings's strong customer orientation. As he recalls it, Dr. Collings had little use for formal organization charts. Whenever the subject of using such charts came up for discussion, Collings would go to the chalkboard and write: "Customer—We all report to him."

Bill Caldwell, assistant general manager during the early days of Dow Corning, remembered Collings as a man of ambition, and above all, a man of action. He recalled the time in the late 1940s when the original plant was barely completed. "With Collings, nothing was ever completed," Caldwell noted. "In a meeting one afternoon Collings observed, 'We should double the size of the plant. We are going to need the capacity, and if we wait until we need it, we're going to be too late. Let's just figure out now what we need to build, what it will cost, and get going'." Around Dow Corning an even more famous story of Collings's risk taking had to do with the erection of the 105 building, a laboratory extension. Collings said to order the steel; he said he would take care of getting the building approved by the board. The steel came earlier than expected, so Collings gave the order to lay the foundation and put up the steel. The board of directors (Figure 5-2) met only four times a year, and he didn't want to wait.

When the board finally met, it failed to approve the new building. The day after the board meeting, one of the members, Dr. Veazey, was touring the Dow Corning plant. "Hey," he said, "Is that the building the board turned down?"

Collings said, "Yes."

Veazey rather gruffly replied, "I guess we'd better OK it next time." Collings had a habit of getting his way.

Dusty Rhodes remembered Collings as a man of vision: "Collings thought that silicones represented a whole new class of materials that would become very important commercially," Rhodes said. "He believed that Dow Corning was building the base for a very large and diverse group of products that would serve many needs. And his enthusiasm was contagious."

Bill Collings's impatience was legendary. "Ship it!" he used to say, his

---

[1]This excerpt and the ones that follow in this section are taken from Dorothy Langdon Yates, *William R. Collings: Dow Corning's Pioneer Leader,* McKay Press, Midland, Mich., 1985.

Figure 5-2. The Dow Corning board of directors, circa 1957 (*left to right*): Dr. William C. Decker; Dr. Earl Bennett (Dow); Dr. Shailer L. Bass, vice president; Amory Houghton, Jr.; Dr. William R. Collings, president and general manager; Dr. Leland I. Doan, chairman of the board; Dr. Edgar C. Britton, secretary; Dr. Carl A. Gerstacker; Mr. Charles D. LaFollette, treasurer; Dr. Eugene C. Sullivan, honorary chairman of the board.

associates remembered. "What are those packages doing on the dock?" The answer would be: "We're going to ship as soon as the paper comes down." Collings's response was always the same: "You don't understand. The most important thing is to send the customer an invoice, and you can't do that until you put it on the truck and worry about the paper later. I don't care what you've got to do to ship. We have the product. You ship it." When the dock workers saw Collings heading in their direction, there was a flurry of activity.

While Collings could be a tough taskmaster, he also had a heart of gold and took a personal interest in the lives of his workers. Norbert Dickmann, executive account manager, recalled: "When Rita and I were married in September of 1954, Dr. Collings came out to the lab the first day I was back at work to offer his congratulations. When our first baby was born he was back again with congratulations." Later, when Dickmann was working in the Minneapolis–St. Paul sales office, he received a call from Collings one Friday afternoon. Collings told him: "This is Bill. Helen and I are in town for a meeting a day early. We're going to help you and Rita celebrate your fifth wedding anniversary tonight"; according to Dickmann, they were "marvelous hosts."

Virginia ("Ginny") Schultz, who worked as Dr. Collings's secretary for a number of years, saw him as a father figure bringing up Dow Corning as one would a child: "His enthusiasm for the success of Dow Corning was an inspiration to all of us to contribute all we could to his hopes and driving spirit. I soon learned that he was interested in all employees, in the sense of family, and would have done all in his power to ensure their happiness and satisfaction in the Dow Corning working environment."

Ms. Schultz recalled that Dr. Collings used to bring huge bouquets of his lilies to the office and ask her to distribute them to the other secretaries. He never overlooked the secretarial staff and would periodically take them on tours of the plant, showing them the laboratories and explaining what was being done so they would feel more a part of the entire enterprise.

When times got tough, Collings's caring nature shone through the brightest. In 1958, the entire chemical industry's business plunged into the midst of a recession, resulting in a need to decrease the labor force. Because of his empathy for all Dow Corning employees, the enforced layoff of 10 percent of employees nearly broke Dr. Collings's spirit, associates remember. Collings did everything possible to retain staff and helped to find jobs in the community and other areas for those who had to be released.

Because of the downturn, university recruiting trips had to be canceled. Collings encouraged Jack Ludington, then in Personnel, to visit every college where Dow Corning had recruited and explain the problem. Ludington's task, while unpleasant, left an impression of honesty and concern that led to exceptionally good relations between the colleges and Dow Corning when business picked up and it was again possible to recruit.

Dr. Collings always had a keen interest in education and the betterment of his employees. He believed strongly in training for all levels of employees. His interest in employee education dated back to his days in the Cellulose Products Department at Dow Chemical, where he developed a course to teach members of the group about cellulose chemistry. The course was dubbed "Kollings Sellulosic Kollege, Where Students Go to Hell for Knowledge." Mock graduation certificates were given to course participants, to further enliven the program.

Dr. Collings's interest in education extended beyond the corporation and into the larger community. In the 1950s, Collings was one of the community leaders who recognized that the Saginaw Valley was the most deprived of the state's highly populated areas so far as higher education was concerned. He became a member of the first small core group organized to work for an area college and recruited many Dow Corning employees to help.

Collings's dream, shared with many others, was to establish a 4-year college in the area eventually. The dream first led to the establishment of Delta College in 1958, a 2-year community college that granted associate degrees. Collings was instrumental in getting the college a 640-acre section of land in a location central to the tricounty area. As a result of his efforts on behalf of the school, he was named to the first board of trustees of Delta College.

When several attempts to change Delta College from a 2-year to a 4-year college failed, Collings was one of those who worked to bring a 4-year institution to the area, helping to raise private funds and becoming a major donor himself. With dogged determination on the part of many people, including Bill Collings, the first classes of the fledgling university were held in September 1964, in space at Delta College. In 1965 the Michigan legislature established Saginaw Valley College as a 4-year state-supported college. The name was later changed to Saginaw Valley State College; still later, it became Saginaw Valley State University. Collings Drive, on the campus, was named for Dr. Collings in recognition of all the work he did for higher education in the Saginaw Valley.

Risk taker, visionary, father figure, friend, civic leader, educator, communicator...the new president of Dow Corning was a well-rounded man, one eminently qualified to lead the company, with wisdom and confidence, through the second decade of its growth.

Product Development and Management

Product Sales Managers

When Dr. Collings assumed the presidency of Dow Corning in 1954, eight branch offices had been established, with 68 salespersons staffing them. Sales stood at $18.5 million, with profits of $1.4 million.

In order to manage the growth of the sales effort effectively, the company had established the position of product sales manager shortly before Dr. Sullivan resigned as president of Dow Corning. Having sales managers for specific products made possible a more focused selling effort and helped to accelerate the growth of the business.

Electrical Industry. Clayt Doremire had been the first product sales manager named. He was to be responsible for Electrical Industry Sales and was aided in this effort by Lee Teichthesen. As pointed out in Chapter 3, Doremire had been responsible for successfully bringing Dow Corning into the electrical industry. There was substantial potential for the growth of silicones in the electrical field, particularly for use in equipment subject to severe stress and extreme temperatures. No one was better-qualified to shepherd that growth than Clayt Doremire, the man responsible for first introducing silicones to the industry.

Consumer Products. George Marx, who had been named consumer products manager, was assisted by Jack Wiley. SIGHT SAVERS® was a major item in the Consumer Products group. Under Marx, the product was expanded beyond the consumer marketplace and introduced to industry, with the help of the market research department. As a result of Marx's efforts, more than 35,000 SIGHT SAVERS® cleaning stations were set up in industrial plants. Other forms of SIGHT SAVERS®, such as a Dispenser-Pak and SIGHT SAVERS® with advertising imprinted, were introduced as a means of expanding the market.

The Consumer Products group handled other items as well: Slipicone, sterilizing fluids, Cornelia Cloths for dusting, SHOE SAVER®, DOW CORNING 4® compound (which was sold to consumers for use in protecting the spark plugs in their outboard motors), and a group of durable textile finishes.

One of the more interesting new consumer products was bouncing putty, known in the marketplace as "SILLY PUTTY®." While Dr. McGregor and I had developed bouncing putty quite early,[2] Dow Corning had never actively pursued the sale of this product. Dr. Collings believed that it was frivolous, that the group should be focusing on more important applications. In addition, the product was difficult to manufacture.

Peter Hodgson of Marketing Inc. had been marketing SILLY PUTTY® as early as 1950, with General Electric as his sole supplier. Dow Corning took a more active role in 1959 and prepared to supply Hodgson with the raw material. The first order was for 5000 pounds, and before long Dow Corning was supplying as much as 20,000 pounds per week of the curious substance. By this time we had revised the original formula, in response to calls from irate mothers who wished to know how to get SILLY PUTTY® out of their children's hair or the living room carpet. The newer version was formulated not to flow into clothing or rugs and was quite successful during the Collings era and beyond.

In 1956, a new building for the production of consumer products was moved to a 4.5-acre site on Paterson Street in Greensboro, North Carolina, at the site of the textile service center set up in the early 1950s. This became Dow Corning's first satellite plant in the United States. The first plant manager was Ed Sprague. After a few years, Bob Vidal took over as site manager. In 1959 an additional 6.4 acres of land, adjacent to the original site, was purchased for the construction of an emulsion plant, a warehouse, and a laboratory to provide technical service to the southern paper, textile, and leather industries.

[2]R. R. McGregor and E. L. Warrick, U.S. Patent 2,431,878, 1947.

Calvin and Hobbes

by Bill Watterson

Release Agents. Don Francisco had been named product manager for Release Agent Sales. In this position, Francisco was responsible not only for the sales of fluids used in release applications, but also for the sales of various silicone compounds, antifoams, and emulsions of all these products. Releases for food products, such as Pan Glaze, were an important part of the group's effort.

SILASTIC®. With the rise of SILASTIC® sales, Ray Naegele was appointed manager of this product area. Naegele was assisted in this effort by Joe Dellaria, Paul Babinski, and Bob Shipps. The group worked closely with the advertising department to increase sales of SILASTIC®, distributing "Silastic Facts" to customers and prospects and developing a periodic newsletter to keep customers informed of new additions to the SILASTIC® product line.

Resin Sales. The final product area formally established under Collings was for sales of resins for nonelectrical uses. Leo Stebleton was charged with directing the group's efforts, which involved sales of resin products for use in paints and glass cloth coatings and in lamination of glass cloth. Bob Hedlund provided technical assistance to Stebleton.

Textile and Leather Treatments

Another important market segment Dow Corning was serving on an ever larger scale was the textile industry. For many years, Dow Corning had been supplying the industry with waterproofing agents and other textile treatments. With the success of Charlie Sanford's promotion of hangtags in garments, an office was set up in New York City solely for

Figure 5-3. *Left to right:* Charlie Sanford listens as Bill Rossiter explains the Sylflex exhibit to him, along with Bob Parkin and Dr. Collings.

the purpose of serving the textile industry in one of its central locations. Nort Foster, from the Washington branch office, was named textile industry manager.

Around this time, in the mid-1950s, the Sylflex leather treatment, applied during the tanning process, was finally put into commercial production, and an all-out sales effort was orchestrated.

Bill Rossiter was given the task of integrating the sales and advertising campaign on this product. At the May supervisor's meeting, Charles Foley of the S. B. Foot Company of Red Wing, Minnesota, and Bill Sweasy, president of the Red Wing Shoe Company, participated with Rossiter in a panel to tell the supervisors of their experiences in treating leather with Sylflex.

This meeting helped to drum up enthusiasm and to get the product off to a successful start (Figure 5-3). Sylflex sales grew steadily and made a nice complement to the SHOE SAVER® product for making shoes water-repellent.

Project Development Center

In 1957, Chet Currie left his post in the Fluids Section of Andy Kauppi's group and started a New Products Department. Currie's group was given responsibility for the market introduction of experimental products that grew out of laboratory research.

Leo Stebleton and Ray Maneri worked under Currie as market development specialists, and each spent about a year looking at a variety of potential product lines: organofunctional chemicals, molding compounds, hydraulic fluids, high-performance lubricants, dental RTV materials, sealing and caulking compounds, and coatings. Most of these lines eventually became successful, but initially Stebleton concentrated on molding compounds and Maneri on sealants.

Maneri conducted a market study during 1957 and 1958 which uncovered a need for higher-performance adhesives, coatings, and sealants in areas such as the construction, aircraft and aerospace, military, appliance, and automotive industries.

Maneri and Reno Lasorsa further concluded that a one-part sealant would be required for the building-construction market; two-part sealants were too difficult for most industries to utilize. They discussed this with the researchers in Midland, who gave little encouragement about the prospect of coming up with an effective one-part sealant. However, in November 1957 Dr. Leonard Bruner, from Dr. Hyde's group in Basic Research, showed Maneri and coworkers what seemed to be a suitable one-part sealant. This was a pastelike RTV rubber formulation that cured on exposure to moisture in the air with the evolution of acetic acid.

After optimizing the formulation, Maneri's group looked for a suitable site for testing it on a larger scale. Roger Kolderman of the Chicago office had been encouraging the group to try new materials on the S. C. Johnson Building in Racine, Wisconsin, which had a history of leakage around the modern horizontal glass tube structure from the time construction was completed. Rumors were that the boardroom was damp after every rainstorm.

Many other companies had tried and failed to caulk the S. C. Johnson Building, a landmark piece of modern architecture designed by Frank Lloyd Wright.

We approached C. E. Folwell, the building manager, about trying our hand at caulking the building, and he gave his permission. The first samples of the new Dow Corning sealant were applied to a portion of the building in February 1958. Applying the sealant in the dead of the Wisconsin winter was not the best idea, and the task was a difficult one. Ordinary caulking materials would have been impossible to apply in cold weather, but the flat temperature slope of silicones made it possible for the workers to finish the job in freezing weather.

By summer, the favorable results were apparent, and the Johnson Building engineers were enthusiastic about caulking the entire building with the new sealant. The development laboratory began scaling up production of the caulk to complete the Johnson Building. The group started with a 1-quart pot and moved to a 1-gallon pot to manufacture the first 100 gallons of product; later in 1958 a better process was developed for manufacturing the sealant in large volumes.

Soon many orders poured into Dow Corning, as word of success with the Johnson Building spread. Extensive new business resulted, and the product was off to a successful start.

The Special Projects group under Maneri organized a three-tiered marketing approach for the new caulking compound. They proposed to develop the sealant in three formulations: a basic building sealant, a mid-range material for general-purpose use, and a top-of-the-line product to meet the special needs of the aerospace industry. One form of the sealant was introduced to the consumer marketplace as Bathtub Caulk. In 1959 a Project Development Center was built on the Midland site to accommodate manufacture of these new one-part sealants, as well as molding compounds.

International Business

While new products were being developed in the Dow Corning labs, the international business that Shailer Bass had begun building during Dr. Sullivan's presidency continued to grow and prosper under Dr. Collings. In May 1955, Ira Hutchison (Figure 5-4) and Howard Fenn, production manager, visited a number of countries in Europe where our associates had established plants, including England, France, Switzerland, Germany, Italy, and Holland. Hutchison wished to show Howard Fenn how effectively these companies had translated our blueprints and technical expertise into successful operations.

Hutchison contrasted the grim and somber attitudes of the Europeans in 1951 with the greatly improved conditions and attitudes he and Fenn witnessed during their 1955 trip abroad. Fenn was impressed with how hard the people were working to remove war damage and rebuild. Everywhere was new construction, both residential and industrial. The plants they visited contained mostly new and modern equipment even though the buildings housing the equipment were old.

A new era of economic competition seemed to be replacing the old cartel system of doing business in Europe. This was clearly demonstrated at Achema, an international trade show of chemical engineering equipment, held in Frankfurt, West Germany. This was a colossal exhibit with more than 22 miles of corridor space. In many instances they found more than a dozen companies exhibiting competitive equipment.

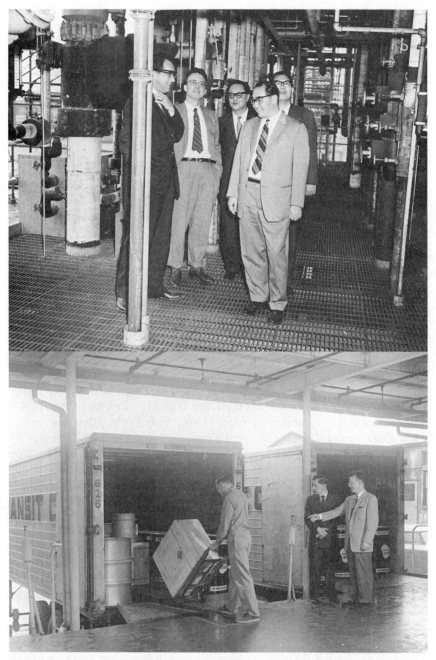

Figure 5-4. *Above:* Dr. Shailer Bass (*left*) and Ira Hutchison tour the plant with the first Japanese visitors at Dow Corning (1958). *Below:* Ira Hutchison observes an early carload shipment to England.

Patent licensing continued as sales expanded in Europe. Farben-fabriken Bayer A. G. was licensed under Dow Corning's German patents in December 1955, and Th. Goldschmidt A. G. was licensed in April 1958. These additional licensees added to the competition for sales in Europe, but, as before, the income from the licenses helped support the growing Dow Corning presence in Europe.

In early 1960, there was a shift in relations with Albright and Wilson. Under a new agreement, Midsil acquired a license under Dow Corning's future patents, and it was agreed the two companies would collaborate in the research area, with the proviso that either party could terminate the research collaboration at any time. This was a step in the direction of Dow Corning's becoming sole owner of Midsil.

By the late 1950s, it was apparent that Dow Corning could greatly improve its opportunities in the international arena by having personnel physically present in overseas markets to provide sales and technical service to distributors and customers. Distributors often were not the best sales agents for Dow Corning, as they handled many product lines, and too often concentrated on pushing products that were easier to sell than were silicones.

Dow Corning International S. A.

As a result of these concerns, early in 1960 Dow Corning International S. A. (DCISA), a trading company, was incorporated in Panama, with headquarters in Nassau. DCISA was given responsibility for sales and technical service in markets outside the United States and Canada. Ira Hutchison was appointed president, and Bob Peele, then auditor of Dow Corning, was appointed treasurer.

To respond to the need for on-site sales and technical service by Dow Corning personnel, DCISA established a branch office in Zurich, Switzerland—the first branch outside the United States. Bob Kroeger was appointed sales manager for DCISA and moved his family to Zurich in the summer of 1960.

Dow Corning A. G.

As the international business grew, it also became obvious that Dow Corning could benefit by establishing a separate corporate framework for the management of the various interests abroad. As a result, around the same time that DCISA was formed, Dow Corning A. G. (DCAG) was incorporated in Basel, Switzerland, to finance and manage some of Dow Corning's overseas interests, including patent licensees and the implementation of technical service contracts.

Sogesil

Earlier in 1960, Dow Corning had joined with two of its European associates, St. Gobain, Italy, and SISS, to form Sogesil (Societe Generale Siliconi e Derivati) located in Milan. Sogesil was established to manufacture a limited line of finished silicone products, mold release and textile emulsions, and to sell and service all Dow Corning and SISS products, as well as its own products, in Italy. Bob Ford, supervisor of Dow Corning's Textile laboratory, was given the responsibility of assisting Sogesil with all production, quality control, and sales problems. He and his family moved to Milan in June 1960.

Japan

Ever since his first visit to Japan, Shailer Bass had been working hard toward establishing a joint venture with the Japanese. He had concluded a joint venture agreement with Sumitomo Chemical in the early 1950s and in 1954 had arranged to form "Nihon Keiso Jushi," a joint venture, with Japan Silicones. However, the Japanese government failed to approve these ventures, and Dow Corning was forced to look for other ways of conducting business in Japan. Shin-Etsu Chemical was licensed in 1957 to make silicones under Dow Corning patents, and Toshiba Electric was licensed to use silicones in electrical equipment. Joint ventures with the Japanese were still years away.

Overseas Personnel

Other Dow Corning employees in overseas positions at that time were Ted Goldmann, who moved to São Paulo, Brazil, in December 1959, and Juan Vinageras, who was hired in Mexico City as our first foreign national. Vinageras had become a member of the International Department soon after it was formed in 1953. He was named manager of Dow Corning de Mexico when the subsidiary was formed in 1961 as a sales company.

In 1961 Dow Corning suffered a great personal and professional loss when Bob Kroeger died in Zurich. After Kroeger's untimely death, Bob Ford moved from Milan to take over management of the Zurich office and was joined in 1962 by Henry Baecker. Ford was replaced in Milan by Reno Lasorsa. Gordon Dean, who had been working in the Midland finance office, became the chief accountant for DCISA at this time.

On the other side of the world, Bill May, who had been a member of our International Department since 1955, moved with his family to Tokyo in 1962. He was to provide sales and technical service to our distributor, Brown McFarlane, and to our latest overseas partner, Fuji Polymer Industries Co. Ltd., which manufactured a line of finished emulsions and silicone rubber, in which Dow Corning now had a significant stake.

Overseas assignments were not always as romantic as they sounded. The May family had a rather unpleasant introduction to the orient. Within a month after moving into their rented quarters in Shibuya, Tokyo, they were burglarized. The culprits were frightened away when the family awoke, but not before they had taken Bill's watch and money. May was due to leave early next morning for a sales trip to Australia, hours before the Tokyo office and banks opened (no automatic teller machines in those days). He made it to Australia with 18 cents in his pocket.

A few months later Charles Dudley and his family moved to Sydney, Australia, to provide sales and technical service to customers through our distributor Swift and Co. Ltd. This arrangement helped to fulfill one of the International Department's stated goals of spreading the business down under.

Collings's Last Visit to Europe

Throughout the Collings years, the overseas business continued to thrive, and Dow Corning gradually expanded and intensified its presence around the globe. In the fall of 1962, shortly before he left the presidency behind, Dr. Collings and his wife made one last trip abroad to observe what had been put in place over the last 2 decades. During the trip, Collings visited almost all the joint venture companies and paused to take pride in their accomplishments. He took many photos during the trip, with the new Polaroid camera he'd just bought (the Europeans were so fascinated with this new toy that Collings had to take duplicate photos to pass out wherever he went). These photos were included in what was to be the last of Dr. Collings's "Me to You" letters, mailed from Europe and expressing his pride at witnessing how far Dow Corning had come, in such a short time, in the international marketplace.

New Businesses

Center for Aid to Medical Research

During the years of Bill Collings's presidency, two major new businesses were formed. One of these grew out of the request of a distraught father whose child was dying.

In the early 1950s, John Holter of Bridgeport, Pennsylvania, wrote to Dow Corning to solicit help to save his baby. The boy had contracted hydrocephalus (water on the brain), and Holter, an engineer, had been trying desperately to save him. He'd invented a small stainless steel valve and needed small-diameter silicone rubber tubing to connect the valve to the brain cavity and the bloodstream near the heart.

Dow Corning quickly supplied the needed tubing, and it was an immediate success; John Holter's baby was saved. Some 10 years later over 600,000 such hydrocephalus shunts had been implanted and were responsible for saving the lives of many children and sparing many others severe pain. These devices remain in place for the person's lifetime and must not react with the body and its fluids. The reasonable biosafety of SILASTIC® silicone rubber was the key to the effectiveness of the shunts.

Word of the success with the Holter valve quickly spread. Once physicians and surgeons learned that the body does not reject silicones, Dow Corning was flooded with requests for new medical products to be used in a host of applications.

Mel Hunter answered this correspondence and began supplying occasional samples to doctors. By 1955, when it became too time-consuming for Hunter to keep up with the correspondence in addition to his role as director of research, Dr. McGregor moved from Mellon Institute to Midland and took up the project where Hunter had left off. Silas Braley, who had come to Midland earlier from my group at Mellon to work in the SILASTIC® laboratory, joined Dr. McGregor in this effort.

As the correspondence continued and grew, Dow Corning formed the Center for Aid to Medical Research in 1959, with Dr. McGregor as director and Silas Braley as executive secretary (Figure 5-5). They were soon joined by Dr. Ethyl Mullison. While the company had not intended to get into the medical products field, and could not foresee a rosy future for it, Dow Corning felt an obligation to continue what it perceived as an important contribution to medical science.

To head off the rising volume of correspondence, McGregor and Braley decided to publish a newsletter that was sent to interested medical personnel around the world. Braley began to attend medical meetings as well, to meet with physicians and surgeons and discuss how silicones might be used in medical applications.

While Dow Corning had been supplying a few samples for medical research, it was not ready to offer finished products to the medical community on a large scale. Bulk SILASTIC® silicone rubber was available to commercial fabricators, but they were not interested in manufacturing small-scale, intricate items for Dow Corning to sell to the medical field, nor were they capable of manufacturing parts in a sterile environment.

Dow Corning faced the choice of discouraging medical research on devices and materials that it could not easily provide on a large-scale ba-

Figure 5-5. Silas Braley (*left*) and Dr. McGregor (*right*), directors of the Center for Aid to Medical Research, show Dr. Collings a Foley catheter, one of Dow's early medical products.

sis, or ensuring that successfully developed products would be available if sufficient demand were generated. The company quickly learned that a great deal of expensive research effort could easily be wasted on interesting but low-potential medical projects.

Dr. Collings asked Dusty Rhodes in Market Research to investigate the problem and recommend a course of action for the company. The decision was reached that Dow Corning would manufacture and sell those medical products, especially fabricated SILASTIC® silicone rubber, for which there appeared to be enough demand to make the effort profitable. Rather than diving into the medical products business, Dow Corning cautiously tested the waters. The first products developed were blocks of silicone rubber and sponge in various degrees of hardness, scleral bucklers, and a small line of silicone rubber tubing. The SILASTIC® rubber blocks and sponge were carved to needed shapes and implanted in the human body by plastic surgeons. The bucklers were used by ophthalmologists for detached retina procedures. The tubing was used on blood pumps and the Holter valve. These products were fabricated in the silicone rubber product engineering laboratory directed by Del Youngs and supervised by Paul Skalnican.

With only a few small-volume medical products, Dow Corning was not in a position to sell and service the widely scattered medical community. There were, however, a number of medical device manufacturers and distributors who had sizable, effective marketing operations, and when contacted, they showed a keen interest in taking on our product line. A distributor agreement was made with one of these firms, Becton-Dickinson.

Applications of technology from the center had made possible a heart-lung machine with a silicone defoamer and a coating for the tubing involved so that clotting of the blood was delayed. A number of heart valves had been developed with assistance from the center. The hydrocephalus valves continued to be used for increasing numbers of children.

SILASTIC®-coated fabric had been used for a variety of "patching" operations—for example, of eardrums and the dura mater (the outermost membrane lining the brain, just beneath the skull). Detached retina cases had been helped with a variety of scleral bucklers and patches. Facial reconstructions had been made in a number of difficult cases.

New products were added to the line at a growing rate. Cooperative research efforts continued between the Center for Aid to Medical Research and some of the best medical researchers throughout the world, doctors in universities and clinics that were fully equipped and staffed to carry out their sophisticated work. The center would regularly receive requests from these doctors for silicone materials and advice in applying the silicones. The center provided access to Dow Corning facilities and expertise at no cost to these doctors. Out of this cooperative arrangement, a number of high-potential product prospects began to emerge. Within a few short years, the medical business was solidly established and steadily growing.

Silicon Business

When I moved to Midland, I was named assistant director of research and Art Barry was named associate director of research, both of us reporting to Mel Hunter. This move placed Dr. Barry and me on the Management Committee which met monthly in Bill Collings's office to discuss research strategy.

During one of these meetings in 1957, Dr. Collings mentioned that Corning Glass Works wanted Dow Corning to respond to a request by Hughes Aircraft for silicon optics to be used in their Falcon heat-seeking missiles. Corning had been making quartz optics for Hughes, but Hughes wanted to increase the sensitivity of the infrared detector by using silicon optics. Collings asked me to go to Los Angeles and visit with Hughes.

Hughes had made a few trial silicon optics and had bought some silicon ingots from Dean Knapic, a small company in Palo Alto, California. Conversations with Hughes engineers made it apparent that Hughes wanted someone of greater commercial capacity to take over the "Knapic" process. Hughes was insistent that I talk to Knapic and arranged for me to visit him in Palo Alto the next morning.

During my visit to Hughes, some of the engineers discussed with me the sad state of the single-crystal silicon business. Yields were poor, seemingly because of a lack of quality control during the crystal-growing process from polycrystal silicon. Most manufacturers of single-crystal silicon were garage operators, as it was a relatively easy thing to set up production on a small scale. However, assuring good quality of the final product was almost impossible in this setting, and as a result, most of the single-crystal silicon produced was poor. The engineers commented to me that Dow Corning might want to look into producing single-crystal silicon in addition to the polycrystalline silicon required for their missiles.

Optical Silicon. The next day I visited Dean Knapic in his small shop in Palo Alto. There he was growing ingots of polycrystal silicon about 3 inches in diameter. Knapic was a spellbinding storyteller and a true promoter. He regaled me with facts and figures and stories about silicon production, bombarding me with so much information that the report I wrote on the flight home occupied most of the 5 hours' flying time.

Knapic had been one of a small group working in California with the Shockley company, which developed early semiconductor devices. The founder of Shockley had been one of the team of three researchers who had received the Nobel prize for physics for the invention of the transistor at Bell Laboratories. Some of these early workers left Shockley to form Fairchild Semiconductor. Others who left Shockley, like Knapic, used their knowledge to grow silicon crystals.

Ultimately, we signed a contract with Knapic to build us a large Czochralski crystal grower to produce large ingots of polycrystalline silicon, for sale to Hughes. Many trips to Palo Alto followed, and the crystal-growing machine was finally built. At that point George Grant, who had managed the Motor Test laboratory and who was an experienced electrical engineer, spent several months growing ingots, many as large as 12 inches in diameter, with the new machine.

Siemens-Westinghouse License. While we were working on the polycrystalline infrared optics for Hughes, Westinghouse approached us with the suggestion that we secure a Westinghouse-Siemens license to make semiconductor-grade polycrystalline silicon and to make "float zone" single-crystal silicon. Westinghouse, a producer of electrical products, wanted to be in the device business and needed good single-crystal silicon as a raw material. But the company was experiencing the same quality problem as Hughes.

Siemens, a German company, had developed a process for growing single-crystal silicon, and Westinghouse was the exclusive licensee for the process in the United States. Westinghouse urged us to acquire a license from Siemens, and a sublicense from Westinghouse, to grow silicon crystals.

Shailer Bass had an intense interest in pursuing the production of silicon. He always wanted to be in the forefront of technology and considered the overtures of Westinghouse an important opportunity to enter into a high-tech business.

By now it was February 1959. I was in Boston attending a meeting on semiconductors, where I met Dr. Enk of Wacker-Chemie, our German associate. We talked about semiconductors, but at that time I was not aware that Wacker-Chemie was a Siemens licensee.

Dr. Bass called me during the Boston meeting and suggested I meet with him at Westinghouse the next day. The following morning, at Westinghouse, we witnessed the production of polycrystalline rods by the Siemens process, involving chemical vapor deposition (Figure 5-6).

These rods were then float-zone refined[3] to make single-crystal silicon of high purity, with impurities in the range of tens of parts per billion. This level of purity, roughly the equivalent of one dust particle in a loaded boxcar, was critical in the manufacturing of semiconductors, a primary use of single-crystal silicon.

Another major use for such pure single crystals was as the active element in rectifying diodes to make direct current out of alternating current. The purer silicon permitted diodes to be made that would withstand 1000 volts across a slice of silicon only a few thousandths of an inch in thickness, to yield direct current in the range of hundreds of amperes. Siemens manufactured a number of these rectifiers.

After observing the silicon production process at Westinghouse, we were impressed with the quality of the procedure, and licensing agreements were signed with Westinghouse and Siemens.

---

[3]Float-zone refining, invented by Bell Laboratories, enables one to lower the level of impurities in single-crystal silicon to a few parts per billion.

Production process

Quartzite is reduced in an electric arc furnace to 98-percent-pure, metallurgical-grade silicon.

$$SiO_2 \; + \; C \longrightarrow Si + CO_2$$

Extensive purification is necessary to meet the ultra-high-purity requirements for semiconductor-grade silicon. The metallurgical-grade silicon is crushed and reacted with anhydrous hydrogen chloride (HCl) to produce trichlorosilane ($HSiCl_3$) in a fluidized bed reactor (FBR).

Additional purification steps are required to allow the trichlorosilane to meet semiconductor-grade quality standards. Electrically active impurities, along with carbon and transition elements, must be removed through advanced chemical separation techniques.

$$Si \; + \; HCl \longrightarrow HSiCl_3 \; + \; H_2$$
(Metallurgical-
Grade Silicon)

Polycrystalline silicon is deposited from purified trichlorosilane in a high-temperature decomposition process. A decomposer contains a mixture of semiconductor-grade trichlorosilane and hydrogen for the deposition of the semiconductor-grade silicon onto an ultra-high-purity silicon substrate.

$$HSiCl_3 \; + \; H_2 \longrightarrow Si \; + \; HCl$$

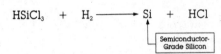
Semiconductor-
Grade Silicon

Employing the same purification technology base, Hemlock Semiconductor Corporation provides high-purity silicon source chemicals:

- semiconductor-grade trichlorosilane
- semiconductor-grade silicon tetrachloride
- semiconductor-grade dichlorosilane
- fiber-optic silicon tetrachloride

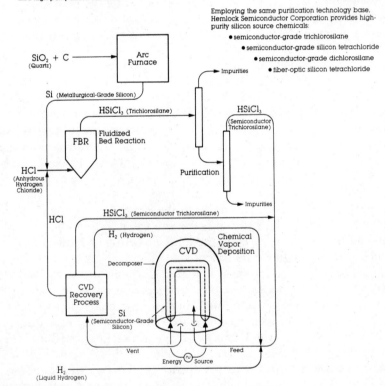

Figure 5-6. The silicon production process.

Trip to Germany. Dr. Bass arranged for a team of four from Dow Corning to visit Germany and observe the Siemens operation in action. Bill Caldwell, Truman Bishop, Bob Rownd, and I made the trip in April 1959. At the same time, we were to visit with representatives of Wacker-Chemie, our German associate, and tour its facilities.

We arrived in Germany some 19 hours after leaving Boston, tired after the long propeller-driven flight. We were joined by Shailer Bass in Munich, Germany, and by the Wacker-Chemie representatives.

We visited Berghausen the next day, where Wacker had its principal chemical plant, its silicone plant, and a new building for the production of silicon. Dr. Enk was our host for the day.

Afterward, we visited the Siemens silicon operations in Pretzfeld. During our stay we also visited the Siemens operation in West Berlin, where we learned a few additional facts about the process, but the bulk of our time was spent in Pretzfeld.

The Siemens deposition, zone refining, and research and production facilities were housed in an old castle with 3-foot-thick walls. There were few buildings left standing in this area after the wartime bombings, and companies set up production in whatever facilities were available. At the castle we were introduced to Dr. Spenke, the head of the silicon operation, and to Dr. Hoffman, his right-hand man.

We spent several days at the Pretzfeld facility, learning all we could about the Siemens process. At the end of our visit, we discussed the order we should place for zone refiners. At that point we all had an unwelcome chance to brush up on our foreign language skills, as our Siemens hosts lapsed into a flurry of German. Fortunately, Dr. Bass was fluent in German and gently reminded the group to speak in our native tongue, not theirs. The order was placed (in English), concluding a successful trip.

Silicon Team. After our visit, we placed orders with Siemens for float-zone refiners but decided to have Bob Rownd design our deposition units. Back at Dow Corning, we formed a team for silicon crystal production. The team worked in a vacant laboratory while other quarters were being built.

Meanwhile we had been searching for someone to make optical parts from the large silicon ingots we were growing. Perkin Elmer finally agreed to make several 4-inch-diameter nose cones and several lenses for us. These were coated with the appropriate optical coating to improve transmission.

Unfortunately, when we approached Hughes about selling the nose cones to the company, we discovered that it had been working on other methods of forming the optics and that our prices were not competitive.

At that point we dropped our large ingot-growing process and concentrated on the Siemens process.

Hyper-Pure Silicon Division. Despite the fact that Hughes did not purchase our silicon nose cones, Shailer Bass was convinced that silicon production was a natural extension of the silicones business and persuaded a reluctant Dr. Collings to go into the business on a large scale. The Hyper-Pure Silicon Division was formed in October 1959, and I was named manager.

The silicon team at this time consisted of Dr. David Fischer, research supervisor, assisted by Vern Flegel, chemist, and Herbert Stewart, physicist; George Grant was manager of process and materials development; Bob Rownd, manager of production, Don Gilson, superintendent of production; Cedric Currin, supervisor of applications engineering, with Al Smith as project leader and Don Kauppi as sales manager. An authorization in the amount of $1,900,000 was approved for the building of a hyper-pure silicon plant.

Our experiences in the addition inside the Midland plant convinced us that we could not carry out sensitive crystal-growing and high-purity deposition processes there. Vibration from trucks passing only a few hundred feet away on the highway could be noticed in the motion of the molten silicon interface and ruined the single-crystal formation. We were also worried about traces of fly ash and chemicals in the air, which might contaminate any high-purity silicon operations.

For these reasons, a country tract of land about 15 miles southeast of Midland was purchased off Fordney Road, roughly 3 miles outside Hemlock, Michigan. This location satisfied the need for isolation from truck vibration and plant contamination. The land purchased was nearly a section (640 acres).

The land was cleared of trees, and a small production building, 50 by 75 feet, was built to house both experimental deposition and zone refining. The building was ready for use in March 1960.

Soon after, the zoners arrived from Germany, and deposition units were built from Bob Rownd's designs. Siemens had developed a fine process, with emphasis on high purity, but it was not able to produce many crystals larger than ¾ inch in diameter. From talking to people at Hughes and Westinghouse, we knew that the demand in this country was for crystals of larger diameter.

Rownd, in particular, believed the deposition units were far too small, and he designed ours to be several times the size of the ones we had seen in Germany. This meant contracting for larger quartz bell jars, which no one had made up to that time. Over the next few years this became a constant problem as we built still larger deposition units and required larger bell jars, which we convinced manufacturers to make, but at great cost to Dow Corning.

Our building began turning out small amounts of polycrystalline silicon product by 1961. Don Kauppi endeavored to sell our product in a market which we entered as number 13.

New Plant. Meanwhile, Truman Bishop took on the task of designing and building our main plant; the Saginaw architectural firm of Prine and Tosach did the layout. The plant was to house a still to purify chlorine, a burner to form high-purity HCl from H_2 and Cl_2, an electrolytic cell (Lurgi) to make the high-purity H_2, and a small fluid bed for the production of trichlorosilane. A number of glass stills were installed to purify this product prior to decomposition.

Demand for product soon outpaced these facilities, and we began to depend on trichlorosilane made and distilled in the Midland plant and brought to Hemlock by truck trailer with a specially designed high-pressure tank.

We moved into the new silicon plant in May 1961, just about 2 years after first learning of the Siemens process. An additional authorization for $1.4 million was required to finish the plant (Figure 5-7).

The silicon business followed a feast-or-famine cycle. When product development and demand were high in the semiconductor industry, our business was excellent; indeed, we often had insufficient capacity to provide all the crystal needed. When the semiconductor business was down from overcapacity, our business was poor and we built inventory. However, the long-term trend was definitely toward expanding demand, and we were convinced we could make a go of the business.

Pricing proved to be a major problem. The market price for single-crystal and polycrystal silicon dropped so regularly that new business plans had to be adopted every few months (the good side to this was that the rapid decline in prices did shake out some of the competition). We had to drop our prices as much as the others, in spite of the higher quality of our product. Fortunately, our high quality did result in a large volume of business which helped us defray our fixed costs, absorb our short-term losses, and, eventually, become profitable.

Innovation. One of our early innovations was the development of one-piece crucible charges, the first step in making single crystals. In this process, silicon pieces were melted in a quartz crucible and a single crystal "seed" was touched to the molten surface and slowly withdrawn to form a larger single crystal.

If small amounts of impurities were added to a polycrystal ("doping"), single crystals with varying levels of resistance to electrical current could

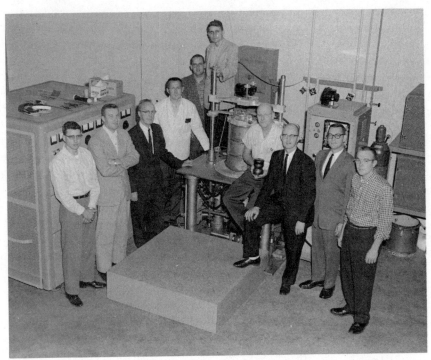

Figure 5-7. Early members of the silicon production team (*left to right*): Vernon Flegel, Dr. David Fischer, Dr. Earl Warrick (*with hand on Czochralski crystal grower*), Don Gilson, F. A. Smith, Cedric Currin, George Grant, Bob Rownd, Don Kauppi, and Herb Stewart.

be produced. Different resistance levels were required for different product applications.

It was a difficult task for customers to add the precise quantities of doping needed, so we began providing this service for them, selling single-crystal silicon that was precisely doped for a particular application. As a result, along with the one-piece charges cut from polycrystalline rods, we began selling small pieces of thin single-crystal silicon rod doped with precise amounts of P-type materials (containing boron) or N-type materials (containing phosphorous) to create the desired level of resistivity.

These crucible charges and predoped silicon rods were an instant success. They were a primary reason why Dow Corning was able to generate a good deal of business despite the fact that we were so late in entering the market.

Buyers in a variety of industries purchased our polycrystalline silicon and helped the business to grow steadily. One of our largest customers was General Motors, which bought our silicon for use in the rectifiers that go into all automobiles to charge the batteries. In fact, GM was so pleased with our product that it agreed to make us its sole supplier of silicon—an unheard-of arrangement for GM, but one which lasted for more than 12 years.

By the end of 1961, we had experienced several cycles of the silicon business, and Dow Corning's board of directors became deeply concerned over losses for the hyper-pure silicon operation. A committee composed of Ralph Hunter (the Dow Chemical chemist who had promoted the silicon idea), Dusty Rhodes, and James Littleton of Corning Glass Works was appointed to make recommendations regarding the future of the silicon business.

After the committee had completed its report, which recommended extensive changes in the business, Dr. Collings asked Howard Fenn, production manager, for his opinion. Fenn told Collings that the report's recommendations were so stringent, it would be virtually impossible to proceed with any hope for success. Dr. Collings asked Fenn to keep track of the production end of the business. Collings then took the matter to the board and got them to agree to keep the business going and give it the time it needed to become profitable.

Shortly after the board agreed to keep the silicon business alive, Truman Bishop, who had been responsible for the construction of the plant, was named production manager when Bob Rownd returned to school to obtain an M.B.A. degree. The silicon business continued to grow, and expansions of the plant were necessary over the next several years to keep up with the growing demand from the semiconductor business. While the business continued to be cyclical, with continued efforts it also became profitable as the volume rose. Eventually we licensed portions of our silicon technology.

Chemical Research

Technology grew rapidly in Dow Corning's second decade. Dr. Speier and his coworkers prepared many new compounds and developed means for placing virtually any organic functional group on carbon attached to silicon. My coworkers and I made basic studies of the radiation resistance of silicone rubber, the preparation of graft copolymers, and the crystallinity of stretched rubber.

Major new fields of products stemmed from technology developed in Midland: fluorosilicone fluids and rubbers, one-component RTV rubbers (Bathtub Caulk), a transparent interlayer for safety glass, soft contact lenses, and masonry water repellents.

During this period, Dow Corning received recognition for its accomplishments in the field of chemical engineering, in the form of an award given by two leading chemical journals.

Chemical Engineering Achievement Award

In 1955, Dow Corning entered a competition for the Chemical Engineering Achievement Award sponsored by *Chemical Week* and *Chemical Engineering* magazines. The award was based on engineering accomplishments, such as new process breakthroughs.

A team of six Dow Corning engineers—Bill Hargreaves, Bill May, Bob Greenhalgh, Earl Beck, Wayne Barrett, and Joe Dellaria—spent most of the summer of 1955 working on the project, including product, process, and application developments in their report. The work was drafted for Dr. Collings and others to preview.

Collings decided the information shown was too valuable to be made public, and a new approach was taken. The new submission covered the unique contribution that chemical engineering was making in all phases of the silicone business: research, process, product, and marketing. The final draft of the report was submitted June 16, 1955, for judging by a panel of 84 educators in the chemical engineering field.

Soon afterward a call came from Sidney Kirkpatrick, editorial director of the magazines, announcing that Dow Corning had won the award. Collings wanted to maximize the publicity he could generate as a result of the award, to make certain that worldwide industry leaders as well as the local community knew of the recognition that his company had received.

The award dinner was to be held in Philadelphia in December 1955, and Collings charged Lou Putnam, advertising manager, and Bob Argyle, public relations manager, with the task of ensuring that the press was well-represented at the dinner. Editors and publishers from all daily newspapers within 50 miles of Dow Corning's home, Midland, Michigan, plus 30 representatives from leading financial and industrial trade papers were guests at the banquet. There were almost 1000 representatives of the chemical industry and profession in attendance.

All the team members who had prepared the entry were invited, as well as researchers from the Corning and Mellon groups. A bronze plaque symbolizing the award (Figure 5-8) was presented to Dr. Collings; after the ceremonies, it was hung in a prominent position in the main hall of the administration building.

Dr. Collings decided that each banquet attendee and each family in Dow Corning should receive a Steuben glass ashtray to commemorate the honor; these mementos are much cherished by those who received them.

Figure 5-8. *Left:* Chemical Engineering Achievement Award plaque. *Below:* Award Presentation Committee, which prepared the nomination (*left to right*): Bill Hargreaves, Bill May, Wayne Barrett, Joe Dellaria, Earl Beck, and Bob Greenhalgh.

Mellon Research

Dr. Speier. Continuing his organofunctional work, John Speier showed that it was possible to add olefins to trichlorosilane by means of low-temperature catalysts in addition to the high-temperature catalysts used by Dr. Barry's group. This was another technique for making the organofunctional compounds Speier was interested in studying.

Speier wanted to see what effect different x groups already on the olefin had on the ability of the olefin to add trichlorosilane; x could be alcohol, acid, aldehyde, or any reactive group. Speier wanted to know how general was the low-temperature reaction.

Leo Somer had shown in early publications that the same additions of olefins to trichlorosilanes could be accomplished at low temperatures using ultraviolet light as the catalyst.[4] Later it had been shown that these additions could be accomplished by yet another method, using triphenylsilane and substituted olefins with benzoyl peroxide as catalyst.[5]

Speier and his coworkers, Jim Webster and Leonard Shorr, began a study of free radical mechanisms for this addition process. They were interested in seeing which functional groups could be present and which silane compounds would add to the olefin—in short, which organofunctional compounds could be produced by this method.[6] The group found that a variety of silanes could be added to olefins. While Dow Corning did not explore the commercial possibilities of most of these compounds, they have become the basis for broad-based research within the chemical industry and in academic circles.

Dr. Speier's researchers spent 4 years studying free radical additions and found that phenylsilane, $C_6H_5SiH_3$, tribromosilane, Br_3SiH, and trichlorosilane, $SiHCl_3$, would add to olefins which did not polymerize in the presence of free radical catalysts. The olefin could contain carboxylate esters, and the double bond could be in either the acid or the alcohol portion of the molecule. Polysiloxanes with adducts were claimed in patents[7] which included the use of the ester group in curing reactions.

John Speier was interested in finding better catalysts than the free radical catalysts his group had been studying for the past 4 years. The literature of patents at this time began to show the use of metals from

[4]L. Somer, *J. Am. Chem. Soc.*, 68:2687 (1947); L. Somer, *J. Am. Chem. Soc.*, 69:188 (1947).

[5]*Gadsby Research*, 3:338 (1950).

[6]J. Speier, J. Webster, and R. Zimmerman, *J. Am. Chem. Soc.*, 78:2278 (1956).

[7]Dow Corning, U.S. Patents 2,925,402, 1960; 3,015,646, 1962.

groups IIIA, IVA, IB and IIB[8] in the periodic table of the elements to catalyze the addition of silane to olefins. Speier disproved much of this literature in subsequent experiments. However, platinum (Pt) did appear to work, and patents[9] had been issued for processes showing that Pt, in various forms and on various substrates, could catalyze the addition of trichlorosilane to simple olefins at moderate temperatures (266°F).

Speier made the thermodynamic calculations[10] which showed that the addition of silane to olefinic double bonds was a favorable process, that is, that the reaction would "go." Speier's group tried platinum on a number of substrates such as carbon and soon showed that 0.06 percent of platinum on carbon would promote the reaction of almost any SiH compound with a number of substituted olefins. Platinum could be used generally to add silanes to olefins.

With this success, the group focused on soluble salts of periodic group VIIIA metals, Fe, Co, Ni, Ru, Rh, Pd, Os, Ir, and Pt, as catalysts. These were all useful, but chloroplatinic acid (H_2PtCl_6) was the most effective. Chloroplatinic acid as $H_2PtCl_6 \backslash 6H_2O$ added to a solution of CH_3HSiCl_2 in pentene-1 at a concentration of 0.0000005 Pt atoms per Si atom rapidly produced a 100 percent yield of the desired adduct.

The patent[11] which was issued covered nearly any SiH compound with nearly any olefinic or acetylenic organic structure. Later, Mel Nelson, in the Midland laboratories, used this reaction as a curing mechanism for an RTV rubber and potting compound. Here the cure was so effective that the chloroplatinic acid alone catalyzed the reaction in seconds. The cure is excellent in that no by-products are formed and no siloxane rearrangement occurs.

Speier's group published some 13 papers over the next 9 years on the use of this catalyzed addition of silanes to olefins.[12] He reviewed the

---

[8]MacKenzie, Spialter, and Schoffman, French Patent 961,876, 1949.

[9]Wagner, U.S. Patent 2,637,738, 1953; Wagner and Strother, U.S. Patent 2,632,013, 1953.

[10]The calculations of the energy of reaction.

[11]J. Speier, U.S. Patent 2,823,218, 1958.

[12]J. Speier, J. Webster, and G. Barnes, *J. Am. Chem. Soc.*, 79:974 (1957); J. Saam and Speier, *J. Am. Chem. Soc.*, 80:4104 (1958); J. Ryan and Speier, *J. Org. Chem.*, 24:2052 (1959); Ryan, G. Menzie, and Speier, *J. Am. Chem. Soc.*, 82:3601 (1960); Saam and Speier, *J. Am. Chem. Soc.*, 83:1351 (1961); A. Smith, Ryan, and Speier, *J. Org. Chem.*, 27:2183 (1962); Ryan and Speier, *J. Am. Chem. Soc.*, 86:895 (1964); H. Bank, Saam, and Speier, *J. Org. Chem.*, 29:792 (1964); M. Musolf and Speier, *J. Org. Chem.*, 29:2519 (1964); M. Stober, Musolf, and Speier, *J. Org. Chem.*, 30:1651 (1965); W. Dennis and Speier, *J. Org. Chem.*, 35:3879 (1970); Ryan and Speier, *J. Org. Chem.*, 31:2698 (1966); Saam and Speier, *J. Org. Chem.*, 24:119 (1959).

subject in *Advances in Organometallic Chemistry.*[13] Later, a book by two Russian authors gave references for more than 2000 published examples of this hydrosilation reaction.[14]

Shorr. Leonard Shorr studied vinylsilanes in the preparation of organofunctional materials. Most reactions eliminated ethylene by cleaving the vinyl group from silicon. He then studied structures such as —SiCCN, which he prepared by a complicated synthesis. In this study he prepared a barbiturate, probably the first instance of production of a silicon-based drug.

Shorr's most useful discoveries centered on the finding that alkyl orthoformates, $(RO)_3CH$, would react with —SiCl to form alkoxysilanes, —Si—OR, compounds that were less toxic and less corrosive than chlorosilanes. The reaction proceeded even in the presence of an —SiH bond. This made possible the preparation of trimethoxysilane, $(C_2H_5O)_3SiH$. This material disproportionated to give a very easy method of making silane, SiH_4. Silane, a gas boiling at $-169.6°F$, is dangerous to handle, as it flames on contact with air. This method of making small amounts of silane out of contact with air made possible a number of syntheses.

Two applications deserve mention. First, an adduct was made of organic rubber in benzene solution, where the trichlorosilane was added to a number of residual double bonds. This adduct later could be deposited from the solution and cured as the chlorines reacted with the water in the air to hydrolyze and form cross-links. Second, a similar adduct was made using linseed oil, in which the double bonds there reacted with the trichlorosilane. This adduct was useful as an addition to other drying oils and paints to give faster cures.

Shorr joined Mary Pat David of the Mellon group to study the modification of commercial products to yield a series of urethane and alkyd resins. Later, a nylon, in which a part of the acid function material was replaced by a siloxane which had hexanoic acid ends, gave a product which, unlike ordinary nylon, had excellent adhesion to glass. This modified nylon had flexural strength and an elastic modulus twice that of commercial nylons. The nylon was tested as an adhesive for copper and glass and proved to be excellent in that use.

A conventional phenyl silicone resin, similar to DOW CORNING® 804

---

[13]J. L. Speier, "Homogeneous Catalysis of Hydrosilation by Transition Metals," *Advances in Organometallic Chemistry*, vol. 17, Academic Press, New York, 1979, pp. 407–447.

[14]E. Y. Lukevits and M. G. Voronkov, *Organic Insertion Reactions of Group IV Elements*, Academy of Sciences, Riga, Latvian SSR, 1964 (published in United States, 1966).

paint resin, was prepared with the ester form of the same end group, $-SiC_6H_{10}COOCH_3$. This resin cured by the addition of a diamine to give a resin whose coatings were more flexible and more solvent-resistant than the normal DOW CORNING® 804 resin. Resins formed with alcohol functional ends, $-SiCH_2CH_2OH$, were treated with an equivalent of toluene diisocyanate. The resulting solution could be coated on glass, iron, or copper to give a hard varnish which was better than DOW CORNING® 804.

After making significant contributions to the research group, Leonard Shorr received his Ph.D. degree from the University of Pittsburgh in 1955. He then decided to go to Israel for a 1-year work experience, but ended up extending the 1 year to 30. He is still in Israel, working for the government.

Mary Pat David, Norm Daughenbaugh, and Ben Eynon continued the organofunctional work after Leonard Shorr left the company. They found that the alcohol trimethoxysilylpropanol, $(CH_3O)_3SiCH_2CH_2CH_2OH$, showed some unusual chemistry. The alcohol hydrolyzed and interacted reversibly to form gels and then fluids which were water-soluble. The results of their studies were published in *Organic Chemistry*.[15]

This silyl alcohol reacted with carboxylic acids at room temperature to give esters such as $-SiCH_2CH_2CH_2OOCCH=CH_2$, an acrylate. Bob Merker of the Mellon group later investigated the copolymerization of these acrylates with acrylate and vinyl monomers. This chemistry permitted the cure of polysiloxanes that contained only a percent or so of acryloxyalkyl groups, by ultraviolet light, free radical catalysts, or heat.

The thought at the time was that such chemistry had potential to modify silicones by adding minor amounts of vinyl polymers, and to modify vinyl polymers with variable amounts of siloxane structures.

Biomedical Research. During the first year of Collings's presidency, the joint research program with Eli Lilly continued. However, toward the end of 1955, the management in Midland feared too much silicone knowledge was being "given away," and the program was dropped.

Mellon Patch. By early 1956 Dow Corning had decided to consolidate all research and development in Midland. The Corning group had moved to Midland in 1950. A new building, 118, was built to house the Mellon group as it moved to Midland—Dr. McGregor in 1955, Dr. Speier and I in 1956. The building became known as the "Mellon

[15]J. L. Speier, M. P. David, and B. Eynon, *J. Org. Chem.*, 25:1637 (1960).

"Eureka! Another sticky, gooey mess!"

Drawing by Vietor; ©1979 The New Yorker Magazine, Inc.

patch," a name it was to retain until it was dedicated as the W. R. Collings Laboratory some years later.

Only three of the Mellon group made the move to Midland; others moved on to new positions elsewhere or remained at Mellon. Bill Piccoli and John Noll took teaching positions in a new college, Monroeville Community College, in a suburb just east of Pittsburgh. Leonard Shorr went to Israel, as mentioned earlier. Mary Pat David took a job as a technical librarian. Frank Fekete went to work for Union Carbide. Dr. Paul Lauterbur left for a position at the State University of New York. Jim Webster took a job with Monsanto Chemical Company in Dayton, Ohio. Bob Merker, Mary Jane Scott, and a few others remained at Mellon, where Dow Corning maintained the fellowship for a few more years.

Speier Group in Midland.   In August 1956, Dr. Speier moved to two laboratories in the Mellon patch in 118 as manager of organic research, along with a doctoral graduate of the University of Iowa, Dr. John Saam. By October they were joined by Gerry Menzie, a former lieutenant commander from the Navy who had flown carrier-based planes throughout World War II and in the Korean war.

In October 1956, John Speier summarized his 13 years of organosilicon research before the Management Committee. He pointed out that his group had invented, patented, and developed new chemical processes to make a large variety of organosilicon compounds and had proved the utility of a variety of organofunctional compounds, such as organic halides, alcohols, amines, acids, amides, phenols, esters, olefins, ethers, aldehydes, urethanes, and ureas.

The files Speier had built over the years contained about 2000 examples of such "chemicals," none more than 10 years old. He pointed out that adding small quantities of these compounds to silicone polymers permitted their cure by organic reagents to give entirely new products with attractive properties. Conversely, incorporation of the compounds into organic polymers permitted them to be cured by inorganic reagents to yield another group of entirely new products with attractive properties. The commercial possibilities for such compounds had not yet been explored, but Dr. Speier felt that the potential was enormous.

Unfortunately, Dr. Collings did not share Speier's enthusiasm for these materials, pointing out that Dow Corning Corporation was a specialty silicone products company and did not intend to change its focus and become a specialty chemicals company.

Dr. Speier was discouraged by this reception, but Shailer Bass encouraged him to continue to exploit this new area, and Bass offered him ongoing support. The body of knowledge which Speier and his coworkers developed is a treasury of information which Dow Corning can draw upon for new commercial applications at the appropriate time.

Speier's group grew by the addition of John Ryan and Gust Kookootsedes in 1958. In 1961, Howard Bank and Marty Musolf joined the group. Ken Lee, Chuck Roth, and Marian Russell were added in 1962. Gerry Gornowicz joined in 1963, and Keith Michael in 1964. In 1965, the group grew even more rapidly, with the addition of Gary LeGrow, Bob Krahnke, Art Smith, Dick Alsgard, and Gary Stark. Samuel Wendel, Alan Alanko, and Anna Cheng joined Speier in 1966. Bill Dennis and Jim Malek came to the group in 1967. Peter Pape and Marvin Coon were added in 1968.

This large group of researchers, crowded into three laboratories at the Midland site, was exceedingly productive. The group had to carry out the functions of a pilot plant as well, scaling up production of each new compound themselves, since the existing pilot plants did not have the equipment or personnel for work of that nature.

Dr. Warrick

Radiation Effects. The opportunity to study the effects of radiation on silicone rubber arose when Dr. A. J. Allen of the University of Pittsburgh made space available to us in the university cyclotron. Samples of a number of commercial silicone rubbers were exposed in a water-cooled cup to the direct beam of 14-MeV deuterons as well as to the secondary radiation produced by the beam's interacting with the cup.

The level of radiation intensity was not measurable directly, so we had no quantitative information, but the effects seemed to be similar to those produced by high-temperature aging. Exposure of a high-molecular-weight polymer to the same radiation produced a high level of cross-linking, which we estimated by swelling measurements. We found a molecular weight between cross-links of M_c 4150, a relatively high degree of vulcanization.

Quantitative measurements were made using three other types of radiation: gamma rays from Co^{60}, 2-MeV electrons from a Van de Graff generator, and x-ray radiation from standard tubes using different target materials.[16]

Polymer samples containing silica were exposed to these levels of radiation, and physical properties were measured. Gamma rays showed an optimum cure somewhere between 5 and 25 Mrep (roentgen equivalent physical). Electrons of 2 MeV gave an optimum cure in the range of 10 to 15 Mrep based on physical properties. Swelling measurements of the "cured" rubbers showed that gamma rays and electrons produced roughly the same number of cross-links based on the energy absorbed. Results of our work on radiation effects were reported in the first of a series of radiation symposia.[17]

Crystallinity. Polydimethylsiloxane rubbers (the great majority of silicone rubbers) were shown by workers at the Bureau of Standards to have the lowest second-order transition temperature ($T_g = -189.4°$) of any rubber measured up to that time.[18] Keith Polmanteer in the Midland laboratories measured Gehman twist angles as samples of silicone rubber were cooled.[19]

---

[16]E. L. Warrick, *Ind. Eng. Chem.*, 47:2388 (1955).

[17]First ARDC Radiation Symposium, Fort Worth, Texas, May 1957.

[18]Also referred to as the "glass transition temperature," the temperature at which a polymer becomes so brittle that it shatters like glass upon heavy impact.

[19]K. E. Polmanteer, P. C. Servais, and G. M. Konkle, *Ind. Eng. Chem.*, 44:1576 (1952). The "Gehman twist angle" is a measure of the recovery of a sample of rubber, after

At Mellon Institute, we studied crystallinity of silicone rubber, which is achieved at the freezing point. We wanted to learn how to develop crystallinity in silicone rubber, because in natural rubber and many synthetics, crystallinity is what gives the material its strength.[20] X-ray studies of stretched samples showed orientation and crystallinity at different degrees of stretch.[21] Crystallinity appeared around −76° F; it was found that this freezing point could be lowered by adding groups to the chain.[22]

Quantitative measurements of the degree of crystallinity were made. Physical measurements on similar samples cooled in stretched positions gave clear indications of crystallinity.[23]

We discovered that, unlike organic rubbers, which show a tension drop as crystallinity occurs, silicone rubber shows a tension rise. With this information we were able to speculate upon the nature of chain structure in silicone rubber. Further evidence of the nature of the chain structure and the reinforcing action of silica fillers was obtained from rheological studies of polydimethylsiloxanes with and without fillers.[24]

Graft Copolymers. From our studies of peroxide vulcanization came the realization that the free radical sites on polydimethylsiloxanes created by benzoyl peroxide could also be sites on which olefin polymerization could occur. The resulting copolymer had chains of the olefin polymer grafted to the base polydimethylsiloxane. Such graft copolymers have distinctly different solubility properties. For example, trifluorochloroethylene polymerizes readily with free radical catalysts in the presence of polydimethylsiloxanes, and one obtains copolymers with fractions which are acetone-soluble, as compared with the toluene-soluble original ungrafted polymer.[25]

When I moved to Midland in August 1956, I was joined by Dr. David J. Fischer and Dr. John F. Zack. There we continued the radiation studies and the graft copolymerization studies begun at Mellon. The radiation studies made use of the Co^{60} source within Dow Chemical. A few

---

stretching, when it is cooled; the lower the temperature, the less the recovery of the rubber. This was a practical measure of crystallinity.

[20]Flame-produced silica mimicked this crystallinity effect, which is why it made silicone rubber stronger.

[21]S. M. Ohlberg, L. E. Alexander, and E. L. Warrick, *J. Polym. Sci.*, 27:1 (1958).

[22]C. E. Weir, W. H. Leser, and L. A. Wood, *J. Res. Nat. Bur. Stand.*, 44:367 (1950).

[23]E. L. Warrick, *J. Polym. Sci.*, 27:19 (1958).

[24]E. L. Warrick, W. A. Piccoli, and F. O. Stark, *J. Am. Chem. Soc.*, 77:5017 (1955).

[25]E. L. Warrick, U.S. Patents 2,958,707, 1960; 2,959,569, 1960.

samples were treated in a nuclear reactor, but the results were not quantified. The results of these studies were reported in several publications.[26]

When I was named manager of the Hyper-Pure Silicon Division in October 1959, I left the field of research. Dave Fischer, John Zack, and others who had joined our group, Dr. Nelson Beck and Roger Chaffee, continued the radiation and grafting studies.

Midland Groups

The expansion of research and development in the second decade was rapid in Midland. Andy Kauppi, still director of product engineering, developed both technical service and new-product development laboratories in every product area. Many of these product-oriented laboratories had counterparts in research. Dr. Hunter managed the research laboratories, the analytical laboratories, and the pilot plant. Because of a shortage of space, it was impossible to segregate research laboratories from those of product development, and there was much overlap between the labs.

During this period the research groups opened several new fields, developing wet-process silica fillers, fluorosilicone polymers, one-component sealants, solventless resins, transparent silicone rubber, and carbon 14 radioactive compounds used for tracing products in toxicological testing. In addition, much work was done for the purpose of improving plant processes. For example, toxicological studies were made on many products, intermediates, and chemicals used in plant processes, to understand their effects and to limit exposure to possible hazards.

Dr. Barry's Group. While Art Barry assumed administrative duties during this second decade, his group continued to study the pseudo-Friedel-Crafts (PFC), or Barry, reaction. Don Hook also continued to study methods of improving the direct process.

---

[26]D. J. Fischer and E. L. Warrick, Second ARDC Radiation Symposium, Columbus, Ohio, October 1957; E. L. Warrick, D. J. Fischer, and J. F. Zack, Jr., Third ARDC Radiation Symposium, Atlanta, Georgia, October 1959; D. J. Fischer, R. G. Chaffee, and V. Flegel, *Rubber Age*, 88:59 (1960); D. J. Fischer, R. G. Chaffee, and E. L. Warrick, *Rubber Age*, 88:77 (1960); J. F. Zack, Jr., E. L. Warrick, and G. Knoll, *J. Chem. Eng. Data*, 6:279 (1961).

Fillers. Barry's group began to explore the production of new silicone rubber fillers, once we had demonstrated that small-particle silicas were reinforcing. One of the first attempts involved hydrolyzing silicon tetrachloride to silica by different routes. Unfortunately, none of these simple hydrolysates proved to be reinforcing. Flame-produced silicas, such as Degussa, proved to be good fillers, but because of the problem of crepe hardening they had to be used with plasticizers. Barry's group and others began looking for ways to prepare silicas that would not require the use of a plasticizer. Ion-exchange resins were available, and it was possible to deionize sodium silicate, "water glass," to form silica sols. Bill Daudt, Les Tyler, and Chuck Lenz worked with these sols and a commercially produced sol, Ludox, from duPont, in an attempt to create new silica fillers from them.

Silica sols were treated with trimethylchlorosilane to block some of the —Si—OH structures with $(CH_3)_3Si$—O—Si—. Sols so treated could be removed from the water to recover the silica. These treated silica fillers proved to be excellent reinforcers which also prevented crepe hardening when used in silicone rubber.

Chuck Lenz showed that Ludox could be hydrophobed with hexamethyldisiloxane, $(CH_3)_3Si$—O—$Si(CH_3)_3$, in the presence of HCl. The resulting silica was quite similar to Ludox treated with trimethylchlorosilane. This process became known as the "pop-out" process because the treated silica literally popped out of the sol. Dr. Tyler's contributions to the pop-out process were patented[27] only after Dow Corning sued the commissioner of patents. This was the only suit ever instituted against the commissioner of patents by Dow Corning in the first 30 years of the company's existence. The patent office simply did not recognize the pop-out process as a unique development, one criterion for issuing a patent, but our arguments in court were persuasive.

The hearing was quite complicated. We had to convince a very busy judge in the Washington, D.C., courts, where the patent case was tried, that the pop-out process was indeed a novel and valuable development that warranted a patent. To do so required educating the judge in the chemistry involved. I was a part of the court team and recall that the next case up after ours involved a group of 100 or so Jehovah's Witnesses, who sat in the back of the courtroom during our hearing and let out a collective groan at every explanation of another chemical procedure. When we finally persuaded the judge of the merits of our case, the back of the courtroom erupted in applause.

A whole series of silica fillers, designated as "X," "BX," "LX," and

---

[27]L. J. Tyler, U.S. Patent 2,863,846, 1958.

"IES," evolved from Lenz's work. All were highly reinforcing and helped to produce stronger SILASTIC® silicone rubbers than were obtainable with other silicas. However, these silicas were more expensive than the fume silicas and could be used only in special applications for which the extra cost would be warranted.

Fluorine Chemistry. Wright Air Development Center (WADC) at Wright Patterson Air Force Base, Dayton, Ohio, had frequently asked Dow Corning to participate in contract research, but Dow Corning was concerned about control of the patents which might issue and for that reason refused the offer.

Air Force officers suggested, as an alternative, that we attend conferences when contractors reported and give WADC the benefit of Dow Corning's expertise. This would give us insight into the field of fluorinated silicone rubber, which Wright was exploring. Both sides would benefit from the exchange, without Dow Corning's giving away any patentable information. Dr. Barry was asked to attend these meetings at WADC.

At one early conference, Paul Tarrant presented his work with George Butler at the University of Florida in Gainesville. Tarrant had prepared methyltrifluoropropyldichlorosilane, the key ingredient in fluorinated rubber, from trifluoropropene and methyldichlorosilane, citing the Barry process as the reaction used. Tarrant had made a few fluids, but in quantities too small for preparing high polymers. However, he had conceived of the idea of preparing oil-resistant siloxanes from these polymers.

Dr. Barry reported on this conference to Shailer Bass and Mel Hunter. Immediately, a project to develop solvent-resistant rubbers, through a process of fluorination, was begun. Barry was assigned responsibility for managing this fluororganosiloxane project, which lasted many years. Art Gordon worked on the project with Dr. Robert Ruh of Dow Chemical. Ruh was already at work on the fluorination of a number of organic compounds of interest to Dow. Despite many attempts, no promising candidates evolved from this project.

At one of the WADC conferences, Art Barry met Dr. Ogden Pierce, who had been working for Dr. Earl McBee at Purdue University on a fluororganosilicon project sponsored by WADC. Shortly thereafter, Dr. Pierce joined Dow Corning to head up a fluorine research group.

Fluorine Laboratory. George Grindahl and Eric Brown assisted Ogden Pierce initially, and George Daniels and Don Hook of Dr. Barry's group were also available to carry out pilot syntheses. As time went on, additional researchers—Wayne Holbrook, Art Gordon, Loren Haluska, Don Smith, Bob Murch, and Jim Black—joined the group.

The researchers began to follow Tarrant's route for fluorinating rubber, with Dr. Barry also participating in the studies. Starting with the addition of carbon tetrachloride, CCl_4, to ethylene, $CH_2{=}CH_2$, they succeeded in following the steps Tarrant had suggested at the research conference.

Meanwhile, WADC asked Dow Corning to convert cyclics that Tarrant had produced into polymers. This proved hopeless, as the amount of material provided by WADC was too small. At this point, Dow Corning asked Dow Chemical and Dr. Ruh to produce 1000 pounds of the starting material, trifluoropropylene ($CF_3CH{=}CH_2$). This bridged the materials gap until Ogden Pierce had his own pilot operation in place.

When the WADC group heard of Dow Corning's progress, they were concerned about the status of Tarrant and his coworkers. We had created the compounds that Tarrant had suggested at one of the research conferences, and they worried that Tarrant would not get the proper credit for his work.

As a result, Shailer Bass and Art Barry made a visit to WADC to discuss the matter and from there went to visit Tarrant in Gainesville. They worked out an agreement to file Tarrant's patent for him and to buy the patent rights. Over the next few days their patent application was written at Dow Corning, and it was issued in 1960.[28]

Tarrant and his coworkers published their findings in 1957.[29] Ogden Pierce and his coworkers developed a patent covering the bis(trifluoropropyl)siloxane polymers.[30]

Considerable research effort was expended in investigating other fluorinated groups on silicon and processes for preparing these materials. One reason for such studies was the group's belief that 50 percent or more of a compound had to be fluorine if the compound were to be solvent-resistant. Solvent-resistant compounds were desired for such products as gaskets surrounding petroleum products. Others outside the Fluorine Laboratory participated in this fluorination study, and Ken Johannson further developed the polymerization techniques which led to a patent.[31]

Eric Brown was the first to prepare rubbers from the trifluoropropyl groups. These rubbers had considerable solvent resistance, barely swelling in contact with gasoline and petroleum oils which would have

[28]P. Tarrant and G. W. Dyckes, U.S. Patent 2,934,549, 1960.

[29]P. Tarrant, G. W. Dyckes, R. Dunmire, and G. B. Butler, *J. Am. Chem. Soc.*, 79:6536–6540 (1957).

[30]O. R. Pierce and G. W. Holbrook, Canadian Patent 570,988, 1959.

[31]O. K. Johannson, Canadian Patent 570,580, 1959.

swelled the normal dimethylsiloxane materials beyond usefulness. The low swell was quite unexpected, because the trifluoropropyl-substituted polymer contained only 36.5 percent fluorine, not the 50 percent or more that was felt to be needed. The first member of this low-swell series of rubber was given the designation "LS-53." Within 5 months it was being actively marketed (Figure 5-9).

After this discovery of a solvent-resistant rubber, the group affixed many other fluorinated groups to silicon, and between silicons, to explore the field thoroughly, developing a number of new compounds in the process. The low-swell rubbers thus developed found use in a variety of seals for aircraft and automotive needs. The low-swell fluids were used as lubricants in high-pressure compressors.

The patents issued to Dow Corning for the development of fluorinated rubbers gave the company a solid market position. It was many years before Dow Corning agreed to license this technology. General Electric Company was licensed in 1976 under the basic patents covering the intermediate cyclic trimer, linear fluids, rubbers, and methods of

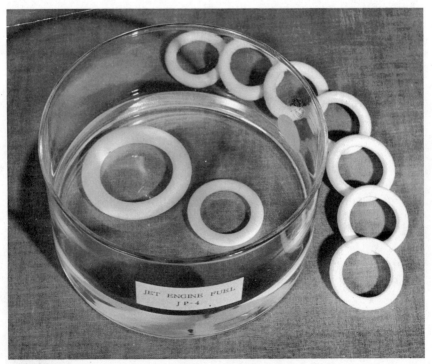

Figure 5-9. O-rings made of fluorinated silicone rubber do not swell in contact with gasoline or other solvents. The larger O-ring in the bowl is made of nonfluorinated silicone rubber.

production, but by this time Dow Corning was well established in the market for fluorinated silicone compounds.

Dr. Hyde's Group. When Frank Hyde moved to Midland, he and a number of others formed the Basic Research Laboratory. After the move, Bill Daudt and Ken Johannson, originally part of Dr. Hyde's group, moved to other laboratories and established programs in their own fields of expertise.

Gust Kookootsedes in Hyde's group studied the preparation of ester and hydroxyl-ended polymers which were used in early two-part (RTV) rubbers. The reaction used in curing was $-O-Si-OC_2H_5 + HO-Si-$ 7 $C_2H_5OH + -O-Si-O-Si-O-$ and was catalyzed by a number of materials. The two components of this RTV system were mixed at room temperature and put in place by trowel or pour. The time to initial cure was usually less than 30 minutes, while a full cure required several hours.

Jack Wehrly in Hyde's group studied emulsion polymerization of dimethylsiloxane cyclics, $[(CH_3)_2Si-O-]_x$, where x might be a number from 3 to 6. This detailed study was a continuation of the work Dr. Hyde had done earlier and led eventually to a process, which was adopted in the plant, for continuous alkaline polymerization of these cyclics.

Hydroxyl-ended polymers were studied in some detail and proved to be useful in preparing silicone rubber foams with Si—H-containing polymers, such as DOW CORNING® 1107. Hydrogen was evolved in the curing and served as the foaming agent. Gust Kookootsedes, Earl Beck, Larry Werner, Len Bruner, and Tom Pooley were all involved in different aspects of these studies.

The preparation of the hydroxyl-ended polymers from chlorine-ended ones was studied by Paul Brown, Len Bruner, and Elmer Schultz. To determine the molecular weight of these polymers, in 1957 Len Bruner converted the hydroxyl ends to acetoxy ends which could be analyzed by simple titration. Bruner's acetoxy-ended polymers were the basis for the development of Dow Corning's first one-part RTV sealant. In 1962, the one-part RTV work was expanded by Ed Sweet, who introduced methylsilyltrioxime, $CH_3Si-[ON=CR_2]_3$ as a curing agent for RTV sealants. The cure of the first one-component RTV eliminated acetic acid, the acid in common vinegar, on exposure to water. Acetic acid was corrosive to many electrical and electronic circuits which needed such a sealant. The new one-part sealant developed by Sweet cured with oxime elimination and was noncorrosive. Sealants were also made of the new trifluoropropylsiloxanes, the LS polymers.

Resin Laboratories.   During these years, the various resin laboratories studied the preparation of silicone alkyds and intermediates that could be used in alkyd paint formulations. Other hybrid organic-silicone resins were prepared: phenolics, epoxies, and, later, acrylates and methacrylates. Various reactive intermediates for preparing these hybrid resins were produced and sold.

Sam Brady and a number of coworkers prepared reactive monophenylsiloxane resins and other mono-substituted resins of low molecular weight as intermediates. Many formulations of these intermediates were brought to market: XZ 6138, XZ 6988, XZ 6168, XZ 4201, and XZ 6118. Hybrid organic resins, which would cure at low temperature, or in some cases on exposure to air, were prepared from these intermediates and were used in many applications. One principal use was in painting hot stacks where heated vent gases caused normal paints to blister and degrade. These resins were also used in painting ships, refineries, and industrial tanks, and many other types of buildings and equipment that were exposed to extreme conditions.

Solventless resins were developed from vinyl-containing siloxanes which were curable with di-t-butyl peroxide. Don Weyenberg had made the first vinyl group containing copolymers and was granted a patent covering the process.[32] Vinyl groups proved to be useful in many ways not immediately envisioned, including as higher-strength rubbers and as special electrical potting resins. These fluid materials were suitable for potting or casting of electrical components to achieve a hard resin encapsulation. These clear-casting resins were prepared by George Helvey, Charles Slemmons, Don Weyenberg, Arnold Buzzard, George Coulman, and John Thomas.

In 1956, Les Tyler summarized the work the group had done on silicone resins used as masonry water repellents. This work ultimately led to a product for treating bricks after they had been fired to make them water-repellent. Later, much work went into waterproofing additives to be used in mixing mortars and concretes.

At one point there was an extensive program to treat concrete bridges and sections of highways to decrease the effect of freezing and thawing on the spalling of concrete. When a water repellency treatment was applied to the concrete, water penetration into small cracks and pores would be reduced and spalling prevented when freezing conditions occurred. However, this use was abandoned when the cost proved to be prohibitive.

SILASTIC® Laboratory.   The first SILASTIC® laboratory was under the supervision of Phil Servais, but after a time George Konkle took charge.

---

[32]D. Weyenberg, U.S. Patent 2,770,634, 1956.

Ray Maneri, also working in the laboratory during this time, investigated the use of vinyl-containing polymers in SILASTIC® 250 formulations. A vinyl-containing material would cure by different means than were normally employed for silicone rubber. The vinyl group permitted the use of lower amounts of peroxide for vulcanization and even the use of other peroxides that normally would be ineffective. Vinyl-containing polymers could be vulcanized by elemental sulfur, a vulcanization agent commonly used with natural and synthetic rubbers. Later, Keith Polmanteer studied the use of vinyl groups in preparing higher-strength silicone rubbers.

Polmanteer also studied the effect of use temperature (i.e., the temperature at which the product would be used) on the tensile strength of silicone rubber versus organic rubber. His studies showed that organic rubber was weaker at high temperatures than was silicone rubber. He also demonstrated that, while the tensile strength of SILASTIC® dropped as the use temperature increased, it was still greater than the strength of any organic rubber tested at the same use temperature. Indeed, a reasonable tensile strength was obtained at 392° F for silicone rubber, far above the temperature at which organic rubbers would remain relatively strong. Polmanteer also showed that fillers, vinyl content, and plasticizers all affected the degree of tensile strength at varying use temperature levels.

The SILASTIC® lab evaluated fillers and fluorine-containing polymers to support research being conducted in other groups. The lab during this period also developed silicone rubber ablatives for use on spacecraft. The Gemini spacecraft went into orbit with DOW CORNING® 325 ablative as its heat shield.

Polmanteer's Research Laboratory. Around this time, Keith Polmanteer left the SILASTIC® development laboratory to establish another SILASTIC® lab, this one exclusively for research.

Transparent Interlayer. The new silica fillers drew Polmanteer's attention, and he began to experiment with them. He showed that some of these could be compounded with polydisubstituted siloxanes containing the proper amount of phenyl to match the refractive index of the reinforcing filler being used. This resulted in a compound that was very transparent at 77F° but which became slightly hazy at temperatures above or below this temperature.

Around this time, in 1954, aerospace companies were looking for windshields for supersonic aircraft, such as the B58 bomber. The windshields of these aircraft needed to withstand heating above 302°F. At supersonic speeds, air friction heats the whole skin of the aircraft, windshield included, above 302°F. A sheet made of the transparent compound Polmanteer developed, when cured between two sheets of glass, forming an "interlayer," resulted in a clear windshield that would withstand the high temperatures caused by air friction (Figure 5-10).

Several different formulations of interlayer material were developed by Polmanteer, John Cretzmeyer, John Erwin, Frank Campbell, Jack Fenner, Tom Laur, Maynard Youngs, Duane Burdick, and Jim Mishler.

Polmanteer and his group set up a pilot plant, run by Duane Burdick, Tom Laur, Jim Mishler, George Kuhlberg, and Tom Martin, to manufacture the interlayer. This included a special polymerization unit with catalyst removal, cyclic removal, and dedicated mixing equipment. The product was a solid success. In all, Polmanteer's group turned out roughly 30,000 pounds of the interlayer over the next 4 years.

Rheological Studies. Polmanteer and his group began a number of rheological measurements on the siloxane polymers used in silicone rubber. These studies were a continuation of work we had performed at

Figure 5-10. Dr. Hunter holds up the new transparent interlayer for inspection by (*right to left*) Dr. Collings, Duane Burdick, Amory Houghton, Jr., and Dr. William Armistead, a Corning executive.

Mellon Institute. Polmanteer's work was published later in a rubber chemistry trade journal.[33]

The group also studied the so-called resin linear polymers, which were block copolymers with resin segments interspersed in a normal linear rubber polymer. The resin segments were formed from the hydrolysis of phenyltrichlorosilane or phenyltrialkoxysilane.

The rubbers resulting from the use of resin linear polymers had high tensile strength even without fillers (900 to 1200 pounds per square inch) and were quite snappy. This meant that the rubbers had low hysteresis loss[34] on stretching, an important characteristic in applications which required repeated stretching. These same rubbers showed improved tear strength as well.

Dr. Johannson's Laboratory. Ken Johannson established a physical chemistry laboratory after moving to Midland. Many fundamental properties were measured, and a number of special materials were prepared.

Bob Holmes, working with Johannson, prepared C^{14}-tagged polydimethylsiloxane fluid. The fluid was given to the Dow Chemical Toxicology Laboratory, which was carrying out a variety of toxicological studies for Dow Corning. This fluid, which could be traced by its radioactivity, was important in demonstrating the biosafety of DOW CORNING® Antifoam A compound and was one factor which helped lead to the approval of the product by the Food and Drug Administration, for use in food applications.

Johannson's group, which consisted of Gloria Stark, John Saylor, Joe Lundquist, and Forrest Stark, also studied the improvement of cyclic dimethylsiloxanes so that higher-molecular-weight polymers could be prepared for silicone rubber. In addition, the group prepared polymers with high phenyl content, for radiation stability tests. It had been shown that higher phenyl content improved the stability of the silicone rubber to radiation by gamma rays, high-voltage electrons, or x-rays.

The treatment of new silicas by cyclic dimethylsiloxanes was studied in order to develop a better understanding of the whole mechanism of reinforcement.

Analytical Laboratory. During the years of Dr. Collings's presidency, the Analytical Laboratory continued its studies of newer and more precise analytical tools. These included extensive use of spectroscopic data

---

[33]K. E. Polmanteer, *Rubber Chem. and Tech.*, 54:1051 (1981).

[34]"Hysteresis" is the failure of a substance that has been changed by some outside force to return to its original state when the force is removed.

of many types and a venture into the new field of gas-liquid chromatography, which soon became a basic tool used in many analyses.

Gas-liquid chromatography came to Midland from Mellon Institute in 1956, courtesy of Dr. Paul Emmett of the Gulf fellowship, who first told us of the use of this technique. With his help and some simple tests, I analyzed a mixture of chlorosilanes by this method. The trials were successful, and on my next trip to Midland I told Mel Hunter and Bob Winger about the technique. Winger immediately began working on the process and over a period of years developed Dow Corning's capability.

By mid-1962, when Dr. Collings stepped down from his role as president of Dow Corning, the company had grown to more than $53 million in annual sales. After guiding the joint venture through its first 2 decades, Collings passed the mantle of leadership to Dr. Shailer Bass.

Upon resignation of his role as president, Dr. Collings was named honorary chairman of the board, in tribute to his many outstanding contributions during Dow Corning's formative years. At the same time, the "Mellon patch" in 118 was renamed the "W. R. Collings Laboratories."

6

Shailer L. Bass: Entrepreneurial Management

We may affirm that nothing great in this world has been accomplished without passion.

G. W. F. HEGEL

Shailer L. Bass

If Dr. William R. Collings was a born leader, Dr. Shailer L. Bass was a natural entrepreneur, always interested in exploring ideas, seeking out new markets, developing new businesses, acquiring new technology. With the inquiring mind of a researcher, Bass systematically pursued the new, the unknown, the possibility, and in the process helped Dow Corning in its formative years to achieve successes that were unusual for a company so young.

Shailer Bass was born the son of a Christian preacher who spent his days on the road, spreading the gospel. The Bass family was one of modest means, at one point even living in a log cabin.

From these humble beginnings, Shailer Bass struck out to make a place for himself in the world, working his way through Butler University by taking a string of part-time jobs. After receiving his undergraduate degree from Butler, he continued part-time teaching and pursued research fellowships to support further schooling.

217

In 1929 Bass obtained a Ph.D. in chemistry at Yale. With sheepskin in hand, he made the trek to Midland, Michigan, along with Howard Fenn and Peter Petrie, in a Model A Ford to join Dow Chemical. Bass had accepted a research position with the company, and Fenn and Petrie joined on as chemical engineers in Dow's Organic Research laboratory. For the first 7 years at Dow, Shailer Bass was a research chemist in Dr. Britton's organic laboratory. It was while working in this lab that he was selected by Bill Collings to become research director of the new Cellulose Products Department. Bass stayed in this position for 8 years, and his training under Collings left him well prepared to assume the position of director of research when the Dow Corning joint venture was formed.

Once he was at Dow Corning, the entrepreneurial talents of Shailer Bass were quickly demonstrated. It was Bass who was responsible for the formulation of DOW CORNING 4® compound, the product that carried the company through the war years. When the war ended, it was Bass who spearheaded the drive for overseas business, developing joint ventures and setting up sales distributors throughout the European area, making Dow Corning an international company at a very tender age. It was Bass who was largely responsible for bringing the high-technology business of silicon production to Dow Corning.

By the time the board of directors named him the third president of Dow Corning at its September 1962 meeting, Dr. Shailer Bass had established himself as a strong leader with an aggressive entrepreneurial management style.

Shailer Bass knew how to motivate his workers. He always sought ways to bring out the best in his employees, to give them an incentive to achieve. One good example of this was his establishment, in 1966, of the President's Sales Club, with membership limited each year to field sales representatives who exceeded their own objectives. Members were rewarded with trips to meetings in warm, desirable locations (although the first meeting was held in Midland, in the midst of a terrible snowstorm) and mementos of their accomplishments. After a time, wives were included in the meetings, and this made the concept even more successful. The sales club begun by Dr. Bass became so popular that it remains in place today.

Shailer Bass was a civic-minded man, involving himself in a variety of activities that contributed to the betterment of the local and national community. Like Collings before him, Bass had an intense interest in education, serving on the Midland school board and helping to shepherd several major expansions of school facilities.

Bass was interested in art education. After voters rejected a tax increase to fund the local school system in 1957, the school board elimi-

Dr. Shailer L. Bass.

nated some art classes in a cost-saving move. At the same time, the Midland Art Council, chaired by Dr. Bass's wife Elizabeth, was struggling to get started and was looking for projects to enhance art education and its application in the very scientific community of Midland.

Dr. Bass suggested a Christmas card contest be initiated for children from elementary and high schools in the area, with prizes awarded and the "best of show" cards used as the official Christmas cards of Dow Corning (Figure 6-1). The contest was an instant success and over the years won national recognition in the form of two awards by community and business organizations.

Dr. Bass was recognized by two colleges for his many contributions to the furthering of education. Butler University, his alma mater, awarded him an honorary degree of doctor of law, and Saginaw Valley College (now Saginaw Valley State University) an honorary doctor of science degree for his many accomplishments in the field of education.

Dr. Bass's concern about education was felt inside Dow Corning as well. Bass was responsible for developing a corporate library in the very

Figure 6-1. Winners of the Christmas card contest, 1957.

earliest days of the company. Thanks to his efforts, in 1945 a library began to take shape. He assigned Pauline Hopfer the task of collecting and cataloguing all books and reports, journals and abstracts, government specifications, photographs, patents, and any other information that might be useful to employees.

In February 1948 the library (which was in 103 building) was officially recognized with the appointment of Ann McNeill as librarian. Over the years this library has become an indispensable tool for the Dow Corning research and development staff. Much of the information has been computerized in recent years, making patent searches and other time-consuming library research far more efficient and far less time-consuming. Dr. Bass's devotion to the community extended beyond the field of education. In the 1960s, he accepted the chairmanship of a successful community drive to raise $1.5 million as the community's share of a $6.5 million center for the arts.

While Dr. Bass worked hard, he also played hard. Bass had a fine sense of humor and always found time to have fun in the midst of his ever-busy schedule. He was not above playing the occasional practical joke; Bass was a prime suspect as the culprit who ruined Dr. McGregor's demonstration of cyclics by pouring end blockers into the formulation.

Shailer Bass knew how to enjoy himself. This was made clear to me during one of our trips to Los Angeles. We completed our work on Friday, and Bass contacted our Mexico sales manager, Juan Vinageras, who was vacationing with his family in the area. We arranged to join the family in a trip to Disneyland on Saturday, and I do believe Shailer had more fun than anyone in the group, including Juan's 7-year-old daughter.

Within Dow Corning and within his community, Dr. Bass was an involved contributor. Even after his retirement in 1971, he continued to seek out new opportunities, building a home on the island of St. John in the Virgin Islands and selling plots of land which he had purchased along with the house.

In June 1964, 2 years into his presidency, Shailer Bass wrote an article on creativity for the *Dow Corning News* in which he quoted Charles Knowles from the *Psalm Book*. This quote, as much as any description of the man, sums up the approach and philosophy, the dedication to discovery and achievement, that made Shailer Bass so successful in his work within Dow Corning and for the larger community: "To make a valuable contribution with my life is the only way I can assure myself I have value."

Reorganization

Shailer Bass's first task in his new role as president was to reorganize the domestic operations of the company, which had become inadequate as Dow Corning continued to grow. The day after he was named president, Bass called a meeting of all managers to discuss the organizational changes taking place and the prospects for the future of the company. At this meeting he asked for the group's support in achieving the goal of doubling the business by 1970.

At the meeting, Bass introduced John Hannigan to the group. Hannigan, a former vice president of Corning Glass Works, had been named executive vice president for domestic affairs.

At this point in the company's evolution, it was felt that considerable restructuring of the business was needed in order for it to continue functioning effectively. It was also felt that the sweeping changes required could be accomplished only by an impartial outsider, and John Hannigan seemed perfectly suited to the task. He had a solid reputation within Corning Glass, where he had achieved great success in managing the Electronic Products Division, the largest of Corning's operations. He would now be responsible for restructuring Dow Corning's domestic operations, reorganizing the company for greater efficiency, profitability, and capacity to manage further growth of U.S. markets.

John Hannigan (who quickly became known as "Jack" to his management associates) moved rapidly to fill his new role. His first action was to restructure the domestic company into five divisions, each with a general manager reporting directly to him:

- Engineering Products—Bill Pedersen
- Medical and Pharmaceutical Products—Dusty Rhodes
- Chemical Products—Earle Smith
- Consumer Products—Bill Rossiter
- Electronic Products—Earl Warrick

Each division was set up as an autonomous business, with the general manager responsible for the production and sale of all divisional products. Plants in each division were set up as profit centers, with plant managers reporting to their respective division managers (Table 6-1). Under the new structure, the regional sales offices continued to function under the management of Charlie Sanford.

Also reporting directly to Hannigan were Olie Blessing, vice president and director of marketing; Bill Caldwell, director of engineering; Howard Fenn, director of manufacturing; Bill Hargreaves, director of planning; Andy Kauppi, technical director; and Bud Lankton, director of industrial relations.

Earlier in the same year, Truman Bishop was named production manager for the Hyper-Pure Silicon Division. Bob Vidal was named manager of the Consumer Products Division with George Marx as marketing manager.

Once the new divisional structure was announced, Hannigan organized a management retreat, a first for Dow Corning, at the northern Michigan resort of Shanty Creek. This was a 3-day planning session attended by management and marketing people from the five new divisions. The retreat represented a new and different experience, involving a large group of Dow Corning managers who had never before been involved in high-level planning.

Hannigan's efforts were rewarded by a strong vote of support from the group, which now felt more personal responsibility for the success of the company. With domestic operations divided into semiautonomous divisions, managers were given more accountability for performance. But it was also easier for them to measure the value of their contributions, and this led to increased morale and a higher level of dedication to improving operations.

Late in 1963, Jack Hannigan left Dow Corning to assume the presidency of Brunswick Corporation. Although his tenure with the com-

Table 6-1. Divisional Structure under John Hannigan

William Pedersen, Engineering Products Division manager
  Sales managers:
    Edward I. Haire, electrical machinery
    Ray S. Naegele, automotive components and appliances
    Michael Nakonechny, finished products
    John Tyner, aerospace and government
    John R. Wehrly, fabricating products

A. W. Rhodes, Medical and Pharmaceutical Division manager
  Gordon McIntyre, sales manager

William Rossiter, Consumer Products Division manager
  Robert Vidal, director of manufacturing and sales

Earle J. Smith, Chemical Products Division manager
  Sales managers:
    Paul E. Grunder, construction
    Ralph B. Ehlers, process aids
    Roger Kolderman, chemical specialties

Dr. Earl L. Warrick, Electronic Products Division manager
  Sales managers:
    John Dexter, silicone materials
    Donald K. Kauppi, hyper-pure silicon

---

pany lasted little more than a year, he had a major influence on its subsequent functioning. During his brief term, Hannigan infused the company with a new spirit of cooperation, engendered a new sense of loyalty and commitment, convinced us all we were going to be "big," and set up a structure that would allow for growth to be managed effectively and profitability increased significantly in the coming years.

Business Ventures

While Jack Hannigan was restructuring domestic operations, Shailer Bass concentrated on new business ventures and on furthering opportunities overseas.

Alpha Molykote Corporation

Dr. Bass saw potential in combining the technology of molybdenum disulfide, MoS_2, with that of silicones. Molybdenum disulfide ("moly") was used as a solid lubricant. Moly had been used in petroleum oils, but the natural temperature limits of the oils prevented many higher-temperature applications. Bass saw the potential high-temperature uses for moly in DOW CORNING 200® silicone fluid.

As a result, in August 1964, Dow Corning purchased Alpha Molykote Corporation, a leading producer of molybdenum disulfide lubricants. Bill Pedersen was named president of Alpha Molykote, while maintaining his duties as general manager of the Engineering Products Division. Ray Naegele was named executive vice president and moved to Stamford, Connecticut, the subsidiary's headquarters.

History.　At the end of World War II, Alfred Sonntag formed Alpha Molykote to produce a variety of lubricant products from raw molybdenum disulfide. Over the years, Sonntag's aggressive marketing efforts had helped to secure a name for Alpha Molykote by demonstrating the "magic" lubricating abilities of molybdenum disulfide. In these demonstrations, Sonntag would drain all the oil, containing a small amount of MOLYKOTE®, from the crankcase of his car. Then he would drive the car away, as an astonished audience looked on. The MOLYKOTE® coated the moving parts of the car so that even though all the oil was drained, the car could be driven for several miles with no damage to the engine. This marketing technique was so effective that MOLYKOTE® gradually developed a name so strong, it threatened to become "generic."

Alfred Hochbaum, a Czechoslovakian entrepreneur who'd helped finance the business, also arranged for the marketing of Alpha Molykote in Europe. By 1960, European Alpha Molykote was growing faster than its American parent. Soon the trade name "MOLYKOTE®" was known worldwide.

When Dow Corning acquired Alpha Molykote in 1964, the European branch was technically and promotionally the world leader in molybdenum disulfide. In Europe, the MOLYKOTE® product was used as a crankcase additive and was prominently used in racing circles. Major companies such as Daimler Benz, Bavarian Motor Werke (BMW), Citröen, and large steel companies were major users of Alpha Molykote products.

There was another reason behind the decision to purchase Alpha Molykote. Shailer Bass felt that Dow Corning's research and development labs could break the stranglehold that Climax Molybdenum held on the lubricant grade of the raw material by developing a synthetic molybdenum disulfide. As it turned out, before the labs were successful in synthesizing the product, European Molykote developed a far less expensive "white" lubricant that relied on only a small amount of the expensive MoS_2 in the formulation.

While synthetic molybdenum disulfide was never developed, a moly-silicone lubricant for high-temperature applications was successful and the acquisition proved to be a sound one. There were side benefits as well; Dow Corning acquired the distributor lines developed by David Nolte, the parent company's sales manager, and these later became important in the marketing of RTV silicone rubber products.

In a labor-intensive business such as Alpha Molykote, people played an extremely important role. Capitalization requirements were low, and competition was intense. Al DiSapio, manager of product development, had been with Sonntag from the beginning and helped Molykote to remain competitive by developing a popular "bonded lubricant" line. These products were mixtures of solid lubricants in a resin. They were cured in place for "lifetime" lubrication or used as a film for the initial wearing in of bearings.

Harry Gerstung and David Gordon of Alpha Molykote and Al Lewis of Dow Corning became well known in the United States for their work on developing new lubricants. They often worked with Marty Devine in the Navy laboratories and with George Kitchen, a lubrication expert in the Bell Laboratories. Initially Dr. Josef Gaensheimer was the most famous member of the technical group, but after a time Dr. Rudiger Holinsky, his protégé, became equally well known around the world.

Ophthalmics

In addition to the acquisition of Alpha Molykote, Bass supported other new business ventures within Dow Corning, including the use of silicone rubber in making soft contact lenses. In the early 1960s Walter Becker, an optometrist and inventor from Pittsburgh, developed the concept of a silicone rubber contact lens. Becker reasoned that the softness and optical clarity associated with silicone rubber, and its established use in related medical applications, would likely make it an excellent material for contacts. He obtained a basic patent on the concept.

Becker brought his patent to Dow Corning in the mid-1960s, hoping to license us to manufacture the lenses he envisioned. Ira Hutchison and Shailer Bass invited Dr. Robert Blackhurst, a local ophthalmologist, to meet with Becker to review his concept. Dow Corning decided not to take a license.

This meeting piqued Dr. Blackhurst's interest, and he in turn discussed the possibility of a licensing arrangement with Joseph Breger, the owner of Muller-Welt Contact Lens Company in Chicago and one of Blackhurst's suppliers of hard contact lenses. Breger obtained rights to the Becker invention and began to develop the technology for making silicone contact lenses. At this point Dow Corning entered the picture once again, supplying many silicone rubber samples to Breger, along with instructions for their use. A major difficulty encountered was that the surface of silicone rubber was not wet by tears, a necessary condition for comfort. Breger found another patented technology for rendering the surface of silicone rubber hydrophilic (easily wet). This technology made possible the development of a primitive form of silicone contact lens.

Silicone lenses have several advantages. Not only are they soft and comfortable on the eye, but they can also be worn for long periods of time, because of the high level of oxygen transmission through the lens to the eye and carbon dioxide transmission from the eye through the lens to the atmosphere (i.e., they "breathe"). By contrast, prolonged wearing of a hard contact lens deprives the surface of the eye of oxygen because of the much lower level of oxygen and carbon dioxide transmission.

About this time, the Food and Drug Administration ruled that contact lenses were drugs and that Breger had to submit to full-scale clinical trials of the lenses, closely supervised and tightly controlled. This greatly complicated Breger's marketing plans. However, he did begin clinical trials and even made a little money selling lenses to the clinical investigators.

Keith Polmanteer, manager of the Silicone Rubber Research laboratory, was one of Breger's primary contacts within Dow Corning and one of the first to wear test lenses. As the relationship with Breger continued, Dow Corning decided to pursue ophthalmics after all. Negotiations were begun during Bass's presidency for the purchase of the silicone soft contact lens portion of Breger's business.

Silicon Sales

Silicon sales at this point fell under my division, Electronic Products. Sales of hyper-pure, semiconductor-grade silicon grew rapidly from the start of operations. Table 6-2 shows the growth from 1960 through 1965. In 1965, roughly 40 tons of hyper-pure silicon was sold—a substantial figure for a pure material.

Czochralski single crystal, grown from melted polycrystal silicon, became important with the rise of integrated circuits and other communication semiconductor devices. This major revolution in device production continuously decreased the size of devices while increasing the number located on one "chip" of silicon. The numbers began in the few hundreds and rapidly moved to thousands and ultimately to millions of devices on one chip.

In order to increase the number of devices on a chip, larger and larger silicon slices had to be developed. Increasing the slice size meant that more chips could be placed on one slice. An example of the large

Table 6-2. Sales of Silicon
(In $1,000s)

Year	Single-crystal Float-zone	CZ*	Polycrystal	Total
1960	$ 19	$ 0	$ 12	$ 31
1961	248	0	109	357
1962	766	0	694	1,460
1963	834	0	1,785	3,810
1964	2,025	432	3,776	6,367
1965	2,765	1,263	5,460	9,488

*Czochralski-grown single crystal.

crystals grown around this time and the slices prepared from them is shown in Figure 6-2.

We were constantly plagued by the fluctuating requirements of the semiconductor industry. When the device manufacturers began increasing the number of devices on a chip, yields were low as they tried to perfect the process. Production of devices often required as many as 40 steps. Each step had a loss, and many steps meant a low overall yield. As the process improved, they could make the same number of devices

Figure 6-2. Single-crystal silicon rod, 3 inches in diameter, and sliced wafers, 15/1000 inch thick.

with less silicon, and demand for polycrystalline products would go down. Consequently, during periods of process development we would have trouble filling orders. At such times, we were able to sign major customers to long-term contracts. When the yields improved, the demand for polycrystal dropped sharply and we would build inventory.

Price declines continued to plague the business (Table 6-3). There was some firming of prices after 1964, but it was still difficult to maintain profitability, as many of the operations were labor-intensive.

Our growing volume of silicon sales did help to offset some of the fixed costs that were draining profits. Because of our reputation for high-quality product, by 1966 Dow Corning had become the largest producer of polycrystal silicon in the world.

Center for Aid to Medical Research

By the time Dr. Bass became president, the Center for Aid to Medical Research had been working with physicians and surgeons for a number of years. During Bass's term, the center continued to grow and thrive along with the rest of the Medical Products Business.

Toward the end of Shailer Bass's presidency, Dr. McGregor, who had been so instrumental in getting the Center for Aid to Medical Research off the ground, was recognized for his achievements when his alma mater, McMasters University in Ontario, granted him an honorary degree of doctor of science in the spring of 1962.

Mac retired in May 1963 and was named director emeritus of the center. Silas Braley became the new director. The executive committee of the board of directors issued a resolution of recognition and honor upon the death of Dr. Rob Roy McGregor on April 8, 1965.

Table 6-3. Prices of Silicon

(Per Pound in Dollars)

| Year | Single-crystal | | Polycrystal |
	Float-zone	CZ*	
1960	$918	$ 0	$325
1961	671	0	111
1962	632	0	75
1963	529	0	62
1964	465	0	54
1965	418	345	59
1966	462	308	55

*Czochralski-grown single crystal.

Medical Products Business

When Ira Hutchison took over the Medical Products Business in 1965, following Dusty Rhodes's departure for Europe, it was serving two clearly identified markets:

1. Hospital/surgical—finished products purchased by physicians and hospitals

2. Pharmaceutical/OEM (original equipment manufacturer)—products used as ingredients in drugs, processing aids, and materials used in fabricating medical products

Included in these product lines were long-term implants, prosthetic items, treatment aids, and operating aids.

The bulk of the growth of the business came in the United States. Foreign markets grew more slowly; the high selling price of silicones, attributable to the added costs of distribution, shipping, taxes, and import duties, slowed expansion overseas.

However, papers given by American surgeons at international conferences helped spread the word. Visits to surgeons by Dow Corning representatives and distributors in foreign countries were also helpful. Eventually, sales of Dow Corning medical products spread to Europe, Japan, and Australia, and ultimately to eastern Europe and the Soviet Union.

Products. The success of the hydrocephalus shunt, Dow Corning's first major medical product, was important for two reasons. First, it was a high-profile product whose sales were solid and helped boost efforts to pursue other medical products. Second, it demonstrated, in a very important application, the reasonable biosafety of silicones. Once physicians around the country recognized the reasonable biosafety of silicones, they began to see potential for a variety of silicone-based medical products. Many new products were developed during the years Shailer Bass was president of Dow Corning (Figure 6-3).

One of these applications was the mammary prosthesis developed by Dr. T. D. Cronin. Beginning in 1960, Dr. Cronin designed several different silicone prostheses, eventually developing a workable design which was then commercialized in the Dow Corning laboratories.

The mammary prosthesis consisted of a SILASTIC® silicone rubber bag filled with a soft, gel-like silicone product. The prosthesis was sterilized before it was packaged, so that it was ready for immediate use in the operating room. The back of the bag later was fitted with a backing of

Dacron polyester fabric, which provided an anchorage for tissue growth.

Facilities Expansion

During the Bass years there was significant expansion of plant in nearly every area of manufacturing. In addition, the groundwork was laid for construction of a new corporate center at the Midland location.

The plant expansion projects required a substantial amount of capital. To finance the expansion, in 1965 the company's first long-term debt was negotiated. Before this, financing had been limited to relatively short-term loans. Charles LaFollette, treasurer of Corning Glass, arranged for many of these early loans, with the help of Earl Bennett

Figure 6-3. Tom Metcalf (*left*), Dave Batdorf (*center*), and world-famous heart surgeon Dr. Michael Debakey examine properties of silicones. Debakey worked with Dow Corning in the 1960s on developing an artificial heart.

and, later, Carl Gerstacker of Dow Chemical. These men were recognized as financial leaders of their time.

Thanks to the diligent efforts of these same men, and particularly to the foresight of Gerstacker, who accurately forecast the inflation coming in the 1970s, Dow Corning was able to secure two long-term (20-year), $10 million loans to help finance the expansion, at interest rates of less than 5 percent. Within months of securing the loans, interest rates began rising sharply.

Sealants Plant

Shortly after arriving at Dow Corning, Jack Hannigan realized the potential of the one-part sealant that was being manufactured in the Project Development Center on Salzburg Road. He felt the product had a strong future and warranted a plant of its own. The board approved plans for construction of such a plant.

A team of managers and engineers selected Elizabethtown, Kentucky, a city of 10,000 located 40 miles south of Louisville, as the site for the new sealants plant. The plant would manufacture all pigmented silicone materials, including one-part sealant in various formulations, two-part RTV sealants, and related materials which were still under development in the Midland laboratories. Land was purchased in March 1963, the same month in which the board approved the project. Hannigan selected Bud Lankton to manage the plant, with Ed Hergenrother as the engineering project manager, in charge of engineering design and construction. By this time Lankton was an experienced production manager who was serving as director of industrial relations. Hannigan sent Lankton to several Corning plants to learn their management system, which he thought would work well in the new sealants plant.

Once in Elizabethtown, Lankton set up a small pilot operation in rented quarters to study the production process and to anticipate problems that might occur in the main plant. Pending completion of the plant, office activities in Elizabethtown were conducted upstairs at the Harding Furniture Store. Construction of the Elizabethtown facility was completed in November 1963. The original plant staff included Clayt Davidson, production superintendent; Dan Hayes, plant accountant; Dave LaVercombe, personnel supervisor; and Bill Ragborg, chief engineer.

Medical Products Plant

At the same time that the sealants plant was authorized, approval was given for construction of a plant for the manufacture of medical and

FDA-regulated silicone products, to be built on the eastern portion of the land in Hemlock near our silicon plant. Jack Hannigan was a driving force behind getting the plant off the ground, for he strongly believed in the potential of the health care business. The new medical products plant was ready for operation in the fall of 1963.

Rubber Compounding Facility

Less than a year later, in June 1964, approval was secured for the construction of a compounding facility for silicone rubber. This plant was to be built on a 5.6-acre site in the Merritt Parkway industrial park near Trumbull, Connecticut.

The compounding plant represented a new direction in manufacturing for Dow Corning. The plant was set up as a "finishing" facility that would take raw materials shipped from Midland and prepare formulations made to customer specifications. Sales, technical service, and development, as well as manufacturing, would be combined at this location, which would heavily emphasize customer service. The rationale behind this move was to place finished silicone rubber bases and compounds closer to eastern markets so that we could compete more effectively with local producers.

The compounding and service center was opened late in 1964, under the joint management of Don Piper, who handled the technical end of the business, and Jack Wilson, who was responsible for marketing. This was the first time Dow Corning had set up a joint management arrangement. It was felt this was required in order to penetrate the heavily competitive east coast markets as rapidly as possible. The idea worked well, and once the business was well established, Ron Moore took over as manager.

A second compounding and service center was built in 1967 on a 7.5-acre site in the Irvine industrial complex in Costa Mesa, California. The center, under the direction of Wally Rousch, was built for the purpose of better serving the high concentration of aerospace and aircraft companies in the southwest.

Carrollton, Kentucky, Plant

It had always been the philosophy of Corning Glass Works that manufacturing plants functioned best when their size was limited to 500 employees. Corning members of Dow Corning's board of directors became concerned in 1964 that the Midland plant would soon exceed that limit, and they suggested a new plant be built outside Midland.

A site search was begun that same year. Because of the favorable experience with the Elizabethtown plant, the search focused primarily on Kentucky; a site in Tennessee was also considered. A suitable site was soon located a few miles east of Carrollton, Kentucky, on the Ohio River. It included two farms and a drive-in theater and totaled 1200 acres. The site was unique in having a cool underground river flowing beneath it, parallel to the adjacent Ohio River. This greatly benefited the plant, as much water was needed for cooling.

The site also encompassed a farm which carried rights to grow tobacco. Dow Corning leased these rights back to the farmer who sold the land for the plant, and this produced substantial income for Dow Corning over the years. The farm had a fine home on it which was remodeled and used as a residence by the first plant manager, Bud Lankton, who moved from the sealants plant to head up the new Carrollton facility.

Two other Dow Corning employees also moved from Elizabethtown to Carrollton to help set up the new operation: Dave LaVercombe, who became personnel supervisor, and Art Busick, safety supervisor. The other members of the original Carrollton plant staff were Wally Dyste, production superintendent; George King, plant accountant; and Jim Klingler, chief engineer.

While the plant was still under construction, the first offices at the site were set up in the old drive-in theater. Interviewing of applicants for plant jobs was conducted in the repair shed of a nearby farm.

When construction was completed, a formal dedication was held on April 28, 1967 (Figure 6-4). In attendance were Shailer Bass; Kathryn Peden, Kentucky commissioner of commerce; Governor Edward T. Breathitt; Gene Louden, president of Carroll County Industrial Foundation; and Bud Lankton, along with other Carrollton business leaders and Dow Corning employees.

Personnel Migrations at the Sealants Plant

With Lankton's move to Carrollton, Bill Hargreaves was named plant manager for Elizabethtown. He left his position in Midland as director of planning and made the move to Kentucky.

The rapid growth of the market and the changing technology led to many production problems. These were compounded by a unionization effort that succeeded and then struck the plant. For the next 3 months the plant was operated by supervisory personnel and other salaried personnel from across the country on a round-the-clock basis. Personnel came from Midland and from the field on 2-week "stints." Settlement of the strike was reached by the end of the summer of 1965.

Bill Pedersen, manager of the Engineering Products Division, went to

Figure 6-4. Carrollton, Kentucky, plant dedication, April 1967.

Harvard's Advanced Management Program training that fall, and Hargreaves became division manager "pro tem," spending 3 to 4 days each week in Midland and the balance in Elizabethtown, with the help of the company plane. The following summer Hargreaves also attended the Harvard AMP program. His staff, consisting of Bill Ragborg, Clayt Davidson, D. M. Hayes, Paul Philbrick, and Mike Jackson, did yeoman's work in filling the site manager's role while carrying on their own duties. Over the years, this process was repeated again and again as top-level managers attended Harvard programs.

Corporate Center

With several new plants in place, early in 1966 an authorization was approved for preliminary engineering studies for a corporate center in Midland, with the intent of separating plant operations from corporate administration. There was also a need to build a more secure facility, now that the company had grown larger. This was clearly demonstrated in mid-1965, when a man appeared in Dr. Bass's office with a shotgun. The man was a former employee who had been dismissed, and he blamed the president.

Fortunately, Dr. Bass was away from the office at the time. Mike Stinton, director of safety and security, persuaded the man to give up his gun, and the incident ended peacefully. Because of the heightened awareness caused by this incident, security was tightened. New personnel badges were issued, and visitors were required to wear temporary badges. The new corporate center would include built-in security systems.

When the studies were completed, approval was given for the purchase of approximately 1200 acres of land in Bay County for a new corporate center, midway between the plant and the Tri City Airport, for easy commuting. Construction of a service building, service lines, roads, and a laboratory for biomedical research was begun in 1967.

International Business

Alpha Molykote Europe

Dow Corning acquired 100 percent ownership of Molykote Europe in April 1967; the 1964 purchase of the U.S. parent company had included only a portion of the European arm of the company. Bob Sauer, an American who worked in Germany and an early acquaintance of Dr. Bass, was selected as comanager along with Frederick Kuhn-Weiss, who held the distribution rights for Molykote in Europe (interestingly, Sauer had earlier been involved with General Electric's silicone effort).

To improve communications with this site, German lessons were given at weekly luncheons in the Trumbull conference room. These were led by Klaus Bouvier, a veteran of the Molykote organization and a Viennese aristocrat by background. Kuhn-Weiss, the owner-partner and driving force behind the company, left shortly after the acquisition, but Sauer stayed on as manager for 5 years.

In addition to the employees of Alpha Molykote, Dow Corning employees who developed silicone lubricants—people such as Maurrie Hommel, Chet Currie, Harry Schiefer, Rhinee Hollitz, and Gene Groenhoff—also played a major role in the success of the company. These product development people constantly worked with the Alpha Molykote team to develop better formulations of their lubricant products.

Canada: Armet Industries

Shortly after the initial agreement with Alpha Molykote was signed, Armet Industries, a Canadian company located in Guelph, Ontario, was acquired, on September 8, 1964. Armet had two divisions involved with paint and rubber fabricating. The rubber-fabricating division used a number of Dow Corning silicone rubbers.

Jim McFadzen, the former owner, was named president of Armet, and Bob Leavitt, a part-owner of the company, was named vice president for manufacturing. Phil Servais, who was by this time working on silicone rubber developments in the Canadian sales office, was named vice president and technical director.

History. Jim McFadzen founded Anchor Paint company in 1936, changing the name to "Armet" (the Greek word for "helmet," with its connotation of strength and durability) after a dispute with a company which had a name similar to Anchor's.

Armet was located in the small Canadian town of Guelph, Ontario, which experienced an industrial boom in 1948. With the company booming along with the town, Armet management in 1951 persuaded McFadzen's father, a rubber chemist, to come out of retirement and start a rubber-fabricating division. By 1964, when Dow Corning purchased the company, this division was marketing over 400 rubber products, 300 of which were silicone rubber compounds. The division also fabricated parts made from other synthetic rubbers, but silicone rubber made up the bulk of the business.

Beginning in 1958, Shailer Bass visited Armet several times. In 1960, he indicated that Dow Corning was interested in buying the business. Other companies were also interested in purchasing Armet, but when the decision to sell was made, Dow Corning was selected because of the fine relationships Bass had established.

In 1964, when Armet was purchased, the company was in a long-term growth pattern, and sales had doubled in the 6 months prior to acquisition. With the acquisition of Armet, Dow Corning solidified its presence in the Canadian marketplace.

Japan: Fuji Kobunshi (Fuji Polymer)

A. R. Brown McFarlane Company had become Dow Corning distributors in Japan in 1950. The company had set up a technical laboratory in Japan in the late 1950s, in an attempt to service the products it distributed. This effort proved to be inadequate, and shortly after Bass became president, Brown McFarlane formed Fuji Polymer, a finishing company that would customize silicone products for the local marketplace. Because manufacturing costs in Japan were exorbitant, Brown

McFarlane hoped that Dow Corning would supply the new company with base materials to be finished in Japan.

With this idea in mind, Dow Corning was offered a 45 percent interest in Fuji Polymer (in Japanese, Fuji Kobunshi Kabushiki Kaisha). Dow Corning accepted the offer. On international restructuring, Bill May in the Tokyo office acted as the liaison between Fuji Polymer and Dow Corning's domestic operations, providing technology to Fuji Polymer to prepare emulsions, paint additives, Guideline tape (for ensuring consistent thickness in winding motors), and silicone rubber formulations.

International Restructuring

In 1965, the board of directors suggested that Dow Corning adopt a more aggressive stance in the international marketplace. In order to gain more control over operations abroad, the board suggested that Dow Corning pursue an independent course wherever possible.

To assess the state of overseas operations, Shailer Bass called in Jim Abegglin of McKinsey and Company, who made a study of Dow Corning's international activities. Abegglin and others concluded that while Dow Corning had achieved a great measure of success in Europe, there were some developments which portended problems unless changes were made.

Out of the McKinsey study came a number of recommendations for changes in the operation of international business, including

- Control of distribution in the European Economic Community (EEC)

- Construction of a wholly owned Dow Corning manufacturing facility in the EEC

- Negotiations with SISS to acquire the business or sell our portion of the joint venture

- Control of Midsil product sales in that market area

- Development of Fuji Polymer into a significant asset

- Development of other Japanese joint ventures and production of basic silicones in Japan

Abegglen recommended that a senior officer take responsibility for international strategy and programs. He further recommended that area managers be appointed for the three major international marketplaces: the European Economic Community, the United Kingdom, and Japan.

The recommendations were accepted, and reorganization began in mid-1965, with the appointment of Bill Caldwell as president and chairman of Dow Corning International, Ltd. (DCIL), a separate entity which would be responsible for all overseas operations. Dusty Rhodes was named to manage the European area, and Bob Peele was assigned responsibility for Japan and the Pacific. These changes were complex and challenging. Locations for operations had to be selected, personnel hired or transferred, and facilities provided. In Europe, many long-standing relationships had to be altered or terminated, and this put a strain on Dow Corning's dealings with its joint venture partners and distributors. In order to minimize the strain, before any changes were made, each of the licensees and distributors was fully informed of Dow Corning's intentions, so that there would be no real surprises.

It was decided that a central administration center should be established in Europe for the general management of the area. Direct-sales operations would be located in each of the four major European market areas: Germany, France, Italy, and the United Kingdom. Distributors would be used in other areas. Brussels was chosen as the European area headquarters.

With this structure in place, key assignments were filled. Nort Foster was named area marketing manager for the European area. Andrew Dunlop was assigned responsibility for direct sales in the United Kingdom. Bruce Boehm would be in charge of Germany. Reno Lasorsa would manage France. Tom Nehil would be responsible for direct sales in Italy.

The months between August 1965 and March 1966, when the reorganization took place, were a period of feverish activity for all of Dow Corning. By the end of the spring of 1966, the new European structure was in place.

A target of $25 million in revenues for Europe by 1970 was established; this represented a 400 percent increase over 1965 sales. In order to achieve this ambitious goal, Dusty Rhodes decided to concentrate on marketing large-volume silicone products which had good interchangeability with those of competitors and which were in many instances superior to their products.

Nationals were hired as technical sales representatives in each of the four major European markets. These salespeople were recruited and trained by the marketing staff in Brussels before being sent to Midland for training in the laboratories. Among these first employees were a number of outstanding people who are in key positions today—Giovanni Bassani, Enrico Locateli, K. Hoeffleman, Klaus Kastens, Fred Friedle, and Robbie Van Tienhoven.

Shin-Etsu Handotai

Once the new European structure was in place, Dow Corning pursued additional business ventures in Japan. Shin-Etsu Chemical Company had been one of a group of Japanese military and electrical companies that explored silicones during the war after discovering them in American fighters and bombers. This had led Shin-Etsu Chemical to acquire a license from General Electric in 1953, and from Dow Corning in 1957, to manufacture silicones in Japan.

Over lunch one day in 1965, Paul Sawada, a Shin-Etsu employee, mentioned to Bill May in Dow Corning's Tokyo office that the company was interested in selling a portion of its high-purity silicon plant. Shin-Etsu needed technology for depositing large-diameter polycrystalline silicon rods and for growing Czochralski crystals. Dow Corning could offer its expertise in both areas. The Hemlock silicon plant could benefit from the single-crystal and polished wafer expertise that Shin-Etsu could provide.

Shortly after that conversation, negotiations began for the formation of a joint venture between Shin-Etsu and Dow Corning, to produce semiconductor-grade silicon. In 1967, the Japanese government approved the joint venture, which was to be called Shin-Etsu Handotai (Shin-Etsu Semiconductor), with Shin-Etsu owning 55 percent of the venture, and Dow Corning 45 percent.

Kihachi Tamura, who at the time was general manager of the Silicone and Electronic Industrial Materials Division of Shin-Etsu Chemical Company, was named president of the new joint venture. He had been active in developing the silicone industry in Japan, in much the same way Dr. Collings had been active in the United States.

A key element in the joint venture agreement was that Dow Corning would build and sell to the joint venture polycrystalline silicon reactors and their power packs. In addition, Dow Corning was to purchase significant quantities of polished silicon wafers from Shin-Etsu. Since Japanese labor was less expensive than domestic labor, this would allow Dow Corning to compete in this very labor-intensive portion of the market in the United States.

Toray Silicone Company Ltd.

While negotiations between Shin-Etsu and Dow Corning were under way, additional Japanese ventures were being pursued. In May 1965, Toyo Rayon met with Dow Corning personnel to discuss the possibility of a joint venture arrangement. Toyo Rayon was represented by S. Yokota, director of new business planning; K. Shohara, manager of planning; and K. Aikawa, manager of the Plastics Planning Department. Ira Hutchison, Bill May, and Jim Abegglen, the McKinsey consultant, were the Dow Corning representatives.

At this time MITI, the government organization, still had the power to approve or deny joint venture agreements, and many producers other than Dow Corning were interested in getting involved in silicone manufacturing. In order not to arouse the competition and have other potential suitors influence MITI, Toyo Rayon and Dow Corning conducted their negotiations in secret. All meetings were held in the Palace Hotel in a room with a fictitious sign on the door. The two parties to the negotiations arrived at different times.

After a year of discussion, a joint venture agreement and licensing agreement were signed. In December 1966, the new joint venture, Toray Silicone Company Ltd., was officially formed, with DCIL owning a 50 percent share. This was a landmark agreement, which made Dow Corning one of the first American companies to obtain an equal partnership in a Japanese company in the postwar years. K. Aikawa was named president, and Robert Peele was named vice president.

A team headed by S. Yokota, and including K. Shohara, S. Ito, and S. Matsuda from Toyo Rayon, visited the United States for the final agreement. They were introduced to Dow Corning management and were shown the facilities in Midland, Elizabethtown, and Carrollton. This was one of many visits between groups from Tokyo and Midland after formation of the joint venture.

Chiba Plant.   Groundbreaking for the new Toray Silicone plant, to be located in Chiba, Japan, took place in June 1967. Gene Ulanowicz, an engineer from Midland, was named site engineer and moved with his family to Japan.

Building in Chiba was quite a challenge, as the plant site was on land created by filling in a portion of Tokyo Bay. Ulanowicz described the ground there as "much worse than mud, with a consistency somewhat like pudding." When he visited the site for the first time, the taxi driver was instructed to drive onto the site. He drove a short distance and became stuck. The taxi settled into the mud up to the frame, and a bulldozer finally had to pull it out.

Despite the difficult building conditions, a compounding plant, an emulsion and polymer plant, and an applications laboratory were completed by mid-1968. In June, Shailer Bass and S. Hirota, president of Toyo Rayon, presided over the opening ceremony (Figure 6-5).

Sydney, Australia

The other portion of Bob Peele's Pacific market area at this time was Australia. Charles Dudley had been sent to Sydney to open markets for silicones in that country. After the international restructuring, Bill

Figure 6-5. Traditional Shinto ceremony to dedicate Toray Silicones plant in Chiba, Japan, June 1967.

Kuhlman was asked to go to Sydney to develop a small production facility.

One early problem in Australia was that Dow Corning was not allowed to bring dimethylsiloxane hydrolysates into the country, unless it paid a stiff tax. Not wanting to do so, Dow Corning shipped 55-gallon drums of dimethyldichlorosilane to Australia by boat, and Kuhlman arranged to hydrolyze this in a small unit erected within the Australian plant of Dow Chemical. Hydrolysates were then shipped to the Sydney facility for finishing.

Finally, after negotiations with the appropriate government agency, the tax restrictions were lifted, and Dow Corning was permitted to ship hydrolysate to Sydney from the United States. A gum[1] polymerization unit was built, and a compounding plant was constructed to develop finished products for silicone rubber customers. With these new facilities in place, Dow Corning would have a much stronger presence in Australia.

---

[1]"Gum" refers to a high polymer.

Seneffe, Belgium

Dow Corning's sales volume grew rapidly in the first few years under the new international structure, and with the growth came new problems which had to be addressed. Public warehousing services were inadequate, leading to errors, damaged containers, and delays in filling orders. Stocks on hand in Europe were often inadequate. Technical service was limited to nonlaboratory activities.

To overcome these problems, European management leased a small laboratory in Brussels where some simple technical procedures could be performed. Even this limited capability was reassuring to European customers, who were concerned about Dow Corning's ability to service its products effectively. A small-scale rubber compounding and sealant packaging facility was established in the expanded MOLYKOTE® plant in Munich, and this helped Dow Corning to customize products for the Europeans.

At the same time, plans were being made for the construction of a full-fledged manufacturing and service facility in Seneffe, Belgium, to address the long-term needs of the European marketplace. Dennis Ziess was the engineer assigned to manage the construction project.

Research and Development

During Dr. Bass's tenure as president of Dow Corning, a number of management changes were made among the research staff. Mel Hunter was named vice president, while retaining his responsibilities as director of research, in 1963, and Les Tyler was named assistant director of research. Chet Currie was named manager of process and product engineering at the same time. In June 1965 Les Tyler was named director of development, and Art Barry was named director of chemical research. During this period, the relatively new product, one-part sealant, became important and expanded its usefulness and the route by which cures could be obtained. Stronger silicone rubber was developed. A new heat-shrink rubber was perfected in the lab and brought into commercial production. A resin project, Pyrobond, received much attention. Basic chemistry studies continued to contribute to our base of knowledge of organosilicon compounds.

Kipping Award

Having received numerous awards for its own contributions to the field of silicone research, during this period Dow Corning established an award of its own. In 1962 the first Frederick Stanley Kipping Award in Organosilicon Chemistry, named after the researcher who contributed so much to the early chemistry of organosilicon compounds, was given by Dow Corning. The award, administered annually by the American Chemical Society, is reserved for academic researchers who make a significant contribution to the growing literature of organosilicon compounds. Henry Gilman, professor of chemistry at Iowa State University, was the recipient of the first Kipping Award. Since then, researchers from all over the world have been honored for outstanding work in silicone research.

Patent Department

With Bill Blackburn's involvement as general counsel, Bob Fleming was named manager of the Patent Department. Fleming was responsible for recruiting and training Patent Department personnel in silicones as well as patent law. During his short tenure as manager of the department, Fleming developed a systematic means by which technical personnel could file information for patents, and he designed an efficient system for classifying and retrieving patents, patterned after that used in the United States patent office. He also developed a method for searching the patent literature, which was eventually computerized for easy access. Together, these actions helped greatly in streamlining the patent process.

In mid-1963, Harry Dingman was named manager of the Patent Department. At the same time, Larry Hobey was named to the international patent section. Dingman had been one of Jim McHard's employees in the early days of the analytical group in the Cellulose Products Division of Dow. He had joined the pilot plant group when Dow Corning moved to its first plant site. When Bill Blackburn came to Midland, he selected Dingman to study law as preparation for working in the patent department. Dingman obtained his law degree at the University of Pittsburgh, returning to Midland afterward to join the patent department.

New-Product Sales

Dow Corning management had realized for some time that much of its growth depended on new-product sales. In 1965, the objective was established that 25 percent of worldwide sales would come from products less than 5 years old. Up to 1962, new-product sales remained between

16 and 19 percent of total sales. From 1962 forward, new-product sales rose almost linearly from 16 percent to 30 percent of annual sales.

The 25 percent objective was reached in 1965, the same year the objective was set. Silicone rubber products (especially high-strength rubbers) were the largest contributors to new-product sales, followed closely by sealants and RTV materials.

While several new products were developed during these years, most were extensions of known technology. Junction coating resins were one exception. As semiconductors developed in the 1950s, it became necessary to coat their active junctions with a material to prevent changes at this sensitive interface. Over the years, most manufacturers began using one of Dow Corning's resins for this purpose.

Junction coating resins became very popular among manufacturers of semiconductor devices. However, our resins were not developed with semiconductor applications in mind, and not all resins worked equally well in junction coatings. Sometimes the resins contained microscopic levels of impurities which caused the silicon chips to perform out of specification.

As a result, we began receiving frantic calls from manufacturers for particular batches of resins which had been effective. Subsequent batches of the same resins caused the chips to perform out of specification.

On many occasions no more of the same lot of resin was available. Hal Clark, supervisor of one of the resin laboratories, conceived the idea of preparing purified grades of the three most popular resins for use in semiconductor applications. These were sold in 1-ounce bottles, resulting in a small but significant business for Dow Corning.

Along with the new products came a new logo for Dow Corning. William Renwick joined Dow Corning in the new position of director of design in November 1963. One of his first activities was to design a new logo. The logo he developed, still in use today, was made of two horizontal bars separated by a small space with the words "Dow Corning" in the upper bar. This replaced the previous kidney-shaped logo, designed by Dr. Collings's daughter, which in turn had replaced the company's original logo of interlinked letters "D" and "C" (Figure 6-6).

Renwick got involved in a different type of design as well. He was fascinated by the new Dow Corning one-part sealant and in particular by a clear version of it. He designed a hexagonally shaped aquarium made of glass plates held together by sealant alone. For a time, Dow Corning considered marketing the aquarium, but it proved too labor-intensive to be worthwhile. However, the sealant itself was repackaged and sold for use in aquarium construction. It sold quite well in this application.

Figure 6-6. Evolution of Dow Corning's logo: (*a*) The first logo, formed of interlinked letters (shown here on Dow Corning's first service award pin), was replaced by the kidney-shaped logo, (*b*), designed by Dr. Collings's daughter. The drums bearing the logo also carry the Dow Corning slogan, "First in Silicones." (*c*) The current logo has been used by the company since 1963.

Bioscience Research Laboratories

As pointed out in Chapter 4, studies of the biological activity of silicones had begun in 1951 with Dr. John Speier's 3-year research program with Eli Lilly Co. Although the program was discontinued because of Dow Corning's concern about giving away too much technology, Drs. Bass and Hunter continued to support the idea of biomedical research conducted internally.

Research was begun again in 1964, as a result of concern over one of Dow Corning's phenylmethyl fluids, DOW CORNING® 555. The fluid, which was used as a cosmetics additive, showed an unexpected biological activity, similar to that of estrogen. The activity was so weak, under conditions of use, that the material represented no apparent hazard. Nevertheless, it was immediately withdrawn from the market, as a precautionary measure.

Dow Corning wanted to be certain that its other products did not possess pharmacological effects under the conditions of prescribed use. To explore these possibilities, Dow Corning moved to develop an in-house biological research capability.

Mel Hunter and Shailer Bass brought Dr. Donald R. Bennett into the corporation in 1965 to establish a bioscience research unit. The first project undertaken was a 3-year search for the active ingredient in DOW CORNING® 555, led by Frank Hyde in collaboration with the newly formed group. Jim McHard and Ed Hobbs joined in the early toxicological investigations of the fluid as well. In addition to this work, the Bioscience Research group began a number of basic studies of biological activity that would continue long past Dr. Bass's presidency.

Sealants

Once the first room-temperature vulcanizing system was developed, a whole series of RTV systems was produced.[2] The oxime curing system, which vulcanized by hydrolysis of the oxime group with moisture from the air, was the first major improvement. The oxime sealant was introduced for use on concrete, since acetoxy did not adhere so well. The oxime sealant was also used in electronic and other applications in which acid would be harmful.

Other curing systems involved the reaction of chain terminal hydroxyl groups with ethyl silicate in the presence of a catalyst, reaction

---

[2]K. E. Polmanteer, *Rubber Chem. and Tech.*, 54:1051 (1981).

of a silane-ended, —Si—H, chain with another chain containing a vinyl group in the presence of a different catalyst, and the reaction of chain terminal hydroxyl groups with a trifunctional silicon compound.

In some instances, the length of the polymer chains was extended by using a bifunctional reactive unit. The strength of the sealants was improved by these techniques.

Similarly, the solvent resistance provided by the use of fluorinated substituents on silicon was also applied to the sealants field for use in aerospace and other areas where resistance to petroleum products was important.

After success with the S. C. Johnson Building, Dow Corning sealants had been applied to a number of major buildings: Lincoln Center and the United Nations Library in New York City; Union Carbide Laboratories in Tarrytown, N.Y.; the CIA building in Alexandria, Virginia; and Michigan Consolidated Gas building in Detroit.

As time passed, some of these buildings developed dirt pickup and staining, especially on porous surfaces such as marble. Laboratory studies using weatherometer tests yielded no solution. At this point, someone in the sealants lab thought of holding a joint under compression for extended periods, to duplicate the actual conditions in a caulked joint. This showed that DOW CORNING 200® silicone fluid was bleeding out of the sealant under compression.

Once the cause of the problem had been identified, Ed Sweet from Dr. Hyde's laboratory and Wayne Dupree from Keith Polmanteer's group built all the polymer into one network. This stopped the staining and minimized dirt pickup around the joint. Techniques were developed to clean buildings which had shown problems, and the sealant continued to sell well in its new formulation.

Aerospace Applications.　A distinctly different use of the sealant was in ablative heat shields. So effective was the sealant in this application that it was used as the heat shield for the Gemini capsule. While the sealant charred from the heat of reentry, it remained as a thermal barrier to protect the capsule and its occupant.

Another aerospace application was the use of two-part sealants to coat solid-fuel rocket nozzles. The silicone sealants solved the problem of "burn through" and provided a big boost to the U.S. space program.

After these sealants proved successful, the same techniques used in developing them were applied to making a polyurethane sealant with a small amount of silicone in it. This product was a moderate success and was used in highway joint sealing.

SILASTIC®

During the Bass years, much work went into the continued study of SILASTIC®. A major improvement in strength came from basic studies of the effects of cross-link placement. A totally new use for the rubber was developed, the shrink-fitting of tubing on connectors and other electrical units. Improvements in many properties also were made.

"Tough Rubber." Silicone rubber began as a rather weak material, but my finding of the reinforcing action of small-particle silica fillers such as Degussa raised the strength considerably, to 1000 pounds per square inch. Studies by Keith Polmanteer showed the possibility of increasing the strength still further by "clustering" the cross-links.[3]

In Polmanteer's system, a "gum" with a low content of vinyl groups was mixed with a low-molecular-weight polymer with vinyl group ends. These vinyl groups would cross-link when peroxides reacted with the groups. The effect of this clustering was to produce a region with a high level of cross-linking (almost gel-like) surrounded by a soft region of low-level cross-linking. The cured rubber was far stronger (1500 pounds per square inch) than my original high-strength rubber and was often referred to as "tough rubber."

Heat-Shrinkable Rubber. Bob Merker, who was in charge of the Mellon Institute fellowship when several of us moved to Midland in 1956, developed a new block copolymer. In this polymer, chains with the normal silicon-oxygen backbone alternated with chains which had phenyl groups between silicon atoms. These were referred to as "silphenylene block copolymers" and were the first silicone thermoplastics.

Compounding these copolymers into silicone rubbers produced the first "heat-shrinkable" (heat-shrink) silicone products. Such rubbers can be heated and stretched. When they are subsequently cooled, they remain in this expanded state until heat is once again applied, whereupon they "shrink."

Don Weyer led a group of chemists and engineers in a project to find a replacement silicone resin and a manufacturing process to develop heat-shrinkable products for aircraft electrical insulation.[4] Manufacturing was set up in 207 building; almost the entire top floor of the building was devoted to the heat-shrink products. Unfortunately, the silphenylene copolymer used in developing heat-shrinkable rubber is

---

[3]K. E. Polmanteer and C. W. Lentz, *Rubber Chem. and Tech.*, 48:795 (1975).

[4]D. E. Weyer, U.S. Patent 3,257,689, 1963.

quite expensive and the market for the product limited. The technology was eventually sold to a large supplier of heat-shrinkable products.

Reversion Resistance. Some applications of silicone rubber required that the rubber be confined in a closed space. In such instances the rubber tended to revert to a softer material, much like the unvulcanized stock. Many studies were made of this phenomenon, until it became clear that water absorbed on fillers or polymers with terminal silanol groups, —Si—OH, was responsible for cutting into the basic siloxane chain to give lower-molecular-weight polymers. Steps taken to dry fillers and to eliminate terminal silanol groups greatly decreased the tendency of rubbers to revert to a fluid state.

Fluorosilicone Rubbers. Studies of the many possible fluorinated groups that could be placed on silicon continued. Eventually we focused on the trifluoropropyl group. Process development for the preparation of the monomer trifluoropropylmethyldichlorosilane, $CF_3CH_2CH_2Si(CH_3)Cl_2$, ultimately settled on the use of gamma radiation from cobalt, Co^{60}, to complete one of the principal steps in the formation of the raw materials. Sealants using the same solvent-resistant base as used for high-consistency rubber were developed for use in aerospace and automotive fields. The work on fluorinating rubber was also extended to fluids. Fabric treatments, using the same fluorinated polymers, were developed. These were not only water-repellent but also oleophobic; that is, they were not "wet" by petroleum oils. Fluids were also developed which proved to be better lubricants than DOW CORNING 200® silicone fluid.

Foam-Filled Tires. Silicone rubber was shown to be highly resilient; that is, it absorbed very little energy on repeated stressing. With this characteristic in mind, Andy Kauppi conceived of the idea of filling an ordinary automobile tire with balls of silicone rubber instead of air. Actual road trials proved this to be a useful concept.

Don Bartos in development carried the idea one step further by extruding a solid rod of silicone rubber, fitting it inside a tire, placing it on a rim, and curing the entire wheel and tire in an oven. The silicone rubber was compounded with a foaming agent to give any desired pressure in the tire.

The resulting foam-filled tire was truly puncture-proof. This was demonstrated at a press conference in New York in May 1968; Bartos drilled ½-inch holes completely through a foam-filled tire mounted on a Jeep and then drove off (Figure 6-7). One of Dow Corning's company

Figure 6-7. Don Bartos, who was responsible for the final development work, drills a hole in a silicone foam–filled tire to demonstrate that the product is puncture-proof.

cars was fitted with foam-filled tires and traveled many miles around the state of Michigan.

Further development showed that organic rubbers could be compounded to give the same high resilience. The technology for producing foam-filled tires was licensed to two companies. Such tires are still used in off-road vehicles and landfill trucks and on farm tractors. When Dr. Bass retired, he was presented with a Jeep with silicone foam–filled tires, for use on the island of St. John, his retirement home.

Resins

Resin studies during the mid-1960s concentrated on hybrid resins—silicone-epoxy and silicone-acrylic resins. The silicone-epoxy was studied to provide a resin powder which might be used in a fluid bed coating system for protecting pipelines distributing gas, oil, or water. Nearly 2 years of research was spent on developing the resin and the necessary catalyst, which was a special version of a so-called Rosenheim silicate developed by Cecil Frye.[5] Ed Plueddemann added siloxane hydrides with platinum catalyst to allylglycidyl ether which contained an epoxy group. This led to the development of a silicone-epoxy resin. The resin was easy to make and displayed the characteristics of organic epoxides.

The final resin product, given the name "Pyrobond," was meant to be applied to steel pipe heated to between 420 and 440°F. The powder fused to the pipe in a coating 7 to 10 mils thick. The coating cured in approximately 20 seconds and was resistant to acids and alkali. It was serviceable from −20 to 275°F and had an adhesive bond of 3000 pounds per square inch.

Ed Plueddemann and Harold Vincent obtained a patent on their system for applying Pyrobond.[6] Unfortunately, the product was not cost-competitive with other resins for this same application, and it was never a commercial success.

Plueddemann showed that the epoxide used in Pyrobond could be converted to a powerful anionic surfactant, and there was some thought given to making a foamless detergent from such surfactants, but the high cost of the silicones ruled out this use.

The silicone-acrylic resin as an emulsion was tested as a finish for wood. Again, the economics of the product limited its usefulness.

Basic Chemistry

A number of studies improved our understanding of silicone chemistry during these years. Comparisons were made between the properties of silicone polymers and the current polymer theories. Random copolymers were compared with regular block copolymers. A new way of polymerizing cyclic dimethylsiloxanes, by means of "living polymer" chains with butyl lithium active ends, was studied.[7] Labeling of polymers with C^{14} made possible the tracing of the location of polymers in the study of dirt pickup and staining by sealants. Substitution of deuterium and tritium for hydrogen helped define bond motions in various spectra.

Analytical Department

The Analytical Department during the Bass years continued its work under Jim McHard. The group provided ongoing support for the pro-

[5]H. L. Vincent, C. L. Frye, and P. E. Opplinger, Advances in Chemistry Series, no. 92, American Chemical Society, 1970, pp. 164–172.

[6]E. Plueddemann and H. Vincent, U.S. Patent 3,461,095, 1969.

[7]C. L. Lee, C. L. Frye, and O. K. Johannson, *Polymer Preprints*, 10(2):1361 (1969).

Drawing by Mankoff; © 1977 The New Yorker Magazine, Inc.

duction process and for our efforts in the lab at learning more about the basics of silicone chemistry. A new type of analysis, spectrographic determination of boron in trichlorosilane, became important as hyperpure silicon production expanded. Gene Kellum and Bob Smith developed the technique, which allowed assay for boron in the 1 to 1000 parts per billion range in trichlorosilane. This enabled evaluation of lots of trichlorosilane to ensure that there were no boron impurities, without the expense of making silicon, preparing a single crystal, and evaluating the crystal.

Organofunctional Chemistry

Dr. John Speier's groups in Mellon Institute, and later in Midland, did much to promote the field of organofunctional silicone compounds during this period. Once the ability to add silane functional compounds, —Si—H, to olefins, CH$_2$=CH—R, had been demonstrated by his groups, others began to add olefins for which R in the above formula contained functionality.

Loren Haluska and Bill Daudt began adding silane functional monomers and polymers to allyl glycol ethers with the objective of defoaming glycol antifreeze. The product did not prove effective in that use. Later we learned that Dr. Donald Bailey of Union Carbide and Carbon Company had used similar compounds to control foam bubble size in polyurethane foams. These materials soon became known as "PUFAs," or polyurethane foam agents. Once we learned of this product, we tried to "play catch-up" in matching Union Carbide's success.

Coupling Agents. During this time, John Speier was part of a research committee which reviewed projects and set goals for the research groups. Dow Corning had been selling organosilicon compounds for treating mineral surfaces to produce better clay fillers for other rubbers, such as those used in tires. A sizable business had developed, especially for treating glass fibers. The business had slumped dramatically, however, because Owens-Corning Fiberglas Company had found a material, A-1100, manufactured by Union Carbide, which could be applied to fiberglass using water rather than solvent.

The Union Carbide product was a pure alkoxyaminopropylsilane. Speier had published papers on the synthesis of such compounds in 1951 but had not shown any utility for them. Union Carbide had found the utility, and a big market for the product.

A patent covering the compound A-1100, the process by which it was made, and aqueous solutions of the compound, was issued to Union Carbide. The patent disclosed, but did not claim, the use of the compound as a coupling agent between glass fibers and resin matrices, leaving Dow Corning room to develop that application.

The research committee placed a high priority on developing a compound similar to A-1100 in order to win back the business it had lost. The development process involved a number of critical steps that caused trouble in manufacturing. One major difficulty was that the reaction tended to place two organofunctional groups on the nitrogen, instead of the desired one. Another route required high-pressure equipment.

Finally, the group tried adding all ingredients to a reactor at one time. The desired product formed, and salts that otherwise would have to be filtered from the mixture merely separated in a solution. No pressure equipment was needed, and the crude mixture could be used directly.

Not only was the group elated, but Owens-Corning Fiberglas Company liked the product as a coupling agent, and soon orders were hard to fill. The product was given the designation "Z-6020." A patent was issued covering the compound and its use on glass fibers.[8]

---

[8]J. L. Speier, U.S. Patent 2,971,864, 1961.

"Mr. Glue."   After the success with Z-6020, Ed Plueddemann began studying a variety of other coupling agents. He analyzed more than 120 different silanes and showed how their structures affected the strength of glass-reinforced resin laminates.

Plueddemann presented a paper at the 1962 meeting of the Society of Plastic Industry, discussing these studies and presenting a theory of how such coupling agents function. He claimed that he could stick anything to anything—and he could.

Plueddemann became the world's foremost expert on coupling agents. In recognition of his contributions in this field, he was given an award for creative invention by the American Chemical Society. Around Dow Corning, Ed Plueddemann is affectionately known as "Mr. Glue" (Figure 6-8).

Uses for Aminosilanes.   A variety of other applications of aminosilanes were developed. Copolymers containing aminosilanes proved to be an excellent waterproofing treatment for boots. These compounds also found use in automobile polishes and in hair care products. Fred

Figure 6-8. Dr. Edwin Plueddemann, one of the world's foremost experts in the area of adhesives, is affectionately referred to around the halls of Dow Corning as "Mr. Glue."

Saunders in Midsil in Wales showed that such fluids were superb treatments for wool, making the fabric almost completely shrink-resistant, even in hot water. Patents also covered the application of these materials in dyeing a variety of textiles.

As research continued, Gust Kookootsedes joined Speier's group and became involved in adding silicon hydrides to methacrylate esters. Samples of copolymers containing this acid functionality and the amine functionality were given to a paper company for use in an especially tough map paper. The copolymer, when used on the paper, provided the matrix for a cellulose composite that was truly tough. The product was patented,[9] but it was never sold, owing to the reluctance of printers to alter their production processes to accommodate it.

Marty Musolf in Speier's group added α-methylstyrene to DOW CORNING® 1107 fluid which contained —Si—H functional groups. Not all the silane hydrogens reacted; he added ethylene to react the few remaining —Si—H units. A sample of the resulting fluid was given to General Motors for testing as a release fluid for rubber gaskets and door seals on cars. The carmaker was enthusiastic, since all previous release materials caused problems; for example, when traces were left on metal parts, paint would not cure properly on the parts. The Dow Corning release fluid solved the problem. The product was patented in 1965.[10]

When Dr. Shailer Bass took over as president, he had set a goal for Dow Corning of doubling the business by 1970. When he stepped down as president in 1967, that goal had already been achieved. From $50 million in 1962, sales had grown to more than $100 million in 1967. The company was profitable throughout all the Bass years. By 1967, annual profits had grown to more than $10 million.

Dr. Bass could look back with pride on the accomplishments of the company under his leadership. With the guidance of Jack Hannigan, the company's domestic operations were dramatically improved. Through the continuing efforts of Shailer Bass in the international marketplace, Dow Corning's global presence was strengthened in several major markets throughout the world. With a shift in emphasis to new-product development, the company was making good use of the base of technology developed during the first 2 decades of research.

Shailer Bass retired from Dow Corning in 1971, after serving the

[9]J. L. Speier, U.S. Patent 3,338,942, 1967.

[10]G. J. Kookootsedes and J. L. Speier, U.S. Patent 3,186,964, 1965.

company for nearly 3 decades. On October 9, 1988, Dow Corning mourned the passing of the man who launched the company into the international marketplace and served as its third president.

7

The Goggin Era: Multidimensional Organization

I believe every right implies a responsibility;
every opportunity, an obligation; every
possession, a duty.   JOHN D. ROCKEFELLER

By the late 1960s it was clear that additional reorganization within Dow Corning would be needed, beyond the changes suggested by Hannigan and implemented by Dr. Bass. Profits were not keeping pace with growing sales and markets, and the company was plagued by a host of problems that inevitably arose as growth accelerated. The board of directors felt that a wholesale restructuring of the company was needed in order to meet the demands of new products, larger volumes of business, and an ever-increasing global presence. Just as the board had elected Jack Hannigan to infuse the company with a new spirit, it was now felt that the company could benefit from another "outsider" with a fresh approach.

The board was worried about several specific problems at this stage in Dow Corning's development, problems that would jeopardize the company's long-term growth and profitability patterns if not addressed:

1. Managers did not have adequate financial information and control of their functional operations. For example, marketing managers did

not know how much it cost to produce a product; prices and profit margins were set by division managers.

2. Cumbersome communications channels existed between key functions, especially manufacturing and marketing, resulting in operating inefficiencies and increased costs.

3. Lack of communications between divisions not only created the antithesis of a corporate team effort but also was wasteful of a precious resource—people.

4. Long-range corporate planning was sporadic and superficial and was leading to overstaffing, duplicated effort, and inefficiency.

5. In the face of stiffening competition, the corporation was insufficiently oriented to the outside world.

To rectify the situation, at a meeting of Dow Chemical executives at the Midland Country Club, Ted Doan, chairman of the Dow board, suggested that Bill Goggin be considered as the "outsider" who would take over where Bass left off and lead the company into the 1970s. Goggin was a 31-year veteran of Dow Chemical, a stellar performer who at the time was heading up the second-largest department of the chemical company.

Dr. William C. Goggin

Goggin had joined Dow Chemical in 1936 with undergraduate degrees in physics, chemistry, and mathematics from Alma College, and a master's degree in electrical engineering from the University of Michigan. He rose quickly within the Dow organization, becoming manager of Organic Plastics Technical Service in 1943.

After the German surrender in World War II, Goggin was granted a leave of absence from Dow to become a consultant to the War Department. As a member of a War Department team, he visited Germany on a project to investigate that country's plastic developments. The team's findings were subsequently published in a book called *German Plastic Practice*. In 1954 he was awarded an honorary degree of doctor of science by Alma College for his many accomplishments in plastics technology.

With his expertise honed, Goggin returned to Dow's Plastics Department and became its general manager in 1958. By 1967, when Ted Doan nominated him to become the fourth president of Dow Corning Corporation, Bill Goggin had built the Plastics Department to $400 million in sales, making it a world leader in plastics.

A decade earlier, the Plastics Department had established the unique business structure which Dow Corning would come to know as the multidimensional organization (MDO). It was this structure, with its emphasis on delegation of responsibility, accountability for cost and profit, and clear and open communication channels, that the board wanted to bring to Dow Corning, in an effort to better manage the company's accelerating growth and to position it for the future.

At a meeting of the Dow Corning board on September 22, 1967, Dr. William C. Goggin was named the new president and chief operating officer of the company. At the same time, Shailer Bass was named chairman of the board and chief executive officer.

When Dr. Goggin stepped into his new role as president, he was relatively unfamiliar with Dow Corning. He had known some of the staff socially and years before had coauthored a paper with Dr. Bass on the electrical properties of cellulose, but that was the extent of his exposure to the company. When he made the move, Goggin wanted to take some of his key people with him. He was told by the board he could have anyone he wanted—so long as they came from Dow Corning. This proved to be a blessing in disguise, as there was a large pool of talent within

Dr. William C. Goggin.

Dow Corning, ripe for development under the able direction of Bill
Goggin.

Dr. Goggin's management philosophy was one that emphasized clarity of purpose, strict accountability, and measurable achievement. This
view grew out of his training and discipline as a researcher in the early
days of his career at Dow. It was nurtured by Ben Branch, chairman of
Dow, and Ted Doan, its president at the time. Goggin was quick to del-
egate authority and assign responsibility; at the same time, he held his
subordinates accountable for the fruits of their labor. Those who knew
Goggin and worked closely with him quickly recognized his penchant
for excellence in all his work.

This drive for excellence, coupled with Dr. Goggin's solid technical
and managerial background at Dow Chemical, would gradually transform Dow Corning into a more efficient, more profitable organization,
with a multidimensional structure so effective for managing growth and
change, ensuring efficiency, and boosting profitability that it is maintained to this day.

The Multidimensional Organization: Evolutionary Steps

Goggin was enthusiastically received at Dow Corning. In the early days
of his presidency, he spoke before a number of management groups
within the company about the new structure he planned gradually to
introduce. This discussion of the elements of the multidimensional organization became known as the "Goggin credo."

The emphasis was on *gradual;* Goggin recognized that the magnitude
of the restructuring he envisioned could be effectively carried out only
as an evolutionary process. In his early speeches to the managers,
Goggin stressed that he would strive to implement changes with a minimum of disruption to the functioning of the company.

As Dr. Goggin explained it, under the new system, responsibility for
costs and profits would be widely dispersed, delegated to the lowest
level of knowledgeable employees. Each product group would be set up
as a profit center. Each function (such as marketing or manufacturing)
would be a cost center. Various support tools, such as a system of "management by objectives," would help to achieve the goals that would be
set under the MDO structure.

One prerequisite for the effective functioning of the new system, and
one that Goggin was to stress again and again in employee meetings,
was open and constant communications throughout the organization.
Another requirement for success was the total dedication on the part of

all managers to seeing the company through the long period of restructuring ahead. Above all, in order for the new system to work, it would require the full participation and commitment of *all* employees, at every level of operations.

Economic Evaluation

A basic component of the MDO concept was a systematic means of evaluating and measuring the value of products and projects. Once Dr. Goggin had explained the MDO structure to employees, he and Jack Ludington, director of industrial relations, developed a formal training course to teach employees the detailed workings of the new system. The course was taught by Win Zacharias and John Churchfield of Dow Chemical.

A group of 20 employees with engineering and M.B.A. degrees formed the first class to participate in the Economic Evaluation courses, which spelled out the criteria by which projects would be evaluated under the MDO structure. Under the new system of evaluation, proposed projects, products, and capital expenditures would have to pass a litmus test, consisting of a variety of financial analyses aimed at determining long-term profitability, before funding would be authorized.

Over the years dozens of professionals and managers participated in the Economic Evaluation course. From the first group, Ed Steinhoff was selected to lead the new Economic Evaluation Department. He worked to install the system throughout the company.

The Board Book

When Bill Goggin arrived at Dow Corning, board of directors meetings were lengthy, taking up the better part of 2 days. The establishment of a common economic language allowed Dr. Goggin to contribute to the efficiency of these meetings. He established a system whereby before every meeting, board members were sent a book that contained letters from the chairman and the president, resolutions, business and area performance data, authorizations with financial support, a treasurer's report, and legal and patent reports, all based on the new common economic language. The net result was that the 2-day meetings were reduced to a few hours.

Establishing the Businesses

With an economic evaluation system put into place, and with Dr. Bass's support and continual urging, Dr. Goggin set about the task of restruc-

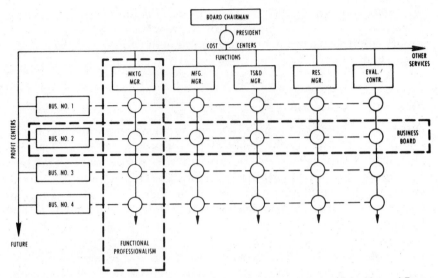

Figure 7-1. The matrix organization concept. *[Reprinted by permission of the* Harvard Business Review. *An exhibit from "How the Multidimensional Structure Works at Dow Corning," by William C. Goggin (January-February 1974, p. 56). Copyright 1973 by the President and Fellows of Harvard College; all rights reserved.]*

turing the businesses. During the first year of his presidency, he retained the existing five-division structure set up by John Hannigan while he gradually developed the support systems needed to accommodate the new structure that would replace the five-division system; this gradual process allowed employees to adjust to the notion of MDO. In June 1968, Goggin restructured the company into a matrix form, the first stage in developing a true multidimensional organization (Figure 7-1).

The matrix was formed by the juxtaposition of "business" and "functional" areas. "Businesses" were formed of specific product lines; "functions" were services, such as manufacturing and marketing, that supported the businesses.

Under the matrix organization, each of the eight businesses was assigned a business manager. Each business also had a "business board" consisting of managers from the functional areas of Marketing, Manufacturing, Technical Service and Development, and Research, as well as an economic evaluator-controller. These functional managers reported to two bosses—a "functional professional" who shared their area of expertise and the business manager of their group.

At this first "matrix" stage, eight businesses were established, as shown in Table 7-1.

Table 7-1. Businesses under the Matrix Organization

Engineering Products Division—Bill Pedersen, manager
  Silicone Rubber Business
    Bob Springmier, manager
      Keith Polmanteer, research manager
      Bob Hedlund, development manager
      Ray Maneri, manufacturing manager
      Ed Haire, marketing manager
  Encapsulants and Sealants Business
    John Dexter, manager
      Frank Hyde, research manager
      Mel Nelson, development manager
      Bill Ragborg, manufacturing manager
      Joe Dellaria, marketing manager
  Specialty Lubricants Business
    Ray Naegele, manager
      Cecil Frye, research manager
      Harry Schiefer, development manager
      Ed Sprague, manufacturing manager
      Clyde Whipple, plant development

Chemical Products Division—Earle Smith, manager
  Resins and Chemicals Business
    Doug Layne, manager
      John Speier, research manager
      George Konkle, development manager
      Don Van Winkle, manufacturing manager
      Byron Culbertson, marketing manager
  Fluids, Emulsions, and Compounds Business
    Les Tyler, manager
      Art Barry, research manager
      George Konkle, development manager
      Don Beshgetoor, manufacturing manager
      Roger Koldermann, marketing manager

Consumer Products Business—Chet Currie, manager
    Joe Keil, research manager
    Dan Pail, development manager
    Dick Gergle, manufacturing manager
    Chuck Lenz, marketing manager

Electronic Products Business—Earl Warrick, manager
    Ted Kern, research manager
    Cedric Currin, development manager
    Truman Bishop, manufacturing manager
    Mike Swantko, marketing manager

Medical Products Business—Ira Hutchison, manager
    Don Bennett, research manager
    Zeke Dennett, development manager
    Henry Pellika, manufacturing manager
    Gordon McIntyre, marketing manager

Corporate Objectives

Once the businesses were established, Goggin and his management team developed a number of corporate objectives to be achieved under the MDO structure. The objectives included:

1. Profit increases of 15 percent per year, compounded
2. Worldwide sales growth of 15 percent per year, compounded
3. Compounded increase in market participation of 1 percent per year
4. Productivity increases of 2 percent per year, compounded
5. Pretax return on investment (ROI) of 30 percent, or after-tax ROI of 15 percent.
6. Minimum 15 percent after-tax ROI on all new capital investment
7. New-product sales equal to 30 percent of total sales
8. Commitment to quality of life and to Dow Corning's being a leading citizen wherever it operates
9. Commitment to safety, to Dow Corning's being consistently ranked among the 10 leaders in the Manufacturing Chemists Association listings

New Business Staging

Dr. Goggin realized that a company which stressed advanced technology must place much emphasis on new-product development and commercialization, thus the emphasis on new-product development as one of the key corporate objectives. Before the introduction of the MDO structure at Dow Corning, an average of 8 years elapsed from the time a new product was conceptualized until it reached the commercialization stage. Goggin realized that the company needed to streamline the commercialization process in order to remain competitive. He assigned Don Weyer, in Technical Service and Development, to address the problem.

Out of this effort a new business staging system was developed over the course of 2 years. The system grew out of work done by the government during the war years, in the area of operations research. The system divided the product life cycle into seven distinct stages, from idea conception through obsolescence (Figure 7-2). With product development organized along these lines, it was possible to see more clearly how a product comes to market and to provide a disciplined, organized approach to the commercialization process.

At each stage of the process, one function has the major role to play

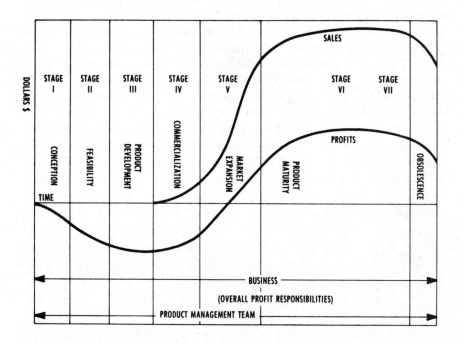

Figure 7-2. The product life cycle. *[Reprinted by permission of the* Harvard Business Review. *An exhibit from "How the Multidimensional Structure Works at Dow Corning," by William C. Goggin (January-February 1974, p. 64). Copyright 1973 by the President and Fellows of Harvard College; all rights reserved.]*

and acts as the project "quarterback." For example, in stage 2 (feasibility), research is the prime mover. When a product moves to stage 4 (commercialization), technical service and development assumes control. In stage 5 (market expansion), it's marketing's ball game. However, in no stage does the lead function have the only input. The new business staging system was and is a team effort, with clearly defined functional responsibilities.

Strike at the Midland Plant

By the spring of 1968, corporate objectives had been set, and the businesses were geared up to pursue operations under the new structure. At this point, Dr. Goggin had to meet another serious challenge: the Midland plant was faced with its first strike in the company's history. On May 21, 1968, the union turned down a company contract, and 750 hourly workers walked off their jobs. The plant continued to be operated by salaried workers, but the strike took its toll on plans to move forward with the MDO restructuring.

The strike dragged on throughout the summer. By early June the two groups were meeting with a federal mediator. Dow Corning had been "lockstep" with Dow on hourly contract matters up to this point, but now it appeared necessary for the joint venture to sever this tie to one of its parents and resolve the strike by establishing its own set of wage guidelines. Jack Ludington, who was then director of industrial relations, led the way in helping to resolve the wage issues. By the end of the summer, accord was finally reached. The new contract was signed August 28, 1968, three months after the strike had begun. The restructuring process could once again proceed.

Ninth Business: New Projects

In order to emphasize new-product development and to ensure that basic products were being used in all possible applications, Goggin announced the formation of a ninth business, New Projects, after the Midland plant strike ended. I was named manager of the business, and Bill Lowery took over my former role as manager of the Electronic Products Business.

The New Projects Business was responsible for products and product applications that were not natural fits for any of the other business groups. One of our first moves was to evaluate the possibilities of old technologies which had never been brought into commercial production. Two of these products, the foam-filled tire and antimicrobial treatments, were brought into production during the time I managed the New Projects group.

The technology to manufacture foam-filled tires was licensed to Goodyear Tire and Rubber Company and to three others. We also approached potential customers about using antimicrobial treatments, which had been developed in Dr. Donald Bennett's Bioscience laboratory, in such applications as hospital gowns and drapes, and in carpets. The idea eventually became very popular, but it took a long time to catch on, because of its novelty (Figure 7-3).

We pursued other projects as well. Henry Scott, working in Dr. Norman Lloyd's research group in Barry, Wales, had developed a technology for cross-linking polyethylene. The resulting product overcame one of the major deficiencies of polyethylene, the fact that it softened and would flow at relatively low temperatures. The cross-linked polyethylene, given the name SIOPLAS® E, did not readily soften or flow. It also resisted stress cracking better than ordinary polyethylene. We licensed the technology to produce this material to a number of manufacturers around the world.

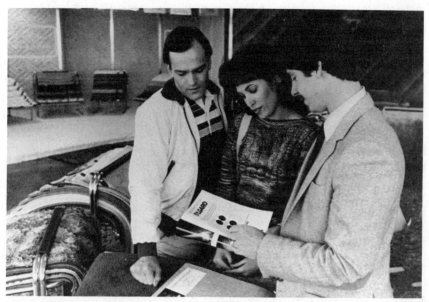

Figure 7-3. Carpet treatment is just one of the many applications of Dow Corning's antimicrobial solutions originally developed in Dr. Donald Bennett's Bioscience Research laboratory.

"What's New"

Dr. Goggin's concern for new technology led him to develop a section of his report to the board of directors which he called "What's New." It was devoted to new developments anywhere within the corporation. By September 1971, Goggin reported on a variety of new developments that included formed-in-place gaskets of RTV silicone rubber for automotive use, high-voltage silicone rubber insulation for use on the high-voltage circuits of television sets, and metalworking lubricants—MOLYKOTE® 3500, for use in hot forging—and gear box lubricants for use in hydraulic systems.

Moon Products

Early in Dr. Goggin's presidency, a unique line of new products was developed for the U.S. space program. An accident on the launch pad that had cost the lives of three astronauts seemed to have been caused by volatiles in products used in the space capsule. To help solve this problem, Dow Corning developed a line of low-volatility, space-grade materials, including fluids, sealants, and rubbers.

As a result, when *Apollo 11* landed on the moon on July 20, 1969, it carried a number of Dow Corning products—sealants, rubber hoses, potting compounds, insulation, and even a half-dollar-sized disk of silicon etched with a goodwill message from leaders around the world. There was an extra thrill for the employees of Dow Corning when *Apollo 11* touched down at Cape Kennedy on July 24, its mission successfully completed.

Further Restructuring: Basic Businesses

In May 1969, Dr. Goggin named Jack Ludington to the newly created post of vice president and general manager of Basic Businesses. Durelle Thomson replaced Ludington as director of industrial relations.

In this new position, Ludington was responsible for management of the five "basic businesses," with their managers reporting directly to him, as follows:

- Fluids, Emulsions, and Compounds (FEC)—Les Tyler
- Resins and Chemicals (R&C)—Doug Layne
- Encapsulants and Sealants (E&S)—John Dexter
- Silicone Rubber—Bob Springmier
- Specialty Lubricants—Ray Naegele

The four other major businesses—Electronic Products (now under Bill Lowery), Consumer Products (under Chet Currie), Medical Products (under Ira Hutchison), and New Projects (under my management)—continued to report directly to Dr. Goggin. Earle Smith and Bill Pedersen had gone on to become comanagers of the Marketing Department at this point.

In June 1971, Ludington announced the formation of a Business Services, Evaluation, and Control Department for Basic Businesses. Larry Reed was named to head the new department, which was to be responsible for providing economic evaluation, planning, financial control, and related services for each of the five basic businesses.

Electronic Products Business

Bill Lowery worked hard to improve the profitability of the silicon business. One step in this direction was to discontinue the single-crystal silicon business in Hemlock and to depend for single crystal on the materials produced by Shin-Etsu Handotai. Another was to sell off many of the Siemens zone refiners and associated power packs.

When Bill Goggin stepped into office, Dow Corning was producing some 4000 products. Elimination of the single-crystal silicon business was part of a broader effort in the early years of Goggin's administration to consolidate and strengthen Dow Corning's product lines by weeding out such marginal products.

When Shin-Etsu Handotai began producing single-crystal silicon in Kuala Lumpur, we sent comanagers to Malaysia to assist the operation. Duane Townley, one of the comanagers, described a problem in the plant, brought on by the "spirits."

Townley found a small crowd of cars and people assembled at the gate of the plant as he returned from a holiday on Christmas eve. The assistant personnel supervisor, Teoh, stepped forward to say that the plant had been shut down for 4 days because of "spirits" which reportedly caused workers to throw fits or go into trances. They had tried several *Bomohs* (witch doctors), performed ceremonies, killed a goat, and sprinkled yellow rice, but the spirits remained. Townley reassured Teoh that they must do what was necessary to pacify the spirits and get the plant rolling again.

The spirits had picked an opportune time to strike. Townley and Tom Kaya, the other codirector, were both out of the country, and the production manager in charge was new and unsure of local customs. He passed leadership on this matter to the Malay managers, who were terrified by spirits, and the problem engulfed the entire plant.

Finally, a frail girl, in a spirit-induced trance, said the spirit needed another goat killed. Production was halted for a day while the goat was slaughtered and incantations recited. No further incidents were reported the first day back at work. Townley posted a letter on the bulletin board, stating that the spirits had been expelled and that any further incidents would be considered personal problems and would be handled with time off for recovery—without pay. The spirits never returned while Townley was in Malaysia.

Medical Products Business

In order to improve the efficiency of the medical products operations, Ira Hutchison consolidated the technical efforts within the business in January 1971. The Technical Service and Development laboratories under Dr. Forrest Stark, the Technical Planning and Evaluation function under Zeke Dennett, and the Center for Aid to Medical Research under

Silas Braley were combined. Dr. Stark was named the manager of the consolidated group, with Dennett and Braley reporting to him.

In 1965, Dusty Rhodes had taken over as European area manager, and Ira Hutchison had been named head of the Medical Products Business. Sales of medical products continued their rapid growth during Hutchison's term of management, increasing from $1 million in 1965 to $30 million when he left the business in 1974. This represented a hefty compounded growth rate of 46 percent per year.

Ophthalmics: SILCON® Lenses.   In 1972, the Medical Products Business acquired Mueller-Welt silicone rubber contact lens business. Negotiations for the purchase of the company, which was originally owned by Joseph Breger, had begun under Dr. Bass's presidency.

The acquisition included facilities in Chicago for the prototype production of silicone lenses and the clinical program begun by Breger. The facilities were small, inadequate, and dispersed throughout several locations in Chicago. One of the first tasks would be to consolidate the facilities and refine the manufacturing process.

The unit formed as a result of the purchase became known as the "SILCON® Lens Project." SILCON® was the trademark that Joseph Breger, the original owner of Mueller-Welt, had established for the silicone contact lens he developed. Ira Hutchison was to manage the business along with his other responsibilities in the medical products area. Don Piper became project leader, and Gene Ulanowicz was named manufacturing manager.

Bioscience Research.   The bioscience research group under Dr. Bennett, while still a separate research entity during the Goggin years, worked on products which ultimately became part of the Medical Products Business. The group continued the search for the source of the biological activity of DOW CORNING® 555 fluid. By 1972 the activity had been identified in an isomer, 2,6-*cis*-diphenylhexamethylcyclotetrasiloxane.[1] Many testing programs on its possible use continued over the next several years. Bioactivity of a number of different compounds was also surveyed.

Drug Delivery.   In addition to searching for the active ingredient in DOW CORNING® 555 fluid, the bioscience group began to investigate the drug delivery field for possible applications of silicone rubber. The group found the silicone elastomers to be highly permeable, and this

---

[1]D. R. Bennett, S. J. Gorzinsky, and J. E. LeBeau, *Toxicol. Appl. Pharmacol.*, 21:55–67 (1972).

led to a variety of patents in the field of drug delivery for fertility control and antibacterial activity.

Silicone Rubber Business

Emulsion Polymerization. Emulsion polymerization of dimethylsiloxane cyclics had been started by Jack Wehrly in Dr. Hyde's laboratory in 1955. His was a complete study of both alkaline and acid catalyst systems, with a wide variety of emulsion-forming surfactants. The advantage of emulsion polymerization was that it made possible the coating of materials with a rubber film, without using solvent.

The lab found a way to make a sealant out of the emulsion polymer. Colloidal silica was added to strengthen the polymer, and curing was effected by the addition of methyltrimethoxysilane and an organic tin compound as catalyst. This gave a curable latex which could be used as a sealant and a construction caulk. Another major use for the latex was in roof coatings which gave smooth, dirt-resistant surfaces.

Later, others showed that the surfactant could also be the catalyst for polymerization, especially if it were a long-chain, aliphatic-substituted benzene sulfonic acid.

Heavy-Duty Tough Rubber. A new class of silicone rubber was developed in Dr. Ronald Zeman's laboratories in the early 1970s. This class of material matched the modulus characteristics and toughness of many organic elastomers. In addition, it had excellent resilience, abrasion resistance, and cut-growth resistance, as well as good molding, calendering, and extrusion characteristics. The first product in this class, SILASTIC® 4600, had a 100 percent modulus of 500 pounds per square inch and a tear strength of 280 pounds per inch. The ability of this new silicone elastomer to withstand mechanical abuse puts it in a class by itself as a high-performance engineering material.

Encapsulants and Sealants Business

High-Strength Sealant. During this time a major effort went into development of a high-strength sealant for aerospace applications and for use in the supersonic transport, the Concorde. A high-strength RTV sealant was developed using a special silica prepared from a silica hydrogel which had been treated with hexamethyldisilazane, $(CH_3)_3$ $SiNHSi(CH_3)_3$, to partially hydrophobe the surface. Such silicas were highly reinforcing. The RTV curing system used the reaction between terminal hydroxyls of high-polymer siloxanes and —SiH groups on a low-polymer fluid. An organic tin compound was used as catalyst. Tensile strengths of up to 1800 pounds per square inch were obtained by this method.

Terraseal®. At the other end of the specification spectrum was a general-purpose terrace sealant, a polyurethane sealant cured through silicones and given the name "Terraseal®." This low-cost sealant was used on terraces and windshields and in general building areas.

Complaints about the slow cure of the one-part Terraseal® led to the development of a two-component polyurethane sealant. This made possible faster initial cures followed by a slower moisture-aided cure. Unfortunately, the cost of the two-part sealant was considerably greater than that of existing two-part urethane sealants. This approach was dropped, and subsequent research was confined to silicone sealants.

Mold Making. A fluid rubber which would cross-link on mild heating was developed. One of the major uses for this fluid rubber was in the making of molds for a variety of casting processes.

The fluid rubber became widely popular within the furniture industry. A furniture maker would take a carved wooden master by a fine woodworker and cover it with fluid silicone rubber. When "set," the mold could be cut off the piece, leaving a cavity into which could be poured a fluid form of a polyester resin. The resin would set in a short time to a woodlike solid-foam piece, recreating the original wooden master.

The mold could be used for several hundred pours and was so detailed that it allowed for the reproduction of the smallest variations in the grain of the wood. The finished pieces could be stained and finished like any standard piece of wood. Silicone rubber molds were (and still are) used in many furniture applications (Figure 7-4).

Resins and Chemicals Business

Ceramics. A molding compound for electronic uses had been developed during the 1950s under the direction of Leo Stebleton. The compound was developed from the same resins used for laminating glass cloth. Resin-coated glass roving, a nonwoven continuous glass fiber, was partially cured and chopped into various fiber lengths and used as the molding compound.

Work on molding compounds was expanded upon in the 1960s when semiconductor manufacturers were demanding a granular compound. Customers such as Motorola and International Resistor were manufac-

Figure 7-4. Molds made of silicone rubber allow for authentic reproduction of the finest details of wood grain furniture.

turing small "nailhead" diodes and resistors which needed to be protected by molding compounds.

The diodes and other semiconductor devices were usually first coated with a silicone "junction coating" resin. The coating protected the devices during subsequent molding and handling. These devices were then embedded in a molding compound, a mixture of silicone resin and finely divided silicon dioxide particles. The operation was carried out in a molding machine in which the molding compound was injected into a hot-mold cavity containing the device. The resin was then cured to provide a hard protective covering for the device.

Another application of the granular molding compound was in aircraft electrical connector inserts. One of the requirements for some of the connectors was the ability to serve continuously at 700 to 900°F. It was obvious to Don Weyer, who was responsible for the research in this area, that the usual fillers could not perform at these temperatures and that calcined fillers were needed. Weyer also found that the silicone resins were slowly decomposing at these very high temperatures and that as they decomposed, a silica residue was left behind. The residue was holding the calcined fillers together in a very hard, brittle mass. The molded test parts were usually bars or disks, and observation showed that there was very little warpage, shrinkage, or loss of detail after firing. The fired bars had a bell-like resonance.

This gave birth to the idea of silicone ceramics. To make such ceramics, a silicone resin is mixed with finely divided particles of silicon dioxide, aluminum oxide, silicon carbide, or other refractory materials and molded to a desired shape in a molding machine. This molded part is then "fired" at very high temperatures to burn away the organic groups on silicon and produce a ceramic part which retains the shape it acquired in the molding operation. This route avoids the costly shaping operations that would otherwise be required on the brittle ceramic mass.

Two patents had been issued to Dow Corning in 1963, but there was no attempt to develop silicone ceramic products for a number of years. Then, after several unsuccessful attempts to commercialize the technology, a decision was made to license this know-how to selected customers. One of the largest applications for the technology was, and still is, the production of hollow metal turbine blades by casting metals that melt at high temperatures into the ceramic molds. These molds contain a core of a silicone–aluminum oxide preformed ceramic. After the metal has been cast around this core, the core is dissolved by treatment with sodium hydroxide. This technique produces hollow turbine blades with precisely formed interior openings.

The Ford Motor Company was interested in exploring the use of Dow Corning ceramics in its gas turbine engines. For its purposes, Ford required a flex strength of 30,000 pounds per square inch. Although the researchers came close (Don Weyer developed a material with a flex strength of 26,000 pounds per square inch), they were unable to develop a strong enough ceramic for Ford during the Goggin years.

Coupling Agents. The work on coupling agents begun by Ed Plueddemann during the mid-1960s was continued in this period. In 1966, a series of aromatic-functional silanes was developed as coupling agents for high-temperature resins.[2] These aromatic silanes are resistant to oxidation in air at temperatures 212°F higher than is the case for standard aliphatic organofunctional silanes. It was also discovered that mixtures of aliphatic silanes with approximately 90 percent phenyltrimethoxysilane gave primer films with comparable heat stability.

[2]E. P. Plueddemann, U.S. Patent 3,481,815, 1969.

In the early 1970s, Ed Plueddemann developed a vinylbenzyl-substituted aminofunctional silane.[3] This material was commercialized as Dow Corning Coupling Agent Z-6032. It is unique among silanes in that it is a coupling agent for virtually all thermosetting and thermoplastic polymers. The tremendous utility of this coupling agent is due to its amine reactivity plus styrene polymerizability. Over time, the product was improved by the addition of a new stabilizer, which prevented gelling in the absence of air.

International Business

The first 2 years of Dr. Goggin's presidency were focused on establishing the basic businesses under the new multidimensional organization. The next dimension to be added was geography. With domestic business being handled by Dr. Goggin, Shailer Bass was free to travel more and to develop the geographical areas of the company around the world.

Pacific Area

In May 1969, Dr. Goggin appointed Arthur ("Bud") Klauser as manager of the Pacific area. Klauser had worked in Japan for a number of years with other companies, and he spoke Japanese fluently. By this time Bill Blackburn had been named vice president and comanager of Toray Silicone Company (Dick Heuerman replaced Blackburn as general counsel). Bill Armstrong was named a director of Shin-Etsu Handotai (SEH) and Bill May came back from Tokyo to assume a new position as technical service manager for the Lubricants Business, reporting to Ray Naegele. Charles Dudley was named manager of the Australasian area (which, at the time, consisted solely of the Australian market).

European Area

SISS. In line with the overall objective of obtaining control of our international distribution channels, efforts were made to purchase St. Gobain's shares in SISS. Added to this desire was the fact that Rhone Polenc had bought out St. Gobain. Since Rhone Polenc was also a com-

---

[3]E. P. Plueddemann, U.S. Patent 3,734,763, 1973.

petitor, Dow Corning would have to either sell its existing shares in the business, or purchase Rhone Polenc's. Dow Corning chose to sell its shares in SISS to Rhone Polenc, for a very favorable sum.

Midsil. As pointed out in Chapter 6, the Midsil joint venture had been experiencing problems for some time. By the late 1960s, conditions had deteriorated to such an extent that Dow Corning pulled all its representatives from the board of Midsil and appointed Bedford Atwood, an acquaintance of Dr. Bass's and an Englishman who was well known in United Kingdom business and government circles, as our sole representative. Atwood did a good job of keeping pressure on Midsil to improve its position in the marketplace, without Dow Corning's direct involvement.

John Hughes, a former Albright and Wilson manager, was in charge of the Midsil operation and had been trying to improve a poor profit performance over the preceding several years. Hughes was in the midst of a redundancy program, trying to reduce the work force of 1200 and to institute general cost-cutting measures. Most of the employees were in the plant area, Barry, Wales, but there were sales offices in England, Austria, the United States, South Africa, and Singapore.

The only solution in the long run was for Dow Corning to take full control of Midsil. Dr. Bass at one time had offered to buy Albright and Wilson's shares in the joint venture for $25 million, and was turned down. As conditions continued to deteriorate, the asking price dropped substantially. Albright and Wilson's shares were purchased in the fall of 1969 for $8.3 million, making Dow Corning sole owner of Midsil.

Dusty Rhodes, as the European area manager, asked for help in assimilating the Midsil organization into the Dow Corning fold. Rhodes alerted the Midsil people that a team from Midland would be making a 2-week visit to discuss personnel, the condition of the plant, and the tasks ahead. Bill Hargreaves led the Dow Corning team, which included Don Watters, Tom Thomson, Ray Maneri, Jack Ludington, Jerry Griffin, and Michael Jackson.

During the visit, the team combed the Midsil site, evaluating the status of the plant and equipment, which was badly deteriorated. They estimated repair costs and capital expenditure requirements. Personnel levels in the plant as well as engineering supervision and maintenance personnel were evaluated. Research and development departments were surveyed for their contributions to new product lines; their utilization of staff, equipment, laboratories, and analytical support; and their quality control. Marketing and sales management sorted out offices, market coverage, and product offerings. Consolidation was a major goal. Technical people surveyed the Midsil product lines to determine which products were duplicates of Dow Corning offerings. At the same time, they tried to evaluate which Midsil products might have a perceived market advantage over Dow Corning's. The finance people were asked to survey their ranks and to develop a plan to convert the Midsil accounting system into that of Dow Corning.

Meanwhile, every effort was made to keep the Midsil people informed of what was being done. The Midland team maintained good relations with the on-site unions, ensuring that no work stoppages occurred during this transition period. Redundancy pay packages were worked out for those whose jobs were eliminated. Meetings were held with the town council, professional societies, and other local agencies with an interest in the local employment situation.

The visiting team was treated well. Over a 2-week period the local restaurant, Water's Edge, ran out of its standard entrées. Thereafter, each evening, the chef would prepare special entrées at the request of the group. Tom Thomson, at dinner on the evening before the group was to depart for Midland, expressed the team's delight over the many fine meals they had enjoyed while in Wales and presented the chef with a bottle of his favorite scotch, Glenfiddich. At the same time, Thomson asked if it would be possible to have a bit of Stilton cheese, a new delicacy to the traveling Americans, to take home with him. The next morning he found a whole wheel of Stilton in his room. Some people wonder to this day how or if he tried to take it home.

At the area headquarters in Brussels, the information gathered by the team was reviewed and a series of recommendations for future operations at Midsil developed. As part of these recommendations, a number of management changes were quickly instituted. Robert Jackson was brought from Midland to manage the finance department. Kermit Campbell was named to direct the laboratories, with the assistance of Dr. Norman Lloyd (who was already on site).

Bud Lankton, manager of the Carrollton plant, was reassigned overseas to manage the Barry site. He was shocked by the appearance of the plant. Rust, chemical leaks, steam leaks, and piles of scrap were everywhere. Since acquisition, there had already been three major reductions of the work force. Morale was low, and employees were understandably nervous.

The situation was disheartening, to say the least—a far cry from the quality operation in Carrollton. During a trip back to Midland shortly after he took over as site manager, a discouraged Lankton commented: "Sometimes I think the best thing to do would be to bulldoze the whole place and start over."

Lankton brought Jim Klingler with him from Carrollton, to manage the engineering and maintenance function at the Barry site. His assignment was to clean up the site, improve safety markedly, decrease the work force (which was still oversized, despite earlier reductions), streamline the product line, and improve productivity and quality. At the same time, he would be responsible for the training of production workers and for overseeing the major capital improvements that would be required to transform the site into a workable operating space.

Progress in the first few months was measured by the tons of scrap iron hauled away and the reduction of lost-time incidents from the five accidents experienced in the first month Lankton was on the job. After 18 months, the Barry plant showed remarkable improvement. Much of the scrap iron was gone, antiquated equipment had been taken out of service, the product line was manageable, and the first major authorization for a new direct-process and hydrolysis train had been prepared and was about to be approved.

In order to generate funds for the major improvements still needed at the Barry plant, Dow Corning floated its first bond issue, with Jerry Griffin heavily involved in the effort. The recession of 1967 had hit Dow Corning hard, along with most manufacturers. The expansion of the Carrollton facilities had further strained the company's financial resources. Dow Corning had been borrowing funds through loans guaranteed by its parent companies. It was evident by now that a longer-term solution was required and that it was time for Dow Corning to become more financially self-sufficient.

The Foreign Investments Act of 1968 had been enacted by Congress to curb the outflow of funds from the United States. The result was a big surge in foreign borrowing by U.S. companies seeking to finance their overseas operations. The Eurobond market developed and flourished in the wake of the act, and in 1971 Dow Corning issued its own Eurobonds, backed by the parent companies.

Dow Banking Corporation had recently formed a 50 percent–owned joint venture called "Eurocapital" with 16 other banks to engage in underwriting Eurobonds. Logically, Dow Corning was viewed as a great opportunity to launch this enterprise. Eurocapital was accepted as a member of a syndicate formed by six banks to issue the Dow Corning bonds. The lead bank was Rothschild of London, and Goldman Sachs, Credit Suisse, Lazard Freres of New York, and Lazard Brothers of London filled out this very prestigious group.

The Eurobond issue provided the financial resources needed to complete the renovation work begun at the Barry site. With the infusion of capital, the dedicated efforts of Bud Lankton, and the recognition that there were many good local employees available to operate a modern facility, the Barry operation was on its way to becoming a fully integrated member of the Dow Corning family.

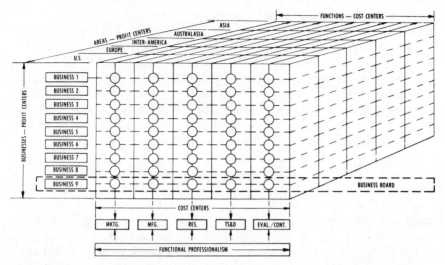

Figure 7-5. The multidimensional organization. *[Reprinted by permission of the* Harvard Business Review. *An exhibit from "How the Multidimensional Structure Works at Dow Corning," by William C. Goggin (January-February 1974, p. 57). Copyright 1973 by the President and Fellows of Harvard College; all rights reserved.]*

Tom Watson and Ian Ross were two of the many local employees who had been especially valuable to Lankton during the time he was working to modernize the Barry site. Once the plant was in good operating shape, it was arranged for Watson to go the Harvard Business School and for Ross to spend some time in Midland gaining additional production experience.

Management Change.   In July 1970, Bill Hargreaves replaced Dusty Rhodes, who had served as European area manager for 5 years. Shortly thereafter, Rhodes was named vice president for engineering and manufacturing.

Bob Sauer, who had managed Alpha Molykote Europe since its acquisition in April 1967, was replaced by Clyde Whipple, who moved to Munich in the fall of 1971.

The Multidimensional Organization: Phase Two

In 1970, the third dimension of the MDO was incorporated into Dow Corning's operating structure (Figure 7-5). In this phase, the geographical areas were organized along the same lines as the domestic operations.

The major thrust outside the United States was in Europe. Bill Hargreaves was responsible for implementing the MDO structure in Europe. A great deal of effort was involved in the overseas restructuring. Employees had to be retrained under the new structure. Many were transferred or redeveloped. Nationals were hired. Doug Layne, director of marketing and business development, oversaw the effort to transform Europe to the MDO structure. This took almost 2 years to implement, and it happened country by country, region by region.

A new financial reporting system was adopted to support the MDO structure. The system, designed by Don Watters, corporate controller, was based on cause-and-effect relationships rather than on a traditional legal entity structure. Each product was assigned to a single business, and credit for each sale went to both the business and the area involved. Both the businesses and the areas were now recognized as profit centers.

Within this reporting system, the financial results of all businesses and of all areas added up to consolidated corporate results. Sales were credited to the business and area where the final trade sale occurred. Semifinished products were "transferred" across business and area lines at direct costs rather than transfer prices. Any effort committed in one business or area in support of another was reflected through appropriate cost allocations.

This system proved to be an effective means of managing the profitability of product lines and geographical subdivisions. It is still in use today.

Dr. Hyde Is Honored

During Bill Goggin's presidency, Dow Corning's pioneering researcher, Dr. James Franklin Hyde, was awarded the prestigious Perkin Medal by the American Section of the Society of Chemical Industry on February 26, 1971, at a ceremony in the Plaza Hotel in New York City (Figure 7-6).

Facilities

Alpha Molykote Plant

When Dr. Goggin became president, the Alpha Molykote operation was still in its original quarters in Stamford, Connecticut. Ray Naegele had

Figure 7-6. Dr. Hyde accepts the coveted Perkin Medal at the Plaza Hotel in New York City, February 26, 1971.

been named executive vice president of the company and Don Piper, chief engineer. By the fall of 1967, Piper moved to head up the custom rubber fabricating plant in Trumbull, Connecticut. Clyde Whipple replaced him as chief engineer for Alpha Molykote.

The Stamford facilities were a sight to behold. The group was operating out of a small building with a two-story office wing and a small, fragmented production facility. The heating and ventilating systems were so poor that no one except Naegele could have an office with four walls; the walls of the other offices stopped about a foot short of the ceiling to allow for ventilation. The office partitions were flimsy and conducted sound readily; as a result, there was little privacy.

The only modification that had been made to the facility was a private shower room built for Frank Todero, the man who operated the sifter which purified the raw molybdenum disulfide powder received from the vendor. Frank was one of the most fastidious, best-dressed people I have ever met, but at the end of his working day he would be coated from head to foot with the black powder. He would step into his private shower room and leave the plant looking as though he had just stepped out of *Gentleman's Quarterly*.

While the Stamford facilities were far below Dow Corning standards, under the new economic evaluation system Clyde Whipple was faced with the problem of justifying investment in new facilities. At the time, the profitability of the Molykote operation was limited, so that some justification beyond the financial was needed.

In order for Bill Goggin to promote authorization of a new facility, Whipple felt he would have to see firsthand the conditions under which the group was working. Goggin accepted Whipple's invitation to visit the facilities. After a brief tour, no further requests or explanations by Whipple were required. Goggin simply told him: "We must get our people out of this mess!"

After Dr. Goggin left Stamford, planning for a new facility went forward. Soon the Molykote operation moved to Trumbull, Connecticut, near the existing rubber compounding plant. Whipple replaced Ed Sprague, who had been lubricants plant manager, and supervised the move. Gus Gosselin, who had been hired from a Connecticut steel company as the facilities and process engineering manager, made sure that the move was accomplished without missing an order or a shipment.

Corporate Center Planning

By the mid-1960s it became obvious that Dow Corning was rapidly outgrowing its Midland plant site, especially the management offices and research and technical service facilities. Management decided to maintain its administrative offices in the Midland, Michigan, area. Don Coultrip and Sandy Sanderson were appointed to form a team to obtain property for a new corporate center that would meet Dow Corning's needs for the coming 30 years.

A site east of the existing Midland site and just inside Bay County was acquired. It consisted of roughly 2 square miles of farmland. Following this, the Bridgeport, Connecticut, architectural firm of Fletcher Thompson (which had designed the finishing plants in Trumbull and Costa Mesa) was chosen to help develop a 30-year plan for the site.

The first facilities planned were a bioscience building, a power plant, and a maintenance building. In early 1968, Dr. Goggin broke ground for these facilities (Figure 7-7). A marketing and administrative office building came next. A novel "open office" concept, involving movable partitions and no doors, was adopted. Construction of this building began late in Goggin's presidency.

Figure 7-7. Groundbreaking for the new corporate center, 1968: (*left to right*) Howard Fenn, Bill Goggin, Shailer Bass, Bill Collings, and Mel Hunter.

Seneffe, Belgium, Plant

As pointed out in Chapter 6, following the relocation of Dow Corning's European headquarters to Brussels, Belgium, there was a pressing need to choose a well-located site for a finishing, warehousing, and distribution facility to service European markets. An open country site had been selected at Seneffe, Belgium, a 45-minute drive south of Brussels. Denny Ziess was the engineer in charge of plant construction, which began immediately after the purchase of the land. The new plant, managed by Clayt Davidson, was dedicated in September 1970.

The first structure was designed to house product finishing for fluids, resins, sealants, and rubbers. Four product laboratories were built to handle technical service and development. A warehouse and site administration offices were included at the site. While the cost of manufacturing in Europe was greater than in the United States (because we couldn't benefit from economies of scale), this was offset by the gains to be realized from being close to the market we were serving.

Figure 7-8. Dedication, Seneffe, Belgium, September 1970: Prince Albert of Liege (*left*) welcomes Bill Goggin, Dusty Rhodes, Howard Fenn, and F. Delmotte, minister, secretary of state for regional development, to Belvedere Palace.

In addition to the Dow Corning executives present at the Seneffe site dedication (Figure 7-8), many Belgian dignitaries attended. Prince Albert of Liege was present, along with E. Vaes, governor of Hainut Province; F. Delmotte, minister, secretary of state for regional development; E. LeBurton, minister of economic affairs; and E. Stievenart, president of IDEA.

Around this time, containerized shipping became available and gave an additional boost to the international side of the business. Now it became possible to load a 40,000-pound container of product in drums and boxes at a domestic plant, seal it, ship it by rail, then send it by ship overseas, and then truck it to Seneffe. Pete Larsen managed these shipping operations from Midland, with the help of Ron Varerewyck and Robert Coppens in Brussels.

More Reorganization

Area Operating Board

Improvement of Dow Corning's short- and long-range planning and budgeting process required accurate information and projections from the various geographical areas of the world. To solicit this information, in the fall of 1971 Bill Goggin instituted Area Operating Board (AOB) meetings. These semiannual, 3-day meetings were attended by key personnel from all the geographic areas around the world. The meetings were integrated into Dow Corning's annual planning and budgeting program. Reports of the latest developments were presented from the various areas throughout the world, and from business and technical departments throughout the company. These meetings contributed to improved communications and better coordination of worldwide efforts within Dow Corning.

Many people who attended the meetings made the trip to Midland in the new corporate jet that was purchased during Dr. Goggin's term as president. Dow Corning's first aircraft had been a two-engine propeller plane. The new jet allowed for rapid transport of key personnel to virtually any part of the United States, and was especially useful for visits to plants in outlying areas.

Corporate Business Board

Around the same time that he established the Area Operating Board, Bill Goggin announced the formation of the Corporate Business Board, to be headed by Goggin and including Howard Fenn, Bob Springmier, Mel Hunter, Jack Ludington, Ray Maneri, Bill Pedersen, Dusty Rhodes, Durelle Thomson, and Don Watters.

The board was responsible for decision making on broad corporate issues that transcended two or more businesses, areas, or functions. Each domestic business manager reported monthly to the board; European and inter-American area managers reported quarterly, and Asian and Australian area managers reported semiannually.

Evaluation System

Toward the end of Bill Goggin's term as president, a comprehensive management evaluation system was installed by Durelle Thomson, head of industrial relations. Under this system, outstanding employees were recognized and moved more rapidly up the ranks of the corporation. As the company grew, such a system was needed in order to better manage Dow Corning's most valuable resource—its talented employees. The program is still retained in its basic form today.

Organizational change, under the best of circumstances, is difficult to accomplish. When Dr. William Goggin took over the presidency of Dow Corning, his charge was to completely restructure an entrenched organization, and to accomplish the restructuring without sacrificing the growth trend and leadership position that Dow Corning had enjoyed for more than 2 decades.

He succeeded. Sales during Goggin's 5-year term as president nearly doubled, rising from roughly $102 million in 1967 to almost $189 million in 1972, a 13 percent compounded growth over the 5-year period. The record of profitability was equally impressive: by 1972, with sales still less than those of the lowest-ranking *Fortune* 500 company, Dow Corning's net income had risen to match the 261st company on the list.[4] The fact that this outstanding performance was recorded in the midst of a companywide, worldwide reorganization effort made it all the more impressive.

In April 1971, Bill Goggin was made chairman and chief executive officer of Dow Corning, when Dr. Bass retired. Goggin continued as chairman until his retirement in 1976.

By the time Bill Goggin relinquished the role of president in June 1972, he could look back on a string of accomplishments in a relatively short period. Dow Corning had regained control over its international operations. A common economic language had been established. With the issuance of Eurobonds, the company was paving the way to financial independence from its parents. Finally, work had begun on a corporate center that would carry the company 30 years into the future.

Most importantly, the multidimensional organization was in place and beginning to function effectively. In the years ahead, the company would continue to grow and thrive under this new structure. So effective is the concept of the multidimensional organization that the fundamental MDO structure introduced by Dr. Goggin in the late 1960s remains in place within Dow Corning today.

On December 15, 1988, Dr. William C. Goggin, Dow Corning's fourth president, passed away.

---

[4]Dow Corning, a privately held company, was not eligible for the list.

8

The Ludington Years: Self-Sufficiency, Consolidation, Growth

To catch Dame Fortune's golden smile,
Assiduous wait upon her;
And gather gear by ev'ry wile
That's justified by honor:
Not for to hide it in a hedge,
Nor for a train-attendant;
But for the glorious privilege
Of being independent.

ROBERT BURNS
"Epistle to a Young Friend"

When Bill Goggin was elected chairman of the board and chief executive officer on June 13, 1972, John S. Ludington was named president and chief operating officer. Jack Ludington was the fifth president of the joint venture, and the first to earn his position by rising through the ranks of Dow Corning.

By the time he was named president, Jack Ludington's career with Dow Corning had spanned 2 decades. He arrived at the company in 1951, after graduating from Albion College with a degree in economics. Ludington began in construction engineering but was soon interrupted by Uncle Sam. After 2 years in the Army, he returned to Dow Corning.

John S. Ludington.

Over the next decade, Ludington worked his way up through the ranks of the corporation, moving from analyst in the Marketing Research Department through a series of jobs in the Industrial Relations Department that culminated in his being named director of the department in 1963. In 1969, under the leadership of Bill Goggin, he was named general manager of the Basic Businesses. In 1971, he became a vice president.

Ludington was unique among the presidents of Dow Corning, not just because he was the first to rise through the ranks, but also because he was the only chief executive whose primary background was nontechnical. His early years in personnel strongly influenced him in his new role. During those years he developed many of the personnel and development systems which are still in use today. Under Ludington's direction, formal salary and wage systems were established. A system of "management by objectives" was introduced. Salary increases were tied to productivity, and "pay for performance" became the rule. Many personnel functions were computerized and standardized at a very early time in the company's history, thanks to Jack Ludington. He helped establish the idea that executives being groomed for top positions should be sent to Harvard, MIT, and Stanford for further executive development. He instituted the notion of developing from within early on, and this has paid big dividends in increased morale and productivity, because the right people were placed in the right jobs.

In Jack Ludington's view, Dow Corning's greatest strength was its people. If there was a single talent that stood out among the many that Ludington brought to the presidency of Dow Corning, it was his ability to recognize and utilize the talents and strengths of employees.

Jack Ludington also worked for the betterment of the community. Over the years, he was involved in a variety of local, state, and national community and business organizations. Director of the American Industrial Health Council, member of the President's Commission on Executive Exchange, member of the board of the Chemical Manufacturers Association, trustee of the Midland Community Center, director of Junior Achievement—these are just a few of the positions through which Ludington made an impact outside the halls of Dow Corning Corporation.

Like Shailer Bass, Ludington had an intense interest in education and did much work over the years to better the schools, including serving as chairman of the board of trustees of his alma mater, Albion College. Ludington has received numerous honorary doctorate degrees from universities and colleges, including Albion College.

Jack Ludington always had his eye on the future. He was continually striving to ensure that Dow Corning remained on the leading edge of change and innovation. Early in his administration, he instituted a system whereby senior executives could act in a consulting capacity until retirement, giving the up-and-comers in the company motivation to achieve and the opportunity to hold positions of major responsibility at an early age. I was one of the first managers to assume a consulting role. Jack felt that this system would provide Dow Corning with a steady stream of new ideas needed to assure continuing growth.

Perhaps the best way to get a real sense of Jack Ludington's style was to observe him at company functions. Coat off, sleeves rolled up, he might be deep in discussion with the engineering staff, or debating the merits of a change with the plant operators, or lending an ear to a group of secretaries, or listening to a technical explanation by an eager young engineer, or singing along with the piano player. Jack liked to mingle with employees of every level and function. He never tired of hearing the ideas and concerns of the people of Dow Corning.

Corporate Self-Sufficiency

An important area of interest to Jack Ludington as president was making Dow Corning more self-sufficient. While steps had been taken in this direction, more independence was needed, particularly in the area of finance.

The first challenge faced in the financial arena was thrust upon the company by outside events. Shortly after Ludington took over as president, the energy crisis, and with it a wave of high inflation, rocked the country and drastically increased Dow Corning's costs.

The cost of raw materials had never increased dramatically. In 1973, almost overnight, many of those costs doubled or even tripled. Silicon, which represented a major portion of raw material costs, went from 20 cents to 60 cents a pound; methyl chloride, another significant contributor to manufacturing costs, tripled. By 1974, with materials costs continuing to soar and profitability beginning to slip, it became obvious that Dow Corning would have to start raising its prices.

An impending price increase might not seem like a major stumbling block, but it came as a shock to a company in which the prevailing mentality had been never to increase prices. After the war ended in 1945, silicone fluids were selling at $20 a pound. Over the next 20-year period they had gradually declined to somewhere around $2 a pound. Each year, prices had been lowered. Now Jack Ludington had to change the company's mentality to accept price increases as inevitable. In 1974, for the first time in the history of the company, prices were raised.

While this had an effect on the short-term competitive position of the company, it simply had to be done in order for Dow Corning to be competitive in the long run. The move to raise prices strengthened the company's financial position and signaled Jack Ludington's intention to make the company more financially independent.

Dow Corning had achieved a fair measure of self-sufficiency by the time Ludington became president. As far back as the late 1940s, the company had set out to recruit its own personnel rather than continue to rely on transfers from Dow or Corning. Once the first Dow Corning plant was built, research and manufacturing functions were handled independently of the parents. While Dow Chemical continued to supply raw materials in the early years, it was not long before Dow Corning began producing many of its own basic chemicals. In the international arena, Dow Corning received assistance from its parents as it established a presence in each new country. But after a short time, it assumed an independent stance.

By the end of the 1960s, only one major hurdle was left before Dow Corning could truly consider itself an independent, self-supporting company. It had to become self-sufficient in the area of finance. With the acquisition of Midsil and the continued rapid growth of the business around the world, it was becoming more evident that the time was ripe for Dow Corning to finance its own growth.

Throughout its history, each time Dow Corning needed an infusion of capital, it had relied on its parents to guarantee its debt. The Eurobond financing of the Barry, Wales, expansion marked a significant move toward financial independence, but the bonds still carried the guarantees of the parent companies. It was now time for Dow Corning to step out on its own.

After 2 years of many discussions among the board of directors, and many meetings of Dow Corning management, in 1975, $60 million in domestic bonds was issued.

There was a competitive risk in proceeding with the bond issue. For the first time in its history, Dow Corning had to make public its financial status. Whereas before, competitors might make educated guesses about the size and strength of the joint venture, now such information was freely available. Other major competitors—General Electric and Union Carbide in the United States; Wacker Chemie, Rhone Polenc, and Bayer in Europe; Shin-Etsu Chemicals in Japan—could combine their silicone operations within their larger organizations. Dow Corning, the only company with principal activities in organosilicon compounds, was the only producer which now disclosed its specific position.

The risk of disclosure was well worth taking. After the 1974 bond issue, Dow Corning continued to grow and prosper. So successful was the move to financial independence that since 1975, Dow Corning has been able to access the debt markets on the basis of its own financial strength.

Recognizing the need to place more emphasis on financial matters from now on, in early 1976 Jack Ludington brought Larry Reed back from Europe, where he had been managing finance for the European area, to become the company's first chief financial officer.

Growth and Development

With the issue of financial independence successfully resolved, Dow Corning began expanding its customer base at home and abroad under Jack Ludington's leadership.

Dow Corning's domestic business continued to grow, and international markets flourished through acquisitions, joint ventures, and the expansion of sales efforts around the globe. This was the most energetic and expansive search for opportunities for Dow Corning since the end of World War II. Ludington's own history during Dow Corning's formative years gave him a broad perspective. He viewed Dow Corning's world of the 1950s and a good share of the 1960s as a country-by-country marketplace. England, Germany, France, Canada, Mexico, Japan—all were separate market opportunities. The decade of the 1960s was the first in which Dow Corning made major strides in establishing a permanent presence outside the United States.

As Dow Corning entered the 1960s, total sales were approaching $40 million. In the United States, two major facilities would come on stream, both in Kentucky: Elizabethtown in 1964 and Carrollton in 1967. There was much activity outside the United States as well:

1960	Dow Corning A.G. in Switzerland formed
1961	Dow Corning de Mexico formed
1962	Dow Corning do Brasil Ltda. formed
	Joint venture formed with Fuji Polymer in Japan
1964	Armet Industries, Guelph, Ontario, purchased
	Dow Corning de Argentina S.A. formed
	Dow Corning Australia formed
1965	Dow Corning GMBH in Germany formed
	Dow Corning Ltd. incorporated in the United Kingdom
1966	Dow Corning France S.A. formed
	Toray Silicone and Shin-Etsu Handotai joint ventures established in Japan
1967	Molykote purchased, Munich
	DC Silicones Inter-America Ltd. formed
1969	Dow Corning S.A. in Belgium formed

The world was changing and coming together. Dow Corning's interests were spreading. Dow Corning had moved forward in its international expansion from a company that distributed products in several countries to a company that had direct representation—and in many cases an equity position—in several major countries. At the same time, individual countries with mutual economic interests were beginning to regionalize their interests. In Europe, the 1960s saw the beginning of the European Economic Community.

Japan and countries in southeast Asia were forming the roots of the Pacific basin—which was to become a dynamic region of the world during the Ludington years.

In the United States, a number of movements that would change the way we think, live, and work had taken hold and had been translated into governmental legislation. There was environmentalism and passage of clean air and clean water legislation and civil rights legislation. Change seemed fast-paced.

Amory Houghton, Sr.

By the time Jack Ludington left his leadership position in the Industrial Relations Department to become general manager of the Basic Businesses in 1969, Dow Corning's multidimensional organization was starting to take shape under Bill Goggin's direction. There were 10 global businesses, and geographic areas also were in the formative stages. There was a concerted effort to build professionalism in our functions and to install a common global "language" called "economic evaluation."

Corporate Center

In 1966, with the blessing of the board of directors, the architectural firm of Fletcher Thompson developed a 30-year plan for a corporate center site. The site was 5 miles east of the original Midland site. It was surrounded by farmland and bordered by two major highways. The bioscience laboratories, the first facilities completed, were occupied in 1969. More new buildings were constructed. By the fall of 1974, 500 employees occupied DC-2, the first administrative building on the site.

The new administrative building was designed according to the open-office concept. Cloth-covered partitions, 5 to 6 feet high, took the place of standard offices and allowed easy reconfiguration of space. No one had a closed, private office in DC-2, including the chairman of the board. Living plants and high ceilings in the office area helped to generate feelings of warmth, openness, and privacy.

The board of directors decided to dedicate the Dow Corning administrative offices at the corporate center to Amory Houghton. He had indicated his desire, early in 1975, to resign from the board because, in his words, he was "approaching middle age"—at 76. Ambassador Houghton (he had been appointed ambassador to France under President Eisenhower) was the last member of the original board of directors of Dow Corning.

The administrative building was dedicated on September 5, 1975. At the dedication ceremony, Carl Gerstacker, chairman of The Dow Chemical Company board, talked about the significant role Ambassador Houghton had played in helping to ensure the success of Dow Corning. "Over the 32 years, you provided the leadership and the spirit of cooperation that has been the cornerstone of Dow Corning's success," Gerstacker said. "Others could do the research, the technical work, the marketing, the production, the finance, but without this vital ingredient that you provided, it wouldn't have worked."

A few short years after the dedication, Dow Corning mourned the passing of one of its most influential pioneer leaders. In February 1981, Amory Houghton died.

Building continued at the corporate center throughout Jack Ludington's presidency. The facilities begun in 1974 for the Technical Service and Development group were completed and occupied in 1977. A second administration building, DC-1, was ready for use in July 1982. The open-office concept was continued in this new building, as it was in all Dow Corning sites worldwide.

The 1970s

Several factors came together in the 1970s to make it perhaps the most fascinating decade in Dow Corning's short history. Annual sales by 1970 were $139 million—a $100 million surge in just 10 years. The early efforts to position Dow Corning in major growth countries were beginning to pay off. A flexible global organization allowed Dow Corning to grow up with and take advantage of the developing regions of the world. Importantly, technology and the information age were coming together to make Dow Corning's world smaller in terms of transportation, information generation, and communications.

In 1971, the year before Jack Ludington became president, Dow Corning achieved 100 percent ownership of Midland Silicones. The Seneffe finishing plant came on stream in Belgium. In 1973, Dow Corning's holding in Fuji Polymer in Japan increased to 100 percent. In 1974, the headquarters moved from the Midland plant site to the new Dow Corning Center. Businesses consolidated from 10 to 6. In 1978, ownership in Toray Silicone increased to 65 percent, and in Brazil, the Campinas plant became operational.

Events of the 1970s continued to reflect the dynamics of change and turbulence. Worldwide terrorism became almost an everyday occurrence. Consumerism in the United States came into its own. Zero population growth was a hot topic, and U.S. inflation rates crept into double digits by the end of the decade. The country was proving that it really could conserve energy when the chips were down, and Japan was starting to teach the world the meaning of the word "quality."

The 1980s: Big Opportunities, Rapid Change

As Dow Corning entered the 1980s, the corporation had reached a point from which it could start to view the world as one big marketplace, and it was well positioned to do so. By 1980, more than half our total business came from geographic regions outside the United States, and worldwide sales were pushing $700 million. An increasing number of customers were, like Dow Corning, multinational organizations that preferred working with suppliers who understood how to meet customer needs on a worldwide scale.

In 1981, Dow Corning formed its first commercial units, reorganized the businesses, and combined Latin America and Canada into the inter-America area. Japan became a single-country area like the United States. Also in 1981, Toray Silicone's Fukui plant was opened, and the major methyl expansion went on stream at Barry, Wales. The year 1982 was one of start-ups: the SECO power plant at the Midland site, the Taiwan finishing plant, and the Fukui rubber plant.

In 1983, Dow Corning acquired Perennator Werk in Wiesbaden, West Germany; formed Lucky-DC Silicones in Korea; began the Health Care Center at Valbonne, France; and opened Dow Corning KK's Yamakita site in Japan. In 1984, a joint venture was formed between Dow Corning, Shin-Etsu Handotai, and Mitsubishi metals; the new company was Hemlock Semiconductor Corporation.

Clearly, it was Jack Ludington's intent to develop and build facilities where they were strategically appropriate. However, when it made better sense to acquire an established company, Dow Corning had the flexibility to pursue growth that way instead. From country by country in the 1950s and 1960s, to regionalization in the 1970s, Dow Corning came into a world marketplace quickly in the 1980s.

By this time the future clearly was predicated on accelerated change that demanded a higher level of quality and service for customers and from suppliers than the company had ever known. As Dow Corning moved into the future, the world around it continued its unabated habit of change. The Koreans and Taiwanese began to challenge the powerful economic success of Japan. Instantaneous world communications and the explosion of the information age continued to accelerate.

A major challenge emerging for Dow Corning as the company approached the mid-1980s was to position itself to take complete advantage of the world marketplace. The challenge was to use the resources and organization put in place during the 1970s and early 1980s to strengthen Dow Corning's ability as a global organization.

If a customer had operations in Amsterdam, Chicago, São Paulo, Sydney, or Osaka, the company had to be able to supply the customer's particular needs, even if the requirements differed from location to location. Clearly by the mid-1980s, Dow Corning had the breadth of technology and manufacturing operations literally to span the globe. The hardware was fundamentally in place.

Cultural Sensitivity

A value Jack Ludington added to this environment was establishing the need for employees to develop a cultural sensitivity to each other and to customers. Without this, the company could not take full advantage of the technical and physical capabilities put in place over the previous 15 years.

What did Jack Ludington mean by "cultural sensitivity"? Language was part of it. Doing business in Germany, with German customers, meant speaking the local language. The same would apply in France, Italy, Brazil, Japan, or any other country.

But to Ludington, cultural sensitivity also meant a growing responsibility to know how to find the best answers to customer needs. He felt it should not seem unusual that a Dow Corning laboratory chemist in Europe, Tokyo, or Midland might have the right answer to a customer need in Canada, Italy, Brazil, or Taiwan.

To take full advantage of the world marketplace, Dow Corning had to recognize English as the universal language of internal operations. Employees needed to be able to discuss, conceptualize, and talk with one another and do it in one language. In a competitive climate, the company couldn't afford to have people working as if they were isolated islands. Customers would not allow it.

There were Japanese companies moving to the United States and Europe, European companies moving to the United States and the Pacific basin, and American firms continuing their moves into the world arena. There continued to be economic, political, and social differences from country to country, but Dow Corning customers lived in a world marketplace and needed to be served wherever they were located.

So Ludington's message was simple: "work" this small world to the customer's advantage. At the same time, be proud of your own citizenship and the particular interests of your native country.

As Dow Corning's chairman and chief executive officer, Jack Ludington built upon the company's traditional strengths and added to them the strength of a global organization. He was absolutely convinced that among the world's silicone producers, Dow Corning had the most effective, integrated global network—on all fronts.

Ludington was convinced that Dow Corning's accelerated success depended on recognition for the company's dominant strength—technology. That is, success would find its broadest commercial application only to the extent that the company was able to understand, appreciate, and act on the needs of its customers, whose product requirements transcended by far Dow Corning's knowledge and capabilities.

Silicone Research

Behind Dow Corning's silicone technology and the development of new products and applications were the continuing efforts of Dow Corning researchers. For most of this period, Les Tyler was director of research. He was named to the position in January 1973, when Mel Hunter moved on to become management consultant. In 1976, Tyler was chosen to head the new Research, Development, and Engineering Services (RDES) function, and Don Weyenberg became head of research, under Tyler.

By the time he stepped down as director of research, Mel Hunter had developed a distinguished record that dated back to 1947, when he first assumed the role of research director from Dr. Bass. During the 37 years he led the research effort for Dow Corning, Dr. Hunter had overseen the development of 1876 patents in the United States, and an even larger number abroad.

In the same year that Dr. Tyler became director of research, the OPEC oil embargo drove up crude oil prices and devastated the world's economy. One of Tyler's first actions in his new role was to initiate two projects to find ways of reducing the energy costs of producing silicones. One project focused on studying less expensive methods of producing silicon for the direct process; the other looked at ways to make the direct process more efficient. While these projects were proceeding, Les Tyler continued to oversee the efforts of the talented group of researchers under his direction.

C Resin

One promising research development came from Harold Clark, in the form of a resin coating for plastics, dubbed "C resin" in recognition of his work in developing the product. The development of C resin was typical of many research discoveries; it was found in the course of searching for something else.

Clark had been asked to look for uses for the large amount of methyltrichlorosilane that was regularly produced as a by-product of the direct process. Fillers had been hydrophobed with trimethylchlorosilane for some time, as a way of eliminating the problem of crepe hardening. Clark reasoned it would be much cheaper to hydrophobe silica fillers with the methyltrichlorosilane, because of its by-product nature, and he succeeded in doing so.

Clark then pursued development of a new silica filler. He knew that silica sols were much cheaper sources of silica filler than were fume silicas from the burning of silicon compounds. He thought he could make a suitable silica sol from the methyltrichlorosilane, but the compound proved to hydrolyze too rapidly for that use. Clark then experimented with a methoxyl derivative of the compound, $CH_3Si(OCH_3)_3$.

He added the methoxyl derivative to a number of commercial sols, and they immediately gelled. But when he made the same addition to acid sols, they remained translucent and did not gel. At this point, Clark realized he might be on the way to developing a new resin. However, on trying to coat a microscope slide with the new material he'd just developed, he found that the mixture would not wet the glass.

Clark set the bottle aside, to observe whether or not it would gel over time. On looking at the material several days later, he found that it would now coat the microscope slide. The coating was transparent, and after a slight bake, it became quite hard, as might be expected of a material so high in silica content. Abrasion tests with a pencil eraser proved that the coating was far more abrasion-resistant than a commercial acrylic plastic sheet found in the laboratory.

The TS&D laboratories had been working with Swedlow, a California company that manufactured plastic sheets used as windows in school buses. The labs hoped to improve on a commercial coating developed by duPont, which Swedlow had been using to a limited extent. Samples of plastic sheets coated with the new C resin were sent to Swedlow, and the company's response was immediate and enthusiastic. The resin-coated surface was much harder than anything seen before.

After Clark developed a method to stabilize the solution and extend its shelf life, Swedlow licensed the technology from Dow Corning and ultimately made its own coating materials. The resin was further refined, and many other applications, including plastic eyeglass lenses, were explored and developed. Under the direction of Bob Vidal, Gary Anderson, Bob McKellar, and Bill Householder, the relationship with

Swedlow grew into a partnership and ultimately a joint venture to expand the commercial uses for this technology.

Silicone-Organic Block Copolymers

In the mid-1960s, monodisperse polydimethylsiloxanes had been made from dimethyl cyclic trimer in Dr. Chi-Long Lee's laboratory, using a weak base catalyst that eliminated the bond-rearranging reaction during the ring-opening polymerization. This technique, coupled with the "living polymer" technique, led to the development during the 1970s of a silicone-organic block copolymer. Polystyrene-polydimethylsiloxane multiblock copolymers were made in Dr. John Saam's laboratory by ring-opening polymerization of dimethyl cyclic trimer with "living" dilithiostyrene. Block copolymers with characteristics ranging from thermoplastic elastomers to polystyrenelike thermoplastics were thus obtained. Molecular parameters regulating physical and mechanical properties were controlled to provide a unique family of thermoplastic material.

Another type of thermoplastic elastomer, polyurethane-polydimethylsiloxane multiblock copolymer, was made in Dr. Gerry Gornowicz's laboratory, using the polycondensation polymerization method. By regulating the copolymer structure, researchers developed copolymers ranging from soft gels to tough elastomeric materials for coating and controlled-release drug applications.

"Did you hear someone say 'Eureka'?"

Reprinted courtesy OMNI Magazine © 1979.

Polyethyleneoxide-polydimethylsiloxane graft copolymers also were produced in Chi-Long Lee's laboratories. Because of the hydrophilic nature of these copolymers, their use in the controlled release of drugs and bioactive compounds has been explored.

Emulsion Polymerization
(Silicone-Based Water Emulsions)

Silicone emulsion polymers have been under investigation at Dow Corning since the 1960s. Polymerization cyclics in aqueous alkaline media in the presence of cationic surfactants were developed by Frank Hyde and Jack Wehrly. Polymerization in aqueous acidic media in the presence of anionic surfactants were produced by Don Findlay and Don Weyenberg. Both led to elastomeric materials, but only the system stabilized with anionic surfactants could be reinforced with colloidal silicas to give useful mechanical properties.

In the late 1970s, D. Huebner and John Saam showed that emulsion polymers formed via the latter route are, paradoxically, formed by a reversible silane condensation polymerization that occurs in aqueous media. Normally this type of polymerization occurs only when water is vigorously removed as the process proceeds.

The silicon emulsion polymers made this way could be readily formulated in emulsion with colloidal silica, catalysts, extending fillers, thickeners, and other materials to give an interesting family of water-based elastomeric films and caulks. John Saam, Christine Schmidt, and Dick Johnson showed that useful properties developed simply upon evaporation of the water. It was also shown by John Saam, Dan Graiver, and Madhu Baile that the polymer particles in the latex were cross-linked and that these bonded together, or with a silica, upon evaporation of the water. An extensive commercialization program was subsequently developed by Schuyler Smith, Christine Schmidt, David Mills, Nick Shephard, and C. Schoenherrout out of the findings of this research.

Professional Research Ladder

In addition to his direct contributions to the research effort, Les Tyler made an important contribution to the research staff during his tenure as director of the department, by developing a professional research ladder similar to typical management ladders. The ladder was constructed so that chemists joining the research department would start at the lowest rung. They could progress up the ladder based on the merits of their research; with each new title came a higher salary bracket.

This was a significant change for the department. Before this, the only way a researcher could advance in salary beyond a certain point was by assuming a management position. Until Dr. Tyler created the new professional research ladder, top researchers often moved into management positions, and this was sometimes detrimental to the research effort. The new system corrected this problem. By 1979, under the new system, some of the highest-paid employees in the department were researchers.

In 1980, with an impressive list of accomplishments behind him, Les Tyler moved on to the position of management consultant. At that time Don Weyenberg became vice president of RDES.

Expansion of Worldwide Research Efforts

Before 1980, most of Dow Corning's basic research was conducted in the United States, although some research was being done outside the country, at Alpha Molykote in Germany, at Barry, Wales, and at Toray Silicone in Japan. One of Jack Ludington's goals was to support organosilicon research efforts at appropriate locations around the world. To that end, a small research group was established in 1980 within Toray Silicone, and in 1983, a Materials Development group was organized to expand the research effort at the Barry, Wales, site.

Ludington and Don Weyenberg also supported the desire to have closer ties to university research. The research groups' contacts with foreign universities were enhanced during the early 1980s. For more than 20 years, Dow Corning had supported graduate work in silicone research at the University of Sussex in the United Kingdom. The program of support was similar to the Pennsylvania State University program in the United States. In the early 1980s, Dow Corning reinforced its commitment to the research effort in England by establishing a research partnership within the School of Molecular Sciences at the University of Sussex.

Dr. Norman Lloyd, European vice president and director of European RDES, helped to establish the partnership, with the aid of Dr. Chris Pearce. Dr. James White of the Barry staff was group leader.

University researchers joined the Dow Corning team in exploring entirely new vistas of silicone chemistry. Over the next few years, the Sussex researchers made many contributions to the understanding of silicones. Included in the group were two researchers who had previ-

ously received Dow Corning's annual Kipping Award, Professors
Michael Lappert and Colin Eaborn.

Technical Achievement Awards

In 1983, Don Weyenberg established an annual award for technical
achievement, to recognize and encourage technical excellence within
the research groups at Dow Corning. The list of recipients of the first
awards bestowed, in 1984, illustrates the breadth and depth of the work
being carried out in the Dow Corning laboratories of the 1980s. In the
United States, Alan Freiberg, Shedric 0. Glover, and David W. Mills
won a team award for improved sealant technology. Gerald A.
Gornowicz won an award for work on new block copolymers; Peter Y.
Lo, for his work on the fundamental understanding of platinum catalysts; Gloria Janik, for development of new silicone gels; the team of
Gale H. Pretzer and Herschel H. Reese, for developing a new manufacturing process; Edward T. Rasmussen, for development of improved
silane process technology; Dr. Chi-Long Lee, for technical leadership;
and David Stickles, for new release technology.

The work of three European researchers was also acknowledged: Dr.
George Sawicki won an award for developing improved defoamers; Dr.
James W. White received honors for new release coatings technology;
and Brian R. Trego was acknowledged for his development of a new
sealant technology.

In Japan, Katsutoshi Mine received an award for his commercialization of new resins. Koichi Aizawa won honors for developing new
antifoam technology.

Health and Safety

From the earliest days, health and safety issues were of paramount importance within Dow Corning. Long before environmental issues came
to the forefront of American consciousness, Shailer Bass, working with
the toxicology laboratories at Dow Chemical, studied the health effects
of silicone fluids, resins, and compounds.

Mike Stinton had been hired early on as director of safety and security, a post he held throughout Jack Ludington's term and beyond.
Stinton developed a worldwide reputation in the field. He wrote proposals and served on manufacturing boards as a consultant on health

and safety matters over the years. His long and broad experience was instrumental to Dow Corning's efforts in this area.

This focus on issues of health and safety had been impressed upon Jack Ludington at a very early age. Before he started his formal career at Dow Corning, Ludington took a summer job with the company during high school. His job was to haul solvents up and down the rows of laboratories. Occasionally he had to empty 40-gallon drums from the solvent shop.

Jim McHard, who managed the Analytical Laboratory, watched this high schooler pour solvents out of the spout, breathing in the fumes. He took the young Jack Ludington aside for 2 hours and put him through a training program on the safe handling of chemicals. This episode made a lasting impression on the future president of the company. During the 12 years of Jack Ludington's presidency, great strides were made in the attention paid to health and safety throughout Dow Corning's operations.

Ecology Committee

One such effort was the formation of an ecology committee by Dr. Hunter in the early 1970s. The committee consisted of Dr. Art Barry and Dr. Ken Johannson in research; Don Bublitz, corporate manager of waste control; Zeke Dennett in manufacturing; Ken Olson, a toxicologist hired from Dow Chemical; Joe Radzius, an attorney in the Legal Department who was familiar with OSHA standards and other health and safety regulations; and Dr. A. Lee Smith in the Analytical Department. The purpose of the committee was to study the potential hazardous effects of materials Dow Corning was shipping by truck or rail, in the event of a leak or spill. Over the years, the committee made a number of recommendations about safe and effective handling of potentially hazardous materials being transported over road and rail.

Ecological studies were performed during this time. Environmental studies were made, in conjunction with Dow Chemical, of the Tittabawassee River, which flowed by the Midland, Michigan, plant. These were performed to ensure that no harmful wastes were in the waters. Analytical techniques were developed to find even trace amounts of silicones in the river.

Similar studies were made in some states where the possibility existed that rivers were receiving runoff containing antitranspirants, used on Douglas fir seedlings to retain water and produce higher yields. Antimicrobial treatments of seeds also were tested as a means of preventing fungus and rot attack.

Also, research by the group showed that DOW CORNING 200® silicone fluid was harmless to the environment. Clays catalyze the degradation of DOW CORNING 200® silicone fluid into volatile cyclics and water-soluble silanols as a first step. The fluid degrades to carbon dioxide and water, leaving a residue of silica.

Health and Safety Board

The Ecology Committee was tightly focused on environmental issues. In 1974, Jack Ludington formed the Health and Safety Board within the company to address and monitor broader issues of health and safety on a continuing basis.

The board was the brainchild of Bill Goggin. During his last years as chairman of the board, Goggin expressed to Ludington his concern that health and safety issues were not receiving the level of attention they deserved. Such issues were handled on an ad hoc basis as specific problems or concerns arose. Goggin wanted to form an ongoing committee to address these issues on a more regular basis.

The group was to include a medical director, a safety director, and leaders in toxicology and epidemiology. The group would meet once a month to make sure that the company remained on top of all issues related to health and safety around the world. It would focus on environmental concerns, addressing these concerns not just from Dow Corning's viewpoint, but from the viewpoints of the customer and the community as well.

To highlight its importance, Goggin indicated that he would act as chairman of the committee until he retired as chairman of the board, at which time Ludington was to take over the leadership role.

The Health and Safety Board was formed in 1974 according to Goggin's plan, and continues its work to this day. During the mid-1970s, the group, particularly Chuck Lentz, worked closely with federal agencies on issues of environmental regulation. As a result, Dow Corning led the way in developing model procedures for addressing environmental issues, some of which were later adopted by the Environmental Protection Agency (EPA). When the Toxic Substance Control Act was passed in 1976, Dow Corning already was complying with its requirements.

An adjunct to the Health and Safety Board was the Health and Environmental Science unit, under the direction of Charles Lentz. The group was formed to study questions and issues developed by the Health and Safety Board.

Yet another effort at increasing safety came in 1977, when the Hazardous Materials Shipping Team was formed. Dick Votaw from Transportation was named chairman. The team was rounded out by representatives from Transportation, Safety and Security, Quality Management, Manufacturing, and Engineering. Among other things, the team studied transportation equipment and made recommendations about the purchase of new equipment—tank trucks, rail hopper cars, rail tank cars, and intermodal equipment—for the safe transportation of silicones and other materials around the country.

Code of Business Conduct

The mid-1970s was a time when congressional reaction to numerous scandals, including Watergate, was being anticipated by the business community. This was also a time when an increasingly large share of Dow Corning's business was coming from outside the United States.

In a letter to employees in May 1976, Jack Ludington said:

> The business community has lost a share of public confidence. I believe business must take overt action to re-establish that lost confidence. I further believe that business freedom can be sustained only to the extent that businesses act responsibly in every sense of the word—morally, ethically and legally.

Thus was born Dow Corning's commitment to a formal business ethics process that has grown and become a staple of the company's culture.

In June 1976, Ludington sent a memo to Dow Corning management in which he said:

> I have formed a special four-person task force comprised of Steve Guittard, Legal, Jerry Griffin, Finance, John Swanson, Communications, and Tom Thomson, Area Management, to give this subject top level attention. They will work with me and all of you, to develop a Corporate Code of Conduct intended to:
>
> • Assure that Dow Corning people are fully informed as to the corporation's view concerning ethical business practices and our responsibility to the public;
> • Reflect our thinking as to what our long-term worldwide policies are and should be;
> • Set high standards for the organization to aim at.

Jack also outlined what he called "area responsibility audits" which would provide "two-way communication relating to the philosophy and practice of how we operate around the world." Committing himself to participate in selective audits, Jack also said in a June 30, 1976, memo something that has proved to be prophetically true for Dow Corning: "I believe the audit procedure can be more important than the written word in reinforcing a proper working environment."

The process established by Ludington in the mid-1970s endured. By the early 1980s, Dow Corning's continuous commitment to the maintenance of high ethical standards—with particular emphasis on the "person-to-person" approach—had become well known and respected throughout the U.S. business community.

The Business Conduct Committee continues to be a four-person committee, with John Swanson remaining on the committee as its secretary and permanent member. The other three members—generally executive managers—serve 2 or 3 years and then leave the committee at different intervals.

Dow Corning's commitment to business ethics was initiated by Jack Ludington as one of his first actions as CEO, and his initiative has positively reinforced Dow Corning's reputation for integrity ever since.

The Quality Initiative

During Jack Ludington's tenure as Dow Corning's president, he initiated a renewed commitment to "quality improvement." In keeping with Ludington's emphasis on service to a global marketplace and adaptation to customer needs, employees, wherever they were, were encouraged to think of quality as being "what the customer says it is."

In 1983, a major training effort was launched to familiarize employees with the quality-improvement process and the merits of natural work groups, quality-improvement teams, and strong emphasis on meeting customer requirements. Mel Nelson, then director of quality management, was quick to remind the uninitiated that "quality improvement" was indeed a process, and not just another program at Dow Corning.

Like other multinational manufacturing companies, Dow Corning was doing much to define and improve the quality of various processes, but it was clearly not enough. What still was missing, customers were telling us, was a true understanding of their needs.

The message was clear. If Dow Corning customers were facing

tougher and tougher competition and were themselves faced with an ever-increasing standard for quality performance, then Dow Corning must also change and improve. Sensitivity to customers' needs—whatever and wherever they might be—started becoming a way of life at Dow Corning.

In many respects the standard for quality performance was constantly changing and was often set by the Japanese. Nevertheless, Dow Corning's objective was truly to perform as a "world-class" company, becoming a partner to customers' success by continually improving product quality and service.

Specifically, this meant reducing product reject rates and increasing shipping performance to meet the customer request date, two issues the company—particularly in the U.S. area—was not accomplishing to the customers' satisfaction. This meant regular work with the plants to collect and analyze data on the improvements, information that must be circulated and displayed for every employee to see.

Through this process, when an employee or customer asked if Dow Corning was making progress on quality improvement, the answer always was available in the data, which were (and are) organized in statistical process control charts. These charts allow the company to determine if it is getting better, staying the same, or declining in its quality initiatives. More importantly, the charts show when to take action to ensure continuous improvement. Continuous improvement was the key when the program was started, and remains so today. The process is never-ending.

In the 1980s, more than ever before, Dow Corning renewed its commitment to partnering with customers. The relationship would be two-way, with Dow Corning understanding customers' businesses and customers understanding Dow Corning.

Taking a Bow

Awards and Honors

Over this period of time, Dow Corning received many accolades for accomplishments by Dow Corning individuals.

Each year, *Industrial Research* magazine presents 100 awards to the manufacturers of products it judges to be technically outstanding. In 1976, Dow Corning received an *IR* 100 Award for its X9-6310 Resin for optical-quality coating. In 1977, Dow Corning received two *IR* 100 Awards, one for the PCB replacement fluid, DOW CORNING® 561, and one for the Sylgard antimicrobial treatment. In 1979 Dow Corning received another *IR* 100 Award for its Highway Sealant 888. In 1982, the Silsoft contact lens was recognized, as was an internal mold release for reactive injection-molded urethane plastics.

Research Honors

During this time, some of Dow Corning's early researchers were honored for their efforts. In 1974, Dr. Hyde received the Thomas Midgely Award, named after an inventor who worked with Henry Ford. This award of the American Chemical Society was given to Dr. Hyde in acknowledgment of his contributions in the field of chemistry related to the automotive industry.

In 1972, *Modern Plastics* and the Society of Plastics Industry established a Plastics Hall of Fame to recognize those scientists who make significant contributions to the technology of plastics. In 1976, Dr. Goggin was inducted into the Plastics Hall of Fame (Figure 8-1) along with six other industry leaders, including the well-known Professor Herman Mark of the Brooklyn Polytechnic Institute. In 1979, Dr. Hyde also was

Figure 8-1. Dr. William C. Goggin, inducted into the Plastics Hall of Fame, 1976.

inducted into the Plastics Hall of Fame. It is to Dow Corning's credit that two of its employees are members of this prestigious group.

In the spring of 1976, I received the Charles Goodyear Award from the Rubber Division of the American Chemical Society at its annual meeting in Minneapolis (Figure 8-2). This was the first award to recognize the development of silicone rubber.

Each year, *Industrial Research* magazine names one researcher "Scientist of the Year" for outstanding achievements in some area of industrial science. In 1977 Dr. John Speier (Figure 8-3) was awarded this honor, at a ceremony held in the Museum of Science and Industry in Chicago, to acknowledge the worldwide impact of his work on the protective action of silazanes.

In 1978 the Gallery of Scientists was erected in DC-1 at the corporate center. In the gallery hang portraits of prominent scientists responsible for the research behind the products of Dow Corning (Figure 8-4). Seven portraits hung in the gallery at the time of its dedication. By the end of 1978, 14 scientists were so honored: Ogden Pierce, Gordon Brown, Gus Constan, Tor Orbeck, John Speier, Keith Polmanteer, John Saam, Cecil Frye, Joe Keil, Ed Plueddemann, Ken Johannson, Hal Clark, Rob Roy McGregor, and Frank Hyde. In 1980, A. Lee Smith, Chi-Long Lee, and Bob LeVier joined the group. John Dexter was added in 1981, and Michael Owen in 1983. Ron Baney, Sam Brady, and

Figure 8-2. Dr. Earl Warrick receiving the Goodyear Medal, 1976.

Figure 8-3. Dr. John Speier, Scientist of the Year, 1977.

Don McVannel were also included in the Gallery. More have been added since then.

Portraits of prominent researchers who moved on to management positions were hung in the separate Gallery of Research. Photographs of Mel Hunter, Art Barry, Les Tyler, Ron Baney, and Sam Brady are on display there, along with my own.

Figure 8-4. A section of Dow Corning's Gallery of Scientists.

Fortieth Anniversary:
A History of Achievement—
A Future of Success

On February 17, 1983, Dow Corning celebrated its fortieth anniversary. A slogan was adopted for the occasion: "A History of Achievement—A Future of Success." An employee band called the "Matrix Madmen" accompanied Jack Ludington (who was well known for his love of singing) as he led hundreds of employees in a chorus of "Happy Birthday." Birthday cakes were served to employees by top management. Lunch prices in the cafeteria were rolled back to 1943. Songs of the 1940s were piped through the sound system, to create the proper mood.

A few of the company's early pioneers, now retired, joined in the celebration: Bill Caldwell, who had been general manager of the Midland plant; Don Coultrip, purchasing manager; Howard Fenn, production manager; and two of the original researchers, Mel Hunter and I.

Special tribute was also given to three local employees who had been with the company since its founding: Harry Dingman, who began his career as a lab technician and was now manager of the Patent Department; Pete Larsen, who worked his way up from lab helper to transportation specialist; and Dr. John Speier, senior research scientist and one of the original Mellon researchers.

The Midland area plants celebrated in a similar manner. The local community joined in as well, with the *Midland Daily News* preparing a special edition of the paper to focus on Dow Corning's "Four Decades of Growth."

In December 1984, Jack Ludington's term as president of Dow Corning came to a close. At that time, Larry Reed was named president and chief operating officer of the corporation, and Ludington continued in the role of chairman of the board and chief executive officer.

During Jack's 12-year tenure as president of Dow Corning, the company continued its very rapid growth, with revenues rising from $188.6 million in 1972 to $855 million in 1984. By 1976, Dow Corning's sales had risen to the level of the *Fortune* 500 list, with profits equal to those of far larger corporations (Table 8-1).

In 1984, after 4 decades and five presidents, Dow Corning was still going strong. During a time when American business was being criticized for its short-sighted emphasis on immediate profits, Dow Corning was an anomaly, maintaining a consistently profitable stance in the present while investing heavily in the future. This emphasis on the future is firmly rooted in the past. During the late 1970s and early 1980s, with inflation rampant and businesses worried about the possibility of an impending recession and even depression, Jack Ludington requested

Table 8-1. Dow Corning Rankings within *Fortune 500*

	1976	1978	1980	1982	1984
Sales	471	435	396	386	338
Profit	245	231	227	218	180

an informal study of companies that survived black Friday and thrived when the great depression lifted. He wanted to know what carried these companies through, what lessons could be learned from them. The study would include two survivors with close ties to Dow Corning—the parent companies, Dow Chemical and Corning Glass Works.

The findings of the study were enlightening, and the philosophy and success of Dow Corning can be read in the results. At Dow Chemical, Willard Dow was forced to shorten working hours in some cases, but he did not lay off workers. At Corning Glass Works, operations were maintained at a steady level while the economy continued to shrink. Neither company reduced its dividends throughout this black period.

More important, both Willard Dow at Dow Chemical and Amory Houghton at Corning dramatically increased their investments in research and development as a percentage of sales during the depression years. In the hard times of the present, both men kept a steady eye on the future.

By the time the depression lifted, Dow Chemical had developed a new manufacturing site in Texas, placed magnesium under production, fought the battle with the European cartel, and created its initial thrust into plastics.

At Corning, researchers developed the popular Pyrex brand of cookware, and television tubes, a big money-maker for the company in the postdepression era, were brought into commercial production. In the heart of the depression, Dr. Eugene Sullivan, who was then director of research and later became president of Corning Glass Works, took the risky step of hiring an organic chemist, Dr. J. Franklin Hyde, to develop new compounds that would combine the best of the glasses and the plastics.

The rest is history.

Epilogue

Since Dow Corning's fortieth anniversary year, growth has continued at a rapid pace. In December 1984, Larry Reed became the company's sixth president. Under his leadership, Dow Corning reached a major milestone in 1986, achieving $1 billion in sales, and is well on the way to its second billion.

How has Dow Corning managed to grow and thrive for more than four decades? A variety of explanations could be offered, but they can be distilled into three major reasons for success.

One key reason is focus. Throughout its history, Dow Corning has maintained a consistent focus on the field of organosilicon chemistry. For more than four decades, the company has never swerved from its original mission, to be "first in silicones."

Another secret of Dow Corning's success is self-sufficiency. The company was strengthened by the decision of its parents, at the time of incorporation, to encourage the joint venture to stand on its own. As a result, the young company was forced to learn, at a tender age, the secrets of survival.

More important, from the very beginning Dow Corning sought to recruit and retain the best and brightest workers. Starting with Dr. J. Franklin Hyde, a parade of employees over the years — chemists, administrators, plant operators, managers, engineers, and a host of others — have contributed to making Dow Corning the solid success it is today.

The world is rapidly evolving into a single marketplace, a global business community that knows no geographical boundaries. To succeed in this environment, Dow Corning will have to differentiate itself from a growing list of competitors around the world. By continuing along the path that led to the present, Dow Corning can ensure its continued success in the competitive world of the future. By strengthening its commitment to quality, by maintaining its focus on silicone products, by retaining its independent stance, Dow Corning will be well prepared to meet the challenges of the future. But in the final analysis, it is the people of Dow Corning who will lead the way. In 1984, the company looked back with pride at four decades of achievement, 40 years of firsts. By continuing to hire, develop, and maintain a talented, dedicated team of employees, Dow Corning can look forward to a future of success—for the next 40 years and beyond.

Index of Names

Abegglin, James, 237, 239
Aikawa, K., 239, 240
Aizawa, Koichi, 302
Alanko, Alan, 203
Albert, Glen E., 151
Albert of Liege, Prince, 284
Allen, A. J., 204
Alsgaard, Richard W., 203
Anderson, Gary E., 298
Andrianov, K. A., 24
Argyle, Robert S., 114, 196
Armstrong, William S., 275
Atwood, Bedford, 276

Babinski, Paul, 177
Bachand, J. G., 123
Baecker, Henry J., 183
Baile, Madhu, 300
Bailey, Donald, 253
Baney, Ronald H., 309, 310
Bank, Howard M., 203
Barrett, Wayne E., 40, 122, 137, 151, 196
Barry, Arthur J., 39–41, 43, 72–77, 124,
    125, 137–139, 149, 187, 198,
    206–209, 242, 263, 303, 310
Bartos, Donald M., 249
Bass, Arlen, 166
Bass, Dolf, 166
Bass, Elizabeth, 219
Bass, Shailer L., 33, 36, 72, 73, 76, 84,
    104–106, 108, 110, 117, 118, 121,
    126, 131, 145, 146, 151, 152, 157,
    166, 167, 171, 180, 183, 189, 191,
    192, 203, 208, 209, 216–259, 261,
    270, 275, 276, 286, 289, 297, 302
Bassani, Giovanni, 238
Beck, Earl W., 151, 196, 211
Beck, Nelson, 206

Becker, Walter, 225
Bennett, Donald R., 246, 263, 266, 270
Bennett, Earl W., 49, 50, 230
Berzelius, Johann, 16
Beshgetoor, Donald L., 144, 151, 263
Bishop, Truman B., 191, 193, 195, 222,
    263
Black, James F., 208
Blackburn, William C., 145–147, 154, 243,
    275
Blackhurst, Robert, 225
Blessing, Olin D., 34, 42, 54, 58, 88, 90,
    97, 101–103, 141, 146, 222
Boehm, A. Bruce, 238
Boeschenstein, Harold, 21, 34
Boomer, Cliff, 72
Bott, Robert P., 111–113
Bottomley, James, 109
Boulton, Harry, 102, 103
Bouvier, Klaus, 235
Brady, Sam A., 212, 309, 310
Braley, Silas A., Jr., 123, 154, 163, 164,
    166, 185, 228, 270
Branch, Ben, 260
Branson, Carl, 54, 55
Breathitt, Edward T., 233
Breger, Joseph, 225, 226, 270
Britton, E. C., 27, 32, 42, 48, 49, 51, 56,
    72, 79, 80, 117, 145, 218
Brooks, Charles, 163
Brown, Eric D., 208, 209
Brown, H. Gordon, 51, 52, 55, 57, 134,
    139, 309
Brown, Harold, 95, 130
Brown, Lawrence H., 123, 150
Brown, Murrel A., 126
Brown, Paul L., 150, 211
Bruner, Leonard, 179, 211

Bublitz, Donald, 303
Burdick, Duane F., 214
Busick, Arthur, 233
Butler, George, 208
Buzzard, Arnold, 212

Caldwell, R. William, 50, 55, 87, 113, 139,
    140, 172, 191, 222, 237, 311
Calingert, George, 75
Campbell, Calvin, 43, 49
Campbell, F. J., 214
Campbell, F. Kermit, 277,
Carlson, Clare, 144
Carothers, Wallace, 18, 19
Chaffee, Roger G., 206
Cheng, Anna, 203
Chipman, A. D., 123,
Christensen, Howard M., 111, 112
Church, James, 154, 163
Church, John E., 59
Churchfield, John, 261
Clark, Harold A., 40, 72, 79, 147, 148,
    150, 244, 297, 298, 309
Clark, Richard, 40, 136, 137
Closs, Joseph P., 109
Cmorik, George, 163
Cole, Glen, 34, 35, 42, 48, 60, 145
Collings, Helen, 106, 173
Collings, William R., 33, 34, 37, 39, 42,
    48–50, 52, 58, 60, 62, 76, 87, 88, 91,
    95–99, 101, 102, 104, 106, 107, 109,
    112–115, 117, 125, 127, 129, 130,
    134, 135, 138–141, 145–147, 160,
    167, 169–218, 239
Conant, J. B., 3
Constan, Gus L., 309
Cookingham, Owen C., 95
Coolidge, W. D., 30
Coon, Marvin, 203
Coppens, Robert, 284
Corsello, Helena, 67, 68, 154, 163
Coulman, George, 212
Coultrip, Donald R., 282, 311
Crafts, J. M., 17, 18
Crane, Eric, 108
Cretzmeyer, John, 214
Cronin, T. D., 229
Culbertson, Byron J., 263
Cunningham, William C., 134, 135
Currie, Chester C., 40, 78, 79, 90,
    118–122, 178, 179, 235, 242, 263,
    268

Currin, Cedric G., 192, 263
Curry, J. W., 154

Daniels, George P., 208
Darwin, Roy, 144
Daubert, Bernard, 157
Daudt, William H., 29, 63, 149, 153, 154,
    207, 211, 252
Daughenbaugh, Norman, 201
David, Mary Pat, 200–202
Davidson, Clayton, 144, 231, 234, 283
Davidson, James B., 123
Dawson, Mary, 58, 111, 112
Day, Mark W., 142
Dean, Gordon L., 83
Dellaria, Joseph F., 177, 196, 263
Delmotte, F., 284
Delong, Richard C., 22, 29, 30, 63, 79
Dennett, Firth (Zeke), 34, 40, 52, 55, 57,
    77, 119, 124–127, 136, 263, 269, 270,
    303
Dennis, William, 203
Depree, Lee, 52, 72
de Vaissiere, Freddie, 109
Devine, Marty, 225
Dexter, John F., 100, 223, 263, 268, 309
Dickmann, Norbert G., 173
Dickmann, Rita, 173
Dingman, Harry D., 57, 72, 151, 243, 311
Disapio, Albert J., 225
Doan, Ted, 258, 260
Domicone, Joseph, 29, 63, 153
Doremire, Clayton A., 97–100, 115, 131,
    175
Dow, Alden, 55
Dow, Willard, 32–35, 37, 39, 42, 43, 48,
    49, 145, 170, 312
Dryzga, Floyd D., 123, 142
Duane, James, 103
Dudley, Charles F., 126, 184, 240, 275
Dulmage, Fred, 51
Dunlop, Andrew M., 238
Dupree, Wayne, 247
Dyste, Wallace F., 233

Eaborn, Colin, 302
Ebelman, J. J., 17
Ehlers, Ralph B. (Dutch), 103, 141, 223
Eisenhower, Dwight, 293
Emmett, Paul, 216
Enk, Dr., 189, 191
Erwin, John, 214

Eynon, Benjamin A., 201

Fashbaugh, Howard D., 142
Fekete, Frank, 163, 202
Fenn, Howard N., 34, 51, 55, 134, 139, 141, 145, 180, 195, 218, 222, 285, 311
Fenner, Jack V., 214
Findlay, Donald E., 300
Fischer, David, 192, 205, 206
Flegel, Vern, 192
Fleming, Robert F., 29, 32, 40, 63, 146, 153, 154, 243
Fletcher, H. James, 40, 57, 78, 136, 151
Flory, Paul J., 69
Foley, Charles, 178
Folwell, C. E., 179
Ford, Robert, 183
Foss, Niles, 114
Foster, Norton C., 178, 238
Fowler, D. Leigh, 31, 32, 146
Francis, Arlene, 126
Francis, Joseph D., 123, 137, 154, 162, 166
Francisco, Donald M., 101, 102, 120, 131, 177
Freeman, Richard, 40
Freiberg, Alan L., 302
Frevel, Ludo, 40, 66
Friedel, Charles, 17, 18
Friedle, Fred, 238
Frye, Cecil L., 152, 251, 263, 309
Fuller, C. S., 73

Gaensheimer, Josef, 225
Gay, Robert, 109
Gergle, Richard C., 118, 263
Gerstacker, Carl A., 231, 294
Gerstung, Harry, 225
Gibson, Clarence E. (Hoot), 125
Gilkey, John W., 34, 72, 149
Gilliam, W. F., 30
Gilman, Henry, 243
Gilson, Donald R., 137, 192
Glover, Shedric O., 302
Goggin, William C., 257–288, 293, 304, 308
Goldmann, Theodore B., 183
Goodwin, John T., 32, 67, 123, 154, 162, 166
Gordon, Arthur F., 34, 148, 208
Gordon, David, 225

Gordon, M. Susan, 123, 149
Gornowicz, Gerald, 203, 299, 302
Gosselin, Gus, 282
Graiver, Daniel, 300
Grant, George, 80, 123, 143, 144, 188, 192
Greenhalgh, Robert E., 196
Gregory, Ray, 109
Greminger, George, 52
Gribanova, O., 24
Griffin, Jerald L., 276, 278, 305
Grindahl, George A., 208
Groening, William, 45
Gruenhof, Gene, 235
Grunder, Paul, 223
Guittard, Stephen W., 305

Haberland, Gerald G., 166
Haebler, Ariel F., 57
Haire, Edward I., 223, 263
Haluska, Loren A., 149, 208, 252
Hannigan, John, 221–223, 231, 232, 255, 257, 262
Hargreaves, William J., 112, 150, 196, 222, 233, 234, 276, 279, 280
Harris, Ray, 112
Hayes, Dan M., Jr., 231, 234
Heckrodt, William, 142
Hedlund, Robert C., 123, 149, 177, 263
Helvey, George, 212
Henry, James, 142
Henson, Francis, 150
Hergenrother, Edward L., 231
Hernette, Andre, 109
Heuerman, Richard, 275
Hildebrand, Thomas, 119
Hirota, S., 240
Hobbs, Edward J., 246
Hobey, Laurence R., 243
Hochbaum, Alfred, 224
Hodgson, Peter, 176
Hoeffleman, Klaus, 238
Hoffman, Dr., 191
Holbrook, G. W., 208
Holinsky, Rudiger, 225
Hollitz, Rhinee, 235
Holm, Richard W., 137
Holmes, Robert E., 215
Holter, John, 185
Hommel, Maurice C., 113, 235
Hook, Donald E., 72, 149, 206, 208
Hopfer, Polly, 220

Horner, Robert, 150
Houghton, Amory, 42, 48, 293, 294, 312
Householder, William, 298
Huber, Burl D., 49, 60, 113
Huebner, D., 300
Hughes, John, 276
Hunter, Melvin J., 33, 39, 40, 57, 69, 72,
    77–79, 118, 124, 136, 143, 145, 147,
    149–152, 185, 187, 206, 208, 216,
    242, 246, 285, 297, 303, 310, 311
Hunter, Ralph, 142, 143, 195
Hutchison, Ira W., 51, 52, 55, 102, 107,
    109–111, 180, 182, 225, 229, 239,
    263–270
Hyde, James Franklin, 3–6, 9, 11, 13, 14,
    20–23, 26, 27, 29–32, 34, 40, 45, 63,
    64, 66, 73, 78, 117, 145, 153, 154,
    179, 211, 246, 247, 263, 271, 280,
    300, 308, 309, 312

Ito, S., 240

Jackson, J. Robert, 142
Jackson, Robert W., 277
Jackson, T. Michael, 234, 276
Janik, Gloria, 302
Johannson, O. Kenneth, 21, 22, 63, 65, 66,
    145, 153, 154, 163, 211, 215, 303, 309
Johnson, Leo, 111
Johnson, Richard, 300

Kastens, Klaus, 238
Kauppi, Donald, 192, 193, 223
Kauppi, Toivo Andrew, 33, 70, 72, 80,
    113, 117, 118, 125, 131, 136, 145,
    178, 206, 222, 249
Kaya, Thomas, 269
Keil, Joseph W., 118, 119, 123, 263, 309
Keller, K. T., 115
Kellum, G. E., 252
Kelly, Thomas F., 137
Kern, Edward, 263
Kime, Donavan D., 40, 122
Kin, Myron (Mike), 80, 94, 122
King, George, 233
King, James, 112
Kipping, Frederick Stanley, 4, 10, 11, 17,
    18, 31, 66, 106, 152
Kirkpatrick, Sydney, 196
Kitchen, George, 225
Klauser, Arthur E. (Bud), 275
Klingler, James, 233, 277

Knapic, Dean, 188
Knight, Fred, 31, 146
Knowles, Charles, 221
Kohl, Charles, 123, 154, 162, 164, 166
Kolb, Arnold F., 150
Kolderman, Roger W., 34, 59, 80, 101,
    102, 117, 179, 223, 263
Konkle, George M., 123, 212, 263
Kookootsedes, Gust J., 203, 211, 255
Koster, Merritt, 123
Krahnke, Robert, 203
Kroeger, Robert G., 109, 111, 182, 183
Kuhlberg, George, 214
Kuhlman, William D., 51, 55, 136, 137,
    241
Kuhn-Weiss, Frederick, 235

Ladenberg, A., 17
LaFollette, Charles D., 49, 50, 94, 95, 230
Langford, Mel, 102
Lankton, C. A. (Bud), 41, 51, 55, 57, 138,
    144, 222, 231, 233, 277–279
Lappert, Michael, 302
Larsen, Pete, 284, 311
Lasorsa, Reno R., 179, 183, 238
Laudenslager, Harry B., 65, 153
Lauer, Thomas, 214
Lauterbur, Paul, 202
LaVercombe, David, 231, 233
Layne, Douglas K., 263, 268, 280
Leavenworth, Max, 101–103
Leavitt, Robert, 236
Leburton, E., 284,
Lee, Chi-Long, 299, 300, 302, 309
Lee, Kenneth, 203
LeGrow, Gary E., 203
Leitheiser, Robert, 152
Lentz, Charles W., 304
Lenz, Charles J., 207, 208, 263
LeVier, Robert R., 309
Lewis, Al, 225
Liebhafsky, H. A., 30
Littleton, James, 195
Lloyd, Norman C., 266, 277, 301
Lo, Peter Y., 302
Locateli, E., 238
Locke, Harold, 57
Louden, Gene, 233
Lowery, William E., 266, 268
Lubbehusen, Joseph H., 92, 94
Ludington, John S. (Jack), 112, 174, 261,
    266, 268, 276, 285, 287–312

Lundquist, Joe, 215
Lyon, John, 144
Lyons, James D., 122, 151

McBee, Earl, 208
Macbeth, George, 11
McFadzen, James, 236
McGregor, Rob Roy, 6, 8, 9, 11, 13, 16,
    17, 20, 26, 27, 31, 36, 67, 68, 70, 117,
    145, 154–157, 160, 163, 176, 185,
    201, 220, 228, 309
McHard, James A., 34, 72, 150, 243, 246,
    251, 303
McIntyre, Gordon E., 103, 223, 263
McKellar, Robert L., 298
McLean, W. M., 123
McNeill, A. R., 150, 220
McSorley, James J., 109
McVannel, Donald E., 310
Malek, James, 203
Maneri, Remo R., 123, 172, 179, 180,
    213, 263, 276, 285
Mark, Herman, 73, 308
Marshall, A. L., 6
Martin, Thomas, 214
Marx, George E., 131, 176, 222
Mason, Jack, 142
Matsuda, S., 240
May, William, 118, 183, 184, 196, 237,
    239, 275
Mayo, F. R., 73
Mease, Edward, 25, 26, 32
Mellon, Andrew, 7
Mellon, Richard, 7
Menzie, Gerald, 203
Merker, Robert, 201, 202, 248
Merrill, E. E., 149
Michael, Keith W., 152, 203
Mills, David, 300, 302
Minard, Rome, 101, 148
Mine, Katsutoshi, 302
Mishler, James, 214
Miska, B. T., 123
Momany, George, 112
Moore, Ron F., 232
Moorhead, Kenneth W., 123, 151
Morrow, Les, 6
Moses, Graham L., 117
Moyle, Clarence, 32, 56, 136
Mullison, Ethyl G., 185
Murch, Robert M., 149, 208
Murnane, George, 35, 39, 41

Musolf, Marty C., 152, 203, 255

Naegele, Ray S., 131, 177, 223, 224, 263,
    268, 275, 280, 281
Nakonechny, Michael, 223
Neff, Mort, 127
Nehil, Thomas, 109, 238
Nelson, Melvin E., 199, 263, 306
Newkirk, Earl, 139
Noll, John, 154, 159, 202
Nolte, David, 225

Olson, Kenneth, 303
Orbeck, Tor, 309
Ostahowski, John H., 151
Owen, Michael J., 309

Pail, Daniel R., 263
Pape, Peter, 203
Paterson, Clifford, 103
Patnode, Winton T., 6
Patterson, Robert P., 43
Pearce, Chris A., 301
Peden, Kathryn, 233
Pedersen, William W., 71, 80–84, 102,
    222–224, 233, 263, 268, 285
Peele, Robert, 182, 238, 240
Pellika, Henry J., 263
Penney, Matt W., 144
Petrie, Peter, 218
Philbrick, Paul, 234
Piccoli, William, 202
Pierce, Ogden, 208, 209, 309
Piper, Donald G., 232, 270, 281
Plueddemann, Edwin P., 251, 254, 274,
    275, 309
Polmanteer, Keith E., 123, 124, 165, 204,
    213–216, 226, 247, 248, 263, 309
Pooley, Thomas, 211
Pretzer, Gale H., 302
Price, C. C., 73
Przybyla, Richard L., 142
Pugh, Duane, 149
Putnam, Louis S., 59, 60, 115, 196

Quehl, Ernest F., 142

Radzius, Joseph, 303
Ragborg, William H., 118, 231, 234, 263
Rasmussen, Edward T., 302
Rauner, Larry, 40, 53, 81, 122
Reed, Lawrence A., 268, 291, 311

Reese, Herschel H., 302
Renwick, William, 244
Rhodes, A. W. (Dusty), 96, 97, 129, 172,
    186, 195, 222, 223, 229, 238, 270,
    276, 279, 285
Rickover, Hyman, 21, 34, 53, 54, 58, 76,
    81, 98
Rising, Walt, 31
Ritter, Eugene W., 48, 49
Roche, Mary Purcell, 29, 63, 66, 153
Rochow, Eugene G., 16, 17, 30, 73–75,
    134
Ross, Donald, 57
Ross, Ian, 279
Rossiter, William, 178, 222, 223
Roth, Charles A., 203
Rousch, Wally, 232
Rownd, Robert, 137, 138, 191, 192, 195
Ruh, Robert, 208, 209
Russell, Marian, 203
Ryan, John, 203

Saam, John, 203, 299, 300, 309
Sanderson, Wayne, 115, 134, 135, 282
Sanford, Charles, 59, 88–90, 101, 126,
    177, 222
Sauer, Robert, 235, 279
Saunders, Fred, 255
Sawada, Paul, 239
Sawicki, George, 302
Saylor, John, 215
Schiefer, Harry, 235, 263
Schmidt, Austin, 142
Schmidt, Christine, 300
Schmidt, H. F., 123
Schneider, Irvin, 101, 102
Schoenherrout, C., 300
Schultz, Elmer, 211
Schultz, Virginia (Ginny), 173, 174
Scott, Henry G., 266
Scott, Mary Jane, 202
Selfridge, Robert, 123, 142
Servais, Phil, 40, 72, 79, 123, 124, 212, 236
Sheeran, William, 112
Shephard, Nick, 300
Shipps, Robert, 177
Shohara, Kiyoshi, 239, 240
Shorr, Leonard, 154, 198, 200–202
Skalnican, Paul, 124, 187
Slemmons, Charles, 212
Smith, A. Lee, 150, 303, 309

Smith, Albert, 192
Smith, Arthur, 203
Smith, Bruce, 109
Smith, D. D.; 208
Smith, Earle J., 40, 79, 102, 103, 122,
    222, 223, 263, 268
Smith, Holland (Bud), 124
Smith, R. C., 252
Smith, Schuyler, 300
Sommer, Leo, 152, 198
Sonntag, Alfred, 224, 225
Speier, John, 67, 70, 71, 77, 154,
    156–162, 164, 166, 195, 198, 199,
    201–203, 246, 252, 253, 255, 263,
    309, 311
Spenke, Dr., 191
Sprague, Edward G., 141, 151, 176, 263,
    282
Sprague, Mary Thayer, 125, 141
Springmier, Robert S., 129, 263, 268, 285
Stark, Forrest, 152, 166, 215, 269, 270
Stark, Gary, 203
Stark, Gloria, 215
Staudinger, Hermann, 18, 19
Stebleton, Leo, 94, 177, 179, 272
Steinhoff, Edward, 261
Stewart, Herbert, 192
Stickles, David, 302
Stievenart, E., 284
Stinton, Mike, 112, 235, 302
Strack, William (Red), 137
Sullivan, Austin, 144
Sullivan, Eugene C., 1–5, 11, 25, 27, 30,
    42, 45, 48, 49, 94, 95, 99, 103, 145,
    166, 167, 170, 175, 180, 312
Swanson, John, 305, 306
Swantko, Mike, 263
Sweasy, William, 178
Sweet, Edward, 211, 247

Tamura, Kihachi, 239
Tarrant, Paul, 208, 209
Taylor, W. C., 3, 4
Teichthesen, Lee, 148, 175
Teoh, 269
Thomas, John, 103, 122, 148, 212
Thomson, Durelle, 150, 268, 276, 277,
    285, 305
Todd, Charles, 118
Todero, Frank, 281
Torok, Julius, 63, 65

Townley, Duane, 269
Trego, Brian R., 302
Tyler, Les, 149, 152, 207, 212, 242, 263,
    268, 297, 300, 301, 310
Tyner, John, 92, 103, 223

Ulanowicz, Gene, 240, 270

Vaes, E., 284
Vallender, Donald, 137
Vandeusen, Jil, 150
Van Dyke, Gerald, 40
Van Tienhoven, Robbie, 238
Van Volkinburg, Leon, 150
Van Winkle, Donald, Jr., 151, 263
Varerewyck, Ron, 284
Veazey, William R., 34, 41, 42, 48, 54, 76,
    145, 172
Vidal, Robert, 118, 176, 222, 223, 298
Vinageras, Juan, 183, 221
Vincent, Harold L., 251
Votaw, Richard, 305
Vukovich, Thomas J., 137

Warrick, Earl L., 6, 8, 9, 11, 13, 40,
    67–71, 73, 84, 145, 154, 163–166,
    176, 187–189, 191, 192, 195, 201,
    204–207, 216, 220–223, 226, 248,
    266–268, 281, 289, 309–311
Watson, Thomas, 279
Watters, Donald, 276, 280, 285
Webb, Arthur, 57, 151
Webster, George, 115

Webster, James, 159, 198, 202
Wehrly, Jack R., 211, 223, 271, 300
Weirauch, Arthur, 95
Wendel, Samuel, 203
Werner, Lawrence, 211
Weyenberg, Donald, 152, 212, 297,
    300–302
Weyer, Donald, 248, 264, 273, 274
Whipple, Clyde, 263, 279, 281, 282
White, James W., 301, 302
Whiting, Jean, 40, 53, 57
Whitmore, Dean Frank, 152
Wiard, William, 90
Wiley, Jack, 176
Williams, Donald, 42
Wilson, Jack, 232
Wing, Howard, 142
Winger, Robert, 150, 216
Winslow, A. F., 30
Witman, R. C., 124, 149
Wohler, Frederick, 16, 17
Woods, Anthony, 101, 102
Wright, Frank Lloyd, 179

Yokota, S., 239, 240
Youngs, Delmar, 101, 123, 124, 187
Youngs, M. L., 214

Zacharias, Win, 261
Zack, John F., 205, 206
Zeman, Ronald, 271
Ziess, Dennis, 242, 283
Zimmerman, Ruth, 154, 158

Subject Index

A. R. Brown McFarlane & Co. Ltd., 108
Acetoxymethyl silicones, 78, 211
Acquisition, 223–224, 235–236, 276, 295
Acrylates, 201
Advertising, 59–60, 113–117
Aerospace application of ablative heat
    shield, 213, 247
Albright and Wilson, Ltd., 104–105
Alkali salts, 153
Alpha Molykote Corporation, 223–225
American Chemical Society (ACS),
    meeting of, 29–30, 42, 171
Amory Houghton Center, 293–294
Analysis:
    boron, 252
    IR spectrometers, 150
Analytical Laboratory, 72, 150, 215–216,
    251–252
Antifoaming, 28, 121–122
Antimicrobial treatments, 266
Area Operating Board (AOB), 284–285
Australia, 240–241
Awards and honors:
    Chemical Engineering Achievement
        Award, 196–197
    Goodyear Award, 309
    IR 100 Awards, 307–308
    Perkin Medal, 280
    Plastics Hall of Fame, 308–309
    Scientist of the Year, 309
    Thomas Midgely Award, 308

Barry process (PFC), 76, 138–139
Basic Businesses, 268
Basic Research group, 154
Bathtub Caulk, 180
Biological activity, 246, 270
Bioscience research groups, 246, 270

Bleeding from sealant, 247
Block copolymers, silicone-organic, 299
Board book, 261
Board of directors, 48
Bond issue, 278
Bond refractions, 166
Book, 156
Boron analysis, 252
Branch offices, 102–103, 238
Bread release, 90–94
Brussels, 238
Businesses under matrix organization:
    Consumer Products, 263
    Electronic Products, 263, 268–269
    Encapsulants and Sealants, 263
    Fluids, Emulsions, and Compounds,
        263, 268
    Medical Products, 263, 269–271
    New Projects, 265, 266
    Resins and Chemicals, 263, 268
    Silicone Rubber, 263, 268
    Specialty Lubricants, 263, 268

C resin, 297–299
Capital funding, 50
Car polish, 120–121
Cellulose Products Department, 33–34,
    39, 41, 72–85, 88, 170
Center for Aid to Medical Research,
    184–186, 228
Ceramics, 272–274
Chemistry:
    organosilicon, 15–18, 152
    polymer, 18–19
    synthetic organic, 16
Chiba plant, 240
Chloroplatinic acid catalyst, 199–200
Chlorosilane Committee, 138

Christmas card contest, 219
2,6–*cis*-diphenylhexamethylcyclote-
   trasiloxane, 270
Code of Business Conduct, 305–306
Commercial units, 295
Competition, 62
Concept, 1–4
Condensation polymers, 19
Connecticut Hard Rubber Company,
   84
Construction, 54–55
Continuous hydrolysis, 148
Cooperative program, Corning and
   Mellon, 13–15
Corning Glass Works, 1–5, 9, 25, 35, 47
Corporate Business Board, 285
Corporate Center, 234–235, 282
   Amory Houghton Center, 293–294
Corporate objectives, 264
Corporate self-sufficiency. 290–291
Coupling agents, 253–254, 274–275
Crepe hardening, 165
Cross-licensing, 74
Crucible charges, 193–194
Crystallinity, 204–205
Cultural sensitivity, 296–297

Decetex 104, 126
Departments;
   advertising, 59–60, 113–117
   engineering, 58
   personnel, 58, 111–113
   sales, 42, 58–59
Depolymerizing high polymers, 154
Diethoxydichlorosilane, 77
Diethyl fluids, 78
Diethyl zinc, 17
Diffusion pump fluids, 78–79, 118
Dimethyldichlorosilane, 22, 51, 73, 75, 79,
   133
Dimethyldiethoxysilane, 41, 52, 145
Dimethylsiloxane:
   cylics, 29, 40, 136
   DOW CORNING 200® fluid, 51, 57, 68, 77,
      88–91, 95, 120, 133–134, 136, 151,
      156, 224, 247, 249
   high-polymer fractions, 40
   linears, 40
   Mellon, 24, 26, 36, 69, 145
   octamer, 40
   trimer, 40, 299

Direct process:
   Barry process (PFC), 76, 138–139
   Big Bertha, 134–135
   early work, 41, 73–74
   fluid bed techniques, 136–137
   tumblers, 134
Director of research, 118, 297
Director of Research, Development, and
   Engineering Services (RDES), 297
Directors, 48
Distillation, 11, 22–23, 40, 52
Divisions:
   Chemical Products, 222–223
   Consumer Products, 222–223
   Electronic Products, 222–223
   Engineering Products, 222–223
   Medical and Pharmaceutical Products,
      222–223
Domestic bonds, 291
Dow Chemical Company, 27, 32–35, 42,
   47
   research progress, 37–41, 43
DOW CORNING® Antifoam A compound, 67,
   121–122, 151, 215
DOW CORNING 4® compound, 36, 39, 43,
   53, 58, 79, 82, 83, 103, 118–119, 121,
   218
DOW CORNING® 33 grease, 82, 83, 85, 139
DOW CORNING® 35 emulsion, 88–90, 97,
   114, 131, 133
DOW CORNING® 41 grease, 84, 85, 139
DOW CORNING 44® grease, 82, 85, 139
DOW CORNING® 55M pneumatic grease, 83
DOW CORNING 200® silicone fluid, 51–52,
   57, 68, 77, 88–91, 95, 120, 133–134,
   136, 151, 156, 224, 247, 249
DOW CORNING 325®, 213
DOW CORNING 510® silicone fluid, 81, 82,
   136
DOW CORNING 550® silicone fluid, 81, 136
DOW CORNING® 555 silicone fluid, 246, 270
DOW CORNING® 561, 307
DOW CORNING® 702 diffusion-pump fluid,
   118
DOW CORNING® 703 diffusion-pump fluid,
   118
DOW CORNING 710® silicone fluid, 81, 84,
   136
DOW CORNING® 801 silicone resin, 81, 136
DOW CORNING® 802 silicone resin, 136
DOW CORNING® 803 resin, 136

DOW CORNING® 804 resin, 136, 200–201
DOW CORNING® 990A additive, 39, 53, 63, 79–81, 123
(*See also* Silicone resin, 990A)
DOW CORNING® 993 resin, 79, 123, 136
DOW CORNING® 996 resin, 136
DOW CORNING® 1107 fluid, 124–126, 137–138, 255
DOW CORNING® 1109 treatment, 126–127
DOW CORNING® 2101 laminating resin, 71, 81
DOW CORNING® 2102 laminating resin, 71, 81
DOW CORNING® 2103 laminating resin, 81, 136
Dow Corning A. G. (DCAG), 182, 292
Dow Corning Division, 42
Dow Corning International, Ltd. (DCIL), 237–238
Dow Corning International S. A. (DCISA), 182
Dow Corning Silicones Ltd., 108
Drug delivery, 270–271

Economic Evaluation courses, 261
Electrical Industry Sales, 100
Elemental silicon plant, 141–144
Eli Lilly and Company, 160, 201
Emulsion polymerization, 154, 211, 300
Entrepreneur, 217–256
Etherless Grignard, 24–25, 27, 32, 40–41, 51, 134, 145
Ethyl silicate, 9–10, 25, 41, 43, 51, 134
(*See also* Tetraethoxysilane)
Ethylmethylsiloxanes, 149
Ethylphenyldichlorosilane, 6, 26–27
Eurobond issue, 278
European Economic Community (EEC), 237
Expansion:
facilities, 230–231
personnel, 111–112
plant, 139–140
research, 301–302
work force, 57–58

Facilities:
Alpha Molykote plant, 280–282
corporate center plans, 282
Seneffe, Belgium, plant, 242, 283–284
(*See also* Plants)

Fiber Products Division, 6
Fiberglas sizes, 78
Fillers, 149, 164, 207–208
First employee, 42
First experiments, 4
First product, 35–37
First silicone resin, 6
First silicone rubber, 70
Fluid bed techniques, 136–137
Fluorination, 162–163
Fluorine chemistry, 208–209
Foam-filled tires, 249–250, 266
40th anniversary, 311
Fortune 500, 311–312
Fractionation, 149

Gallery of Research, 310
Gallery of Scientists, 309–310
General counsel, 147, 243, 275
General Electric Company, 6, 29–30, 41
Gibson Island High Polymer Conference, 73–74
Glass block, 9
Glass-fiber sizes, 78
Global organization, 279–280
Graft copolymers, 205, 300
Greases, 79, 81–85
Grignard:
etherless, 24–25, 27, 32, 40–41, 51, 134, 145
in situ (etherless, *above*)
and Kipping, 18
machine, 22, 39
normal, 11, 18, 23–24, 26–27, 29, 41, 51, 133–134
production, 133
Gripmitt, 129–130
Growth and development, 292–293

Health and safety, 302–305
ecology committee, 303–304
Health and Safety Board, 304–305
Heat shield for Gemini, 247
Hexafluoroxylyl silicones, 163
High-strength rubber, 164–165
Highway Sealant 888, 308
Honors (*see* Awards and honors)
Hybrid resins, 212, 250–251
Hydrocephalus shunt, 229
Hydroxyl-ended polymers, 154, 166, 211
Hyper-Pure Silicon Division, 192–195

Ignition sealing compound, 36–37
Inhibitors for oxidation, 70
Insulation of electric motors, 21
Interference, patent, 74
Intermediates, 212
International beginnings:
  Bass's trip to Europe, 103–104
  Bass's visit to Japan, 108
  Canada, 108
  Collings's trip to Europe, 106–107, 184
  first joint venture, SISS, 105
  foreign distributors, 104–105
  International Department, 109–111
  Kipping's visit, 106
  Latin America, 111
  second joint venture, Midsil, 105
  Wacker-Chemie, 105–106
International business, 180–182, 235–237
  Alpha Molykote, 223–225
  Argentina, 292
  Armet Industries, 235–236, 292
  Australia, 292
  Brazil, 292
  European area, 238, 275–280
  Fuji Polymer, 236–237, 292
  Germany, 292
  Health Care Center at Valbonne, 295
  Hemlock Semiconductor Corporation,
    295
  Lucky-DC Silicones in Korea, 295
  Mexico, 292
  Midsil, 105, 276–279
  Pacific area, 238, 275
  Perennator Werk in Wiesbaden, 295
  restructuring, 237–242
  Shin-Etsu Handotai, 238–239
  SISS, 105, 237, 275–276
  Toray Silicone Company Ltd., 239–240,
    292
  United Kingdom, 292

Japan, 183, 238–240
Johannson's laboratory, 215
Joint program, 14–15
Joint venture, 34–35, 41–45
Junction coating resins, 244

Kipping, Frederick Stanley;
  Bass's visit with, 106
  papers of, 10, 106
  Kipping Award, 242–243
    winners, 243

Korean war, 151

Laboratories, 19–25, 45
Latin America, 111
Leather treatment, 80, 177
Library, 220
Licensing, 74
Lithium, 29
Living polymers, 299
Logo, 244–245
Lubrication, 23, 36

Macbeth Evans Company, 9
McKinsey and Company, 237
Magnesium, 53–54
Mammary prosthesis, 229–230
Management evaluation system, 285
Management retreat, 222
Manager of foreign technical service,
  107
Manager of organic research, 202–203
Marketing research, 95–97
  "Technical Bulletin," 97
Matrix organization, 262
"Me To You" letters, 106
Medical Products Business, 186–187,
  229–230
Mellon Institute, 7–9, 23–26, 40, 47,
  154–166, 198–201
"Mellon patch," 201–202
Methoxysilanes, 148, 200
Methyl bromide, 25
Methyl chloride, 74
Methyl silicon trichloride, 73
  (See also Methyltrichlorosilane)
Methylchlorosilanes, 22–23, 30, 74
Methyldichlorosilane, 77, 137
Methyltrichlorosilane, 22, 73, 75, 135
Midsil, 105, 276–279
"Mr. Glue," 254
Molecular weights, 77, 149
Molybdenum disulfide, 223–224
MOLYKOTE®, 224
MOLYKOTE® 3500, 267
Moon products, 267–268
Motor Test laboratory, 80, 123
Multidimensional organization (MDO),
  259–268
  Matrix organization, 262, 263
  phase two of, 279–280

Navy, 21

New business staging, 264
  product life cycle, 264–265
New business ventures:
  Alpha Molykote Corporation, 223–225
  Armet Industries, 235–236
  Fuji Polymer, 236–237
  Hemlock Semiconductor Corporation, 295
  Lucky-DC Silicones in Korea, 295
  Midsil, 105, 276–279
  opthalmics, 225–226, 270
  Perennator Werk in Wiesbaden, 295
  Shin-Etsu Handotai, 238–239
  Toray Silicone Company Ltd., 239–240
New product sales, 243–244
New Products Department, 178–180
Ninth business, 266

Officers, 48–49
Operating agreements, 49
Opthalmics, 225–226, 270
Organofunctional silanes:
  addition to olefins, 198–200, 252–253
  alcohols, 157–158
  amines, 159–160, 254–255
Organofunctional silicones, 156–160, 203
Organosilicon compounds, 14, 17
Owens-Corning Fiberglass, 21
Oxidation resistance, 69–70
Oxygen, resistance to, 28–29

PA fluid, 124, 165
Pan Glaze, 90–94, 97, 114, 136
Paper treatments, 119–120, 126
Patent Department, 243
Patent effort, 31–32
Patent interference, 74
Patents, 145–147
Pennsylvania State University, 152–153
Perkin Medal, 280
Peroxides, 71
Personnel:
  evaluation system, 285
  expansion, 111
  overseas, 183–184
  supervisory training, 112–113
PFC (pseudo-Friedel-Crafts) process, 76, 138–139
Phenylmethylsiloxanes, 78–79
Phenylsilicon compounds, 60–62
Phenyltrichlorosilane, 27, 76, 138–139
Photochlorinator, 157

Physical chemistry laboratory, 215
Pilot plants:
  Mellon, 25–27
  Midland, 151
Pioneers of progress, 145
Plants:
  Alpha Molykote, 280–282
  Carrollton, Kentucky, 232–233
  Chiba, Japan, 240
  Elizabethtown, Kentucky, 231, 233–234
  first, 53
  Greensboro, North Carolina, 140–141
  medical products, 231–232
  Midland, 53
    methyl chloride, 141–142, 144
    SILASTIC®, 141–142
    silicon, 141–144
  pilot (see Pilot plants)
  rubber compounding facility:
    Costa Mesa, California, 232
    Trumbull, Connecticut, 232
  sealants, 231
  Seneffe, Belgium, 242, 283–284
  Sydney, Australia, 240–241
Plasticizer (PA), 165
Platinum catalyst, 199–200
Polyamides (nylons), 19
Polydimethylsiloxane:
  cyclics, 28, 48
  DOW CORNING 200® fluid, 77
  fluid, 24, 28–29, 35, 145
  linears, 40
Polymerization studies:
  cyclic siloxanes, 65–66, 153
  emulsion, 154
  living polymers, 299
  sulfuric acid, 67, 163
Polysilanes, 147–148
Polyvinyl acetate resin, 5, 9
Postwar products:
  DOW CORNING® 35 emulsion, 88–90, 97, 114, 131, 133
  electrical products, 97–100
    Dow Corning as distributor of, 99
  Pan Glaze, 90–94, 97, 114, 136
  SIGHT SAVERS®, 95–97, 114, 120, 127, 131, 136, 141
  SILASTIC®, 100, 131, 136, 139, 141–142, 149–150, 155, 159, 164, 177, 185–187, 208, 213, 229, 248
Silsoft contact lens, 308
Potassium fluosilicate, 16

President:
  first, E. C. Sullivan, 48–49
  second, W. R. Collings, 169–216
  third, S. L. Bass, 216–256
  fourth, W. C. Goggin, 258–286
  fifth, J. S. Ludington, 287–312
  sixth, L. A. Reed, 311
President's Sales Club, 218
Product engineering laboratories:
  Fluids laboratory, 118–122
  Leather Treatment laboratory, 126–127
  Motor Test laboratory, 80, 123
  Resin laboratories, 122–123
  SILASTIC* laboratory, 123–124, 185,
    212–215, 226
  Textile Treatment laboratory, 124–126
Product manager:
  consumer, 131, 176
  electrical, 131, 175
  mold release fluids, 131, 177
  resin, 177
  SILASTIC*, 131, 177
  textile industry, 177–178
Production, 50–53, 55–58, 136, 138–139
Professional research ladder, 300–301
Profits, 60, 312
Project Development Center, 178–180
Protecting active hydroxyls, 158–160
Pseudo-Friedel-Crafts (PFC) process, 76,
  138–139
Publications, 30–31, 117
Publicity, 62–63
Pyrobond, 241

Quality initiative, 306–307

Radiation effects, 204
Rearrangement, methylchlorosilanes, 75,
  135–136, 149
Release fluids, paintable, 255
Reorganization, 221–223, 257
  divisions, 222–223
Report of progress, 43, 49–50, 60–63
Research:
  agenda, 14–15
  meeting, 43
  professional ladder, 300–301
  progress:
    Corning, 63–66
    Dow, 72–80
    Mellon Institute, 66–72
  technical achievement awards, 302

Research (*Cont.*):
  worldwide expansion, 301–302
Restructuring, 268
Rewind shops, 98–99
Rockerfeller Center window, 5
RTV rubber, 153–154, 179, 211

Sales, 166–167, 255, 286, 294–295
Sales force, 58–59, 101–103
Sealant:
  high-strength, 271
  one-part, 179–180, 211, 246–247
  RTVs, 211
  two-part, 211
Sealants plant, 231
  strike at, 233–234
Shin-Etsu Chemical Company, 108,
  238–239
Shin-Etsu Handotai, 238–239
SHOE SAVER*, 126, 128, 147, 178
SIGHT SAVERS*, 95–97, 120, 127, 131, 141
Siemens-Westinghouse license, 189–191
Silane, 17, 200
Silane addition to olefins:
  high-temperature, 76–77
  catalysts, 198–200, 252–253
SILASTIC*, 100, 131, 136, 139, 141–142,
  149–150, 155, 159, 164, 177,
  185–187, 208, 213, 229, 248
  coated glass tape, 100, 114
  first, 84–85
  foamed pad, 129–130
  fluorosilicone rubber, 249
  heat-shrinkable rubber, 248–249
  laboratory, 212–213
  medical products, 186–187
  R tape, 100
  research laboratory, 123–124, 185,
    213–215, 226
  reversion resistance, 249
  tough rubber, 248, 271
SILASTIC* 250, 124, 149, 164–165, 213,
  248
SILASTIC* 4600, 271
Silazanes, 159–160
SILCON* lenses, 270
Silicates (silicon esters), 17
Silicon:
  elemental, 41, 74
  optical, 188
  semiconductor, 187–195
  sales, 226–228

Silicon carbide, 41
Silicon tetrachloride (SiCl₄ 16, 17, 22, 41,
    43, 52, 57, 73, 75
Silicone:
  compounds, DOW CORNING 4*, 35–37, 39,
      42–43, 53, 58, 79, 82, 83, 103,
      118–119, 121, 218
  emulsion, DOW CORNING* 35, 88–90, 97,
      114, 131, 133
  fluids:
    diffusion pump, 78–79, 118
    DOW CORNING 200* silicone fluid,
        51–52, 57, 68, 77, 88–91, 95,
        120, 133–134, 136, 151, 156,
        224, 247, 249
    DOW CORNING 510*, 81, 82, 136
    DOW CORNING 550*, 81, 136
    DOW CORNING 710*, 81, 84, 136
    Mellon, 24
    phenyl containing, 81
    tagged, 215
  greases, 79, 81–85
  organic block copolymers, 299
  putty, 166
  resin;
    C, 297–299
    DOW CORNING* 801, 81, 136
    DOW CORNING* 802, 136
    DOW CORNING* 803, 136
    DOW CORNING* 804, 136, 200–201
    DOW CORNING* 993, 79, 123, 136
    DOW CORNING* 996, 136
    DOW CORNING* 2103, 81, 136
    first, 6
    laminating, 71, 81
    Mellon, 11, 23
    mono-tri, 68–71
    990A (Hyde), 6, 20–21, 26, 35, 39, 43
    paint, 81
    solventless, 212
  rubber:
    ablatives, 213
    crystallinity, 204–205
    early, 70
    emulsion polymerization, 154, 211,
        271
    first, 70
    first RTV, 153–154
    fluorosilicone, 249
    foams, 211
    heat shrinkable, 248–249
    high-strength, 165

Silicone, rubber (*Cont.*):
  LS-53, 210
  mold making, 272
  plasticizer (PA), 165
  program, 71–72
  Research Laboratory, 213–215, 226
  reversion resistance, 249
  rheology, 214–215
  sealants, 271–272
  SILASTIC* 250, 124, 149, 164–165, 213,
      248
  tough rubber, 248, 271
  transparent interlayer, 213–214
  vulcanization, 70–71, 156, 162, 213,
      246–247
Silicones, 5–6, 10, 17–18
  sales, 166–167, 255, 286, 294–295
SILLY PUTTY*, 28, 176–177
Silmethylene, 162
Siloxanes, trifluoropropyl, 209–211
Silsoft contact lens, 308
Silyl-substituted amines, 159
SIOPLAS* E, 266
SISS, 105, 109, 237, 275–276
Sodium fluosilicate, 29
Sogesil, 183
Solvent-resistant rubbers, 210–211
Solventless resins, 212
Specialty products:
  Gripmitts, 129–130
  Stove Toppers, 130
Spirits, expelling of, 269
Start-up (official), 48, 57
Strike:
  Elizabethtown plant, 233
  Midland plant, 265–266
Studies, cooperative, 13–15
Sulfuric acid polymerization, 67, 163
Supervisory training, 112–113
Support services:
  advertising, 59–60, 113–117
    traveling display, 115–117
  engineering, 58
  personnel, 50, 111–113
Survival story, 312
Sylflex, 126–127, 178
Sylgard antimicrobial treatment, 307
Sylkyd 50, 148, 151
Sylkyd 60, 148, 151
Synthetic organic chemistry, 16

Technical achievement awards, 302

TERRASEAL®, 272
Tetraethoxysilane, 9–10, 25, 41, 43, 51, 134
  (*See also* Ethyl silicate)
Tetraethylsilane, 17
Textile treatment, 177
Tire-mold release, 88–90
Toray Silicone Company Ltd., 239–240
Toyo Rayon, 239–240
Toxicology studies, 121, 151–152, 215
Transparent interlayer, 213–214
Traveling display, 115–117
Trichlorosilane, 17, 73, 138, 200, 252
Trifluoropropylene, 209
Trifluorotolyl silicones, 163
Trimethoxysilane, 200
Trimethoxysilylpropanol, 201
Trimethylchlorosilane, 22, 75, 135, 145
Trimethylethoxysilane, 145

Union Carbide, 9, 253
University of Sussex, 301–302

Vinyl acetate copolymer, 9
Viscosity index, 28
Viscosity measurements, 77
Vulcanization, 70–71, 156, 162, 213,
  246–247

Wacker-Chemie, 105–106
Waterproofing, 79–80, 254
Water repellency, 40–41, 64–65, 77
Water-repellent products, 137–138,
  212
"What's New," 267
Wool treatment, 254–255
World War II, 32, 36–37, 85, 87

X-ray studies, 40, 66

Yarn, fiberglas size of, 78

Z-6020, 253
Z-6032, 275

About the Author

Dr. Earl L. Warrick is the creator of silicone rubber and holds 44 U.S. and numerous foreign patents. During his 33 years with Dow Corning, Dr. Warrick was one of the company's most prominent scientists, rising to the position of Assistant Director of Research. He was awarded the Goodyear Medal by the American Chemical Society in 1976 for his discovery and development of silicone rubber.